# Africa Since 1940
## The Past of the Present

Frederick Cooper's latest book on the history of decolonization and independence in Africa initiates a new textbook series: New Approaches to African History. His book will help readers understand the historical processes which have shaped Africa's current position in the world. Covering the last half-century, it bridges the divide between colonial and post-colonial history, allowing readers to see just what political independence did and did not signify. The book follows the "development question" across time, seeing how first colonial regimes and then African governments sought to transform African societies in their own ways. Readers will see how men and women, peasants and workers, religious leaders and local leaders found space within the crevices of state power to refashion the way they lived, worked, and interacted with each other. And they will see that the effort to turn colonial territories into independent nation-states was only one of the ways in which radical political and social movements imagined their future and how deeply the claims of such movements continued to challenge states after independence. By looking at the post-war era as a whole, one can begin to understand the succession of crises that colonial and post-colonial states faced without getting into a sterile debate over whether a colonial "legacy" or the failings of African governments are the cause of Africa's current situation.

Frederick Cooper is Professor of African History at New York University and former Chair of the Department of History at the University of Michigan. He is a well known and much admired figure in African studies worldwide. His recent publications include *Decolonization and African Society*, published by Cambridge University Press in 1996, plus numerous articles on labor, social movements, decolonization, and development.

*New Approaches to African History*

*Series Editor*
Martin Klein, *University of Toronto*

New approaches to African history is designed to introduce students to current findings and new ideas in African history. Though each book treats a particular case, and is able to stand alone, the format allows the studies to be used as modules in general courses on African history and world history. The cases represent a wide range of topics. Each volume summarises the state of knowledge on a particular subject for a student who is new to the field. However, the aim is not simply to present reviews of the literature, it is also to introduce debates on historiographical or substantive issues, and may argue for particular points of view. The aim of the series is to stimulate debate, to challenge students and general readers. The series is not committed to any particular school of thought.

# Africa Since 1940

*The Past of the Present*

Frederick Cooper

CAMBRIDGE
UNIVERSITY PRESS

PUBLISHED BY THE PRESS SYNDICATE OF THE UNIVERSITY OF CAMBRIDGE
The Pitt Building, Trumpington Street, Cambridge, United Kingdom

CAMBRIDGE UNIVERSITY PRESS
The Edinburgh Building, Cambridge CB2 2RU, UK
40 West 20th Street, New York, NY 10011-4211, USA
477 Williamstown Road, Port Melbourne, VIC 3207, Australia
Ruiz de Alarcón 13, 28014 Madrid, Spain
Dock House, The Waterfront, Cape Town 8001, South Africa

http://www.cambridge.org

First published 2002

Printed in the United Kingdom at the University Press, Cambridge

*Typeface* Plantin 10/12 pt.    *System* LaTeX 2$_\varepsilon$   [TB]

*A catalogue record for this book is available from the British Library*

ISBN 0 521 77241 9 hardback
ISBN 0 521 77600 7 paperback
African edition ISBN 0 521 53307 4

# Contents

# Plates

# Figures

# Maps

# · Tables

x

# Preface

It is now forty years since the exciting, hopeful days when most French, British, and Belgian colonies emerged as independent states. Still, much writing on politics, development, or other aspects of contemporary Africa treats this period, or the post-World War II era generally, more as background than as a subject for consideration, while most textbooks and many courses in African history treat this period more as an epilogue than as a full part of the continent's history. The present book attempts to meet the needs of general readers, students, and teachers who would like to do more than that, who want to look at the past of the present in a more coherent way. The dividing line between colonial and independence eras is sometimes thought of so axiomatically that no one asks just what difference acquiring sovereignty made – especially given the continued inequalities of the world order – and just what processes unfolded over a longer time frame. In many ways, the time of World War II (really the late 1930s through the late 1940s) is as important a break point as the moment of independence. More precisely, different aspects of African history present different rhythms and ruptures, different continuities, adaptations, and innovations – a theme developed in the "Interlude". The book is organized to promote discussion of such issues. *Africa Since 1940* is thus intended for readers with an interest in both history and current affairs, to encourage the former to look farther forward – to see that history doesn't come to an end point – and the latter to look farther backward – to see that the unfolding of processes over time is essential to understanding the present. I have written this book both within and against the genre of a textbook. Within, because it is intended for readers, students and others, who seek an introduction to a subject and who are not presumed to have prior knowledge of it, and against, because I have eschewed both the comprehensiveness and the blandness characteristic of textbooks. In putting themes ahead of coverage, readers may find that a part of Africa that particularly interests them, say Ethiopia, is neglected, but they should find that it is easier to obtain specific information elsewhere than it is to find a framework through which to analyze and debate the post-war period as a whole. The choice of examples is shaped both by what I know – and there is more to know about Africa than any one scholar can assimilate – and by what works well within the thematic structure and space constraints of the book. Such choices should not be taken to mean that one part of Africa is more interesting or important than any other. *Africa Since 1940* is as much an interpretive essay as a textbook, and its contents are intended more to provoke discussion than to be learned. It is argumentative and even opinionated, but I know of no other way to write African history than to do so from my own point of view and to acknowledge that it is one among many ways of approaching the subject.

Each chapter is followed by a short list of suggested readings. However, a more comprehensive bibliography, keyed to the chapters of this book, is available on Cambridge University Press's website at http://uk.cambridge.org/resources/0521776007. In addition to allowing a longer bibliography than the constraints of print allow, use of the web allows for periodic updating as new scholarship appears.

It was Martin Klein's innovative idea for a series of modular texts on different themes of African history that inspired me to write this book, and my attempt to make it accessible to students of political science, development, and perhaps world history as well is, I think, compatible with Marty's goals for the series. I am grateful to Marty and to his advisory committee for several rounds of suggestions on my prospectus and the draft of the book. I would also like to thank Mamadou Diouf, Devra Coren, Nancy Hunt, Andrew Ivaska, David Newbury, Luise White, and Jennifer Widner for their helpful critiques of earlier drafts.

Devra Coren's skills in building and using databases and presenting them graphically deserve the credit for the figures and tables presented in chapter 5. I am grateful to Agence France Presse, Documentation Française, Bettmann/CORBIS, and the Eliot Elisofan Photographic Archive of the National Museum of African Art of the Smithsonian Institution for permission to reproduce photographs. I am also grateful to the staff of the Map Room at the University of Michigan Library, and particularly Karl Longstreth and Chad Weinberg, for working with me on the maps.

Map 1 Africa: countries and cities, *c*. 2000

# 1    Introduction: from colonies to Third World

On April 27, 1994, black South Africans, for the first times in their lives, voted in an election to decide who would govern their country. The lines at polling stations snaked around many blocks. It had been over thirty years since African political movements had been banned, and the leader of the strongest of them, Nelson Mandela, had spent twenty-seven of those years in prison. Most activists and observers inside and outside South Africa had thought that the "apartheid" regime, with its explicit policy promoting white supremacy, had become so deeply entrenched and its supporters so attached to their privileges that only a revolution would dislodge it. In a world that, some thirty to forty years earlier, had begun to tear down colonial empires and denounce governments which practiced racial segregation, South Africa had become a pariah, subject to boycotts of investment, travel, and trade. Now it was being redeemed, taking its place among nations which respected civil rights and democratic processes. This was indeed a revolution – whose final act was peaceful.

Three weeks earlier, a part of the vast press corps assembled to observe the electoral revolution in South Africa had been called away to report on another sort of event in another part of Africa. On April 6, what the press described as a "tribal bloodbath" began in Kigali, capital of Rwanda. It started when the plane carrying the country's President, returning from peace discussions in Arusha, Tanzania, was shot down. The government was dominated by people who called themselves "Hutu," which most of the press assumed was a "tribe" that had long been engaged in rivalry and eventually civil war with another "tribe," known as the "Tutsi." Indeed, a significant number of Tutsi had fled from periodic massacres over the previous decades, and a group of exiles were invading Rwanda from neighboring Uganda to fight for a place for Tutsi in Rwandan government and society. The Tanzanian discussions were an attempt to resolve the conflict. But on the night of the plane crash there began the systematic slaughter of Tutsi by the Hutu-dominated army, by local militias, and apparently by angry mobs.

The killing spread throughout Rwanda, and it soon became clear that this was more than an outburst of hatred; it was an attempt to destroy the entire Tutsi population, from babies to elders. When it ended, some months later, around 700,000 Tutsi had died, a large portion of the Tutsi population, as had numerous Hutu who had opposed the genocidal leaders. It only ended because the Hutu-dominated army, deeply involved in the genocide, became too demoralized to fight the invading army, which captured Kigali and moved to take control over the rest of the territory. The "Tutsi" military victory now produced a wave of "Hutu" refugees into neighboring Zaire. By the fall of 1994, many of the soldiers, militiamen, and thugs responsible for the genocide had joined fleeing children, women, and men in the refugee camps. The genocidal militias were intimidating other refugees into participating in raids on Rwanda. Violence would soon envelop the much larger country of Zaire as well.

## The past of the present

At first glance, these two events of April 1994 seem like opposites, as Africa's two possible fates – either dissolving into "tribal" or "ethnic" violence or uniting under a liberal democratic system. Certainly that is how newspapers and other media in the United States and western Europe portrayed the events at the time. Looked at as a snapshot, in April 1994, such a perspective is understandable. But if one looks to earlier periods in time, what happened in South Africa and Rwanda becomes more complicated, less easily decipherable. That South Africa has come to be governed by institutions familiar in the west – an elected parliament and a system of courts – does not mean that those institutions function in the same way as they do in western Europe or North America or that people do not form other kinds of affiliations, view their lives through other kinds of lenses, and imagine their society through categories distinct from those of the west. Nor is it helpful to think of the Rwandan catastrophe as the result of the age-old division of Africa into neatly separate cultures, each a distinctive and exclusive community with a long history of conflict with people who are "different," unable to function within western-style institutions because such institutions do not fit the reality of Africa. History does not inevitably lead all peoples of the world to "rise" to western political forms, or to "fall" into tribal bloodbaths.

This book explores the period when the rule of European colonial powers over most of the African continent began to fall apart, when Africans mobilized to claim new futures, when the day-to-day realities of life in cities and villages changed rapidly, and when new states had to come to grips with the meaning of sovereignty and the limits of state power faced

1 South Africa's first non-racial election, April 1994. A poster of Nelson Mandela, candidate of the ANC, behind a military vehicle – of the type typically used to control "township violence" – in the black township of Rammulotsi.

2 Genocide and looting, Rwanda, April 11, 1994. A looter removes a bedframe from a house whose murdered inhabitants lie on the ground behind him, Kigali, Rwanda.

with the social realities within their borders and their even less control-lable position in the world economy and global power relations. It is a book about possibilities which people made for themselves as members of rural communities, as migrants to cities and as the builders of social or-ganizations, political movements, and new forms of cultural expression. It is also about the ways many of those openings closed down.

. This book cuts across the conventional dividing point between colonial and post-colonial African history, a division which conceals as much as it reveals. Focusing on such a dividing point either makes the break seem too neat – as if colonialism was turned off like a light switch – or suggests too much continuity, positing continued western dominance of the world economy and the continued presence in African states of "western" in-stitutions as a mere change of personnel within a structure of power that remains colonial. We do not have to make a dichotomous choice be-tween continuity or change. Indeed, the institutions of colonial states, from crop marketing to law courts, did not operate as their designers intended, but were being appropriated, contested, and transformed even while European flags still flew over colonial capitals. Acquiring formal sovereignty was an important element in the historical dynamics of the last half-century, but not the only one. Family life and religious expres-sion also changed substantially in Africa, but not necessarily in rhythm with changes in political organization.

Most important, one needs to understand how the cracks that appeared in the edifice of colonial power after World War II gave a wide range of people – wage laborers, peasants, students, traders, and educated pro-fessionals – a chance to articulate their aspirations, be they the hope of having clean, piped water in a rural village or of taking an honorable place in global political institutions. A distinguished Ghanaian historian, Adu Boahen, begins an article about the 1950s by writing "It was certainly great to be alive in those days..." – a phrase which conveys not only the excitement of being part of a generation that could shape its own future but also a sense that "those days" were better than the ones which followed.

The colonial state that failed in the 1950s was colonialism at its most intrusively ambitious, and the independent states that took over had to take over the failure of colonial development as well: even if the mineral and agricultural production of Africa had increased in the post-war years, the African farmer and worker had not become the predictable and or-derly producer officials dreamed of. New African governments inherited both the narrow, export-oriented infrastructure which developmentalist colonialism had not yet transcended and the limited markets for produc-ers of raw material which the post-war boom in the global economy had only temporarily improved. But now they had to pay for the increasingly ponderous administrative structure that 1950s colonial development had put in place and, more important, to meet the heightened expectations of people who now hoped that the state might really be theirs.

The historical sequence outlined in the first chapters of this book brought into being states that had all the trappings recognized around the world as "sovereignty." But the particular characteristics of those states were consequences of the sequence, not merely the sovereignty. Colonial states had been gatekeeper states. They had weak instruments for entering into the social and cultural realm over which they presided, but they stood astride the intersection of the colonial territory and the outside world. Their main source of revenue was duties on goods that entered and left its ports; they could decide who could leave for education and what kinds of educational institutions could come in; they established rules and licenses that defined who could engage in internal and external commerce. Africans tried to build networks that got around the state's control over access to the outside world and to build economic and social networks inside the territory which were beyond the state's reach. In the 1940s and 1950s, the formal channels of access to officially recognized economic channels, both inside and outside, seemed to be opening wider to Africans. Social, political, and cultural associational life within African territories became richer and links with outside organizations more diverse. The gate was becoming wider, but only so far.

The development effort of late colonial regimes never did provide the basis for a strong national economy; economies remained externally oriented and the state's economic power remained concentrated at the gate between inside and outside. Meanwhile, African leaders' own experience of mobilization *against* the state gave them an acute sense of how vulnerable the power they had inherited was. The mixed success of colonial and post-colonial development efforts did not give leaders the confidence that economic development would lead to a generalized prosperity for which they could get credit and flourishing domestic activity which would provide government revenue. Most rulers realized early on that their own interests were served by the same strategy of gatekeeping that had served the colonial state before World War II: limited channels for advancement that officials controlled were less risky than broad ones which could become nuclei for opposition. But the post-colonial gatekeeper state, lacking the external coercive capacity of its predecessor, was a vulnerable state, not a strong one. The stakes of controlling the gate were so high that various groups tried to grab it – officers or noncommissioned officers in the army, regional power brokers. A regime not so dependent on gatekeeping benefits from the fact that its opponents can afford to lose; they have other avenues for wealth and other loci for power. Gatekeeper states are in danger for the simple reason that rulers temporarily in control of the gate want to stay there. Hence ruling elites tended to use patronage, coercion, scapegoating of opponents, and other resources to reinforce their position, narrowing the channels of access even further. By looking at the post-war era as a whole, one can begin to explain the succession of crises that colonial and postcolonial states faced, without getting into a sterile debate over whether a colonial "legacy" or the incompetence of African governments is to blame. Africa's present did not emerge from an abrupt proclamation of independence, but from a long, convoluted, and still ongoing process.

· When understood in time perspective, the two stories of April 1994 illustrate the openings and possibilities and the closures and dangers of politics in Africa during the last half-century. Let us start to look backward at the history behind the more painful of the two, Rwanda. The murderous violence that erupted on April 6 was not a spontaneous outburst of ancient hatreds; it was planned. It was prepared by a modern institution, a government with its bureaucratic and military apparatus, using modern means of communications and modern forms of propaganda. The hatred in Rwanda was real enough, but it was hatred with a history, not a natural attribute of cultural difference. Indeed, cultural difference in Rwanda was relatively minimal: Hutu and Tutsi speak the same language; most are Catholic. Rwandans and westerners often think that there are ideal physical features of each group – Tutsi tall and slender, Hutu short and broad. But in fact appearance poorly distinguishes them.

Indeed, one of the horrifying features of the genocide was that militias, unable to tell a Tutsi when they saw one, demanded that people produce identification cards that listed their ethnic group and then killed people who were labeled Tutsi or who refused to produce a card. In the years before the mass killings, a shadowy organization of elite Hutu, connected to the government leaders, had systematically organized a propaganda campaign – especially over the radio – against Tutsi. Apparently, many Hutu still had to be convinced that there was a Tutsi conspiracy against them, and social pressure had to be carefully organized, village by village, to bring people into line. Thousands of Hutu did not accept this, and when the genocide began Hutu judged to be overly sympathetic to Tutsi were themselves frequently killed, while other Hutu acted with courage to save Tutsi neighbors.

One has to push back further. There was a "Tutsi" threat – to the government, at least. It had its origins in earlier violence. In 1959 and again the early 1970s, there were pogroms against Tutsi which caused thousands of them to flee to Uganda. Some of them became allies of the Ugandan rebel leader Yoweri Museveni, as he worked in the 1980s to take over a state submerged in the chaos left by the dictatorship of Idi Amin Dada and his brutal successors. President Museveni was grateful for their assistance, but eager that they go home. The Rwandan Patriotic Army trained in Uganda, attacked Rwanda in 1990, and attacked more vigorously in 1993; whether their objective was to take over Rwanda or to be reintegrated into "their" country was in dispute. In 1994, mediators from inside and outside Africa tried to settle the conflict and devise a power-sharing arrangement that would provide security to both Hutu and Tutsi. That was why President Habyarimana took his fatal flight in April: he had attended discussions aimed at resolving the conflict. He may have been killed by "Hutu Power" extremists for fear that he would compromise and in order to provoke an already-planned slaughter. Within hours of the crash, the hunt for Tutsi had engulfed the capital, and it soon spread. Whenever local people and local officials weren't enthusiastic enough in their bloody endeavor, the Rwandan army stepped in to run the killing machine.

We need to push back further. The radio campaign did not build up hatred from nothing. Rwanda had been a Belgian colony since 1918, having been originally colonized by Germany at the end of the nineteenth century, then turned over to Belgium after Germany lost World War I. Belgian officials conceived of Tutsi as natural aristocrats, as less "African" than the Hutu. Only Tutsi were accepted as chiefs under colonial supervision; missionaries were more likely to welcome them into schools and convert them to Catholicism. Belgian officials decided that they needed to know who *was* Tutsi and Hutu, and so they classified people into one or the other and made them carry identification cards. It took work to turn difference and inequality into group boundaries, into ethnicity.

We can push back still further. German and Belgian understanding of Rwandan history was inaccurate, but it was not made up out of whole cloth. Rwanda, like other kingdoms in the Great Lakes of East Africa, was highly differentiated. There was much movement of peoples in Rwanda's fertile hills and a blending of people who lived by hunting and gathering, by keeping cattle, and by agriculture. Some, largely European, versions of Rwandan history have Tutsi pastoralists migrating as a people from the north and conquering agricultural peoples, but there is little evidence to support such a story. More likely, a variety of migratory streams intersected and overlapped, and as particular kinship groups claimed power, they developed their myths of origin and historical narratives to justify their power. Rather than a history of conflict following from the fact of distinction, social distinctions were a product of a complex history.

Several kingdoms developed in the area. Most royal families were Tutsi – although most Tutsi were not rulers – but royal men married women who were both Tutsi and Hutu, so that genetically the categories meant less and less, if they ever meant much at all. Wealthy people owned cattle, and the wealthiest claimed to be Tutsi, but many Hutu became cattle owners and many of them began to think of themselves and be accepted as Tutsi. The nearest English word to describe what Tutsi meant in pre-European Rwanda is "aristocracy" – but it was an aristocracy linked to ordinary people via marriage, cattle-exchange, and a common way of life. This does not mean it was an egalitarian society; the difference between owning many cattle and owning few was important. Nor was it a peaceful society. Violent conflict, however, rarely pit Tutsi against Hutu, but took place between rival kingdoms each of which consisted of both Tutsi and Hutu.

If we look back far enough, then, we see that "difference" is part of the story that led to April 1994, but we do not find a long history of "the Tutsi" in conflict with "the Hutu." Interaction *and* differentiation are both important. When did polarization become acute? The answer appears to be, in the 1950s, as the political structures of the colonial era unravelled. Belgian favoritism toward Tutsi, and particularly Tutsi chiefs, was increasingly complicated when Belgium began to be challenged on its own terms by Rwandans who had a western education, who were Christian, and who were asking why they should be excluded from a voice in their own affairs. Because schools had discriminated in favor of Tutsi, the anti-colonial movement began among people so classified. Belgium, and also the Catholic Church, began to favor Hutu, who were now alleged to represent an "authentic Africa" against the pretentious Tutsi. In 1957, a "Hutu Manifesto" accused Tutsi of monopolizing power, land, and education. The riots of 1959 were part an uprising of peasants with genuine grievances – who were most likely to be Hutu – and part ethnic pogrom. Belgium did little to prepare a peaceful transfer of political institutions into the hands of Africans. But French and British colonies were moving rapidly toward self-government and independence, and Belgium could not escape the trends – a topic which will be the focus of much of this book.

The independence of Rwanda in 1962 was for most Rwandans an eagerly sought moment of liberation from colonial rule. But many Tutsi feared that they would now become a minority group, in danger from a resentful Hutu majority, whose representatives had won the first elections. Many Hutu, on the other hand, feared that Tutsi were conspiring to keep by devious methods that which they could not retain through free elections. The pogroms and the elections chased Tutsi leaders from the political scene and created the first wave of Tutsi exiles.

The ensuing Rwandan regime, like many others in Africa, was highly clientelistic and focused on delivering state-controlled assets to supporters. Like other regimes of that era, it was ineffective and insecure, and it was thrown out in 1973 in a military coup led by Juvenal Habyarimana, who would remain in power until his murder twenty-one years later. This regime proved to be as corrupt and ineffectual as its predecessor, but it received considerable support from France and other donors. When export crop prices fell and the International Monetary Fund (IMF) made the government tighten its belt in the 1980s, government supporters felt they were not getting the spoils they deserved. Some groups tried to organize opposition, but Hutu extremists linked to Habyarimana scapegoated Tutsi and worked harder to exclude them from Rwandan society. Then came the invasion of a Tutsi refugee army in 1990, itself the consequence of past waves of killings and expulsions of Tutsi. The government army (aided by France) grew in response, and Hutu extremists instigated killings, organized local militias, and generated anti-Tutsi propaganda. International organizations tried in 1993 to engineer a peace settlement. Whereas some Hutu leaders, perhaps including Habyarimana himself, entered negotiations hoping that power sharing would ease a desperate situation, others were thinking of another, final, solution.

In the neighboring Belgian colony of Burundi, a similar power struggle within a similar social structure had taken place, but there it was a Tutsi minority who emerged on top. Large-scale killings occurred in Burundi, and there it was Hutu who were the main victims and who often became refugees. In both cases, the decolonization process brought to power governments that were insecure and anxious: in Rwanda led by a section of Hutu, in Burundi by a section of Tutsi. In both cases, oppressive government action and widespread anxiety were cross-cut by often close relationships across the Tutsi–Hutu divide and by uncertainty over who, exactly, was a Tutsi and who a Hutu. In the months before April 1994, the sowers of hatred still had work to do.

I have begun by looking back, step by step, to see the layers of historical complexity leading up to the events of 1994. We began with what might look simple (and did to most foreign journalists) – a tribal bloodbath, old hatreds coming to the surface. We have found something more complicated: a history of interaction as much as of distinction, and a murderous trajectory that was less a burst of ethnic enmity than a genocide organized by a ruling clique.

Let us look back into South African history, briefly now, but in more detail in chapter 6. One can trace the peaceful revolution of 1994 back to the founding of the African National Congress (ANC) in 1912 and find a durable thread: the belief that multiracial democracy was the ideal polity for South Africa. But the negotiated end of white power emerged not just from principled, democratic opposition, but also from a wave of violence that neither the ANC nor other African political groups could control, notably from the mid-1980s to the very eve of the 1994 election, as well as from a range of political movements, not all of which fit the liberal democratic mold. The white regime also turns out to be more complicated than simply die-hard racists from a by-gone era. The apartheid regime was pragmatic and sophisticated, and in the era when late colonial and independent governments elsewhere in Africa were striving – with mixed results – to achieve "development," it presided over the most thorough industrialization of any African economy, producing great wealth and a European standard of living for its white population. These South African pasts will not easily be consigned to history, for the linkage of wealth for some to the impoverishment of many remains very much a part of post-1994 South Africa, even if a portion of the once-excluded African population is now in a position of authority and affluence.

In 1940, segregation, denial of political voice, and economic disenfranchisement did not distinguish South Africa from colonial Africa. But in the 1960s, South Africa had become a pariah in much of the world. It took a great deal of political and ideological labor to make colonial domination appear abnormal and unacceptable to people who did not live under its yoke, and it was this process which began the isolation of South Africa's white regime. After 1994, the social and economic inequalities of South African society appear all too normal, and the question of whether the extremes of poverty and inequality throughout Africa will become a burning, world-wide concern, as did colonialism and apartheid, remains open.

Nothing in South Africa's past determined that it would one day be governed by a non-racialist, democratically elected party. When the ANC was founded in 1912, its program of peaceful protest, petition, and the evocation of democratic principles was one of several ways in which Africans expressed themselves. Alongside this liberal constitutionalist conception of freedom was a Christian one, profoundly influenced by a century of missionary activity, and part of that tendency, influenced by African-American missionaries, linked Christianity to racial unity and redemption. Others operated within the frameworks of Xhosa, Zulu, and other ethnicity-based African political units seeking, for example, to mobilize behind a chief who would represent the solidarity of what people perceived to be their community. By the 1920s, the back-to-Africa politics of Jamaican-born, US-based Marcus Garvey linked South Africa to a Black Atlantic world via black sailors who stopped in South African ports, while other versions of Pan-Africanism came out of educational and cultural linkages to African Americans. A single rural district in the 1920s might witness all these varieties of political mobilization.

Even as the ANC successfully linked its struggle to that of labor unions and militant city dwellers in the post-war years – and with renewed vigor in the 1970s – migrant workers with less permanent roots in the cities, often dependent on rural brethren and rural chiefs for access to land when they returned, sometimes espoused militant ideologies of "tribal identity." By the 1980s, the clashes were not simply between different ways of thinking about solidarity, but between different networks of people, rival organizations. In Johannesburg "comrades" – youth associated with the ANC – sometimes fought, with bloody consequences, "impis" – young men associated with the Zulu cultural/political organization Inkatha. In South Africa, as in Rwanda, "tribal" rivalries were not part of the landscape; they were a product of history, of the realities of ethnic connections and their manipulation by the South African regime. Much as one might think of racism as forcing all Africans into a single category and producing a united struggle which reached its successful climax in April 1994, the struggle generated rivalries as much as affinities, internecine killings as much as armed struggle against the apartheid regime.

Looking backwards from 1994, the peaceful election appears even more remarkable than it did at first glance. Elections do matter: they channel political action in certain ways, and if that in some sense narrows the possibilities of how people act together, it can discourage some of the more deadly forms of rivalry, too. But the history of how resources – land, gold mines, factories, urban real estate – got into the hands of particular people and the consequences of such unequal access is a deep one, and that history did not suddenly turn a new page on April 27.

## • The many Africas: locating a space

At any one moment, Africa appears as a mixture of diverse languages and diverse cultures; indeed, linguistically alone, it is the most varied continent on earth. It is only by looking over time that "Africa" begins to appear. But what is it that emerges? As a land mass, Africa goes from the Cape of Good Hope to the Nile Delta, embracing Morocco as much as Mozambique. But many people in that continental space, as well as most Americans and Europeans, do not think of it as unified, and make a clear distinction between "North Africa" and "Sub-Saharan Africa" or "Black Africa." The dividing line is often seen in racial terms: Africa is the place where blacks are from. The Ghanaian philosopher Kwame Anthony Appiah has posed the question of how one conceives of "Africa" if one doesn't accept the validity of classifying the world's population into racial groups – something biological scientists see as without basis. Africans are as different from each other as they are from anybody else, and it is only by elevating skin color to supreme importance that one can stipulate that Africans are a unique race. But can all of the people who live south of the Sahara Desert be considered a people, if not a race? Or does the fact that about a third of these people are Muslim mean that, after all, they should be classified together with their fellow Muslims of North Africa, whether or not the latter perceive themselves as Africans? Does the alleged strength of kinship ties among Africans, the widespread respect people from the Zulu to the Wolof give to elders and to ancestors, and the centrality of face-to-face social relations in village settings, define a cultural collectivity that is continent wide – and which has influenced peoples of African descent in Brazil, Cuba, and the United States? Or is what all Africans share with each other also shared with most "peasant" communities? Does what people call "culture" in Africa or elsewhere represent durable and shared traits or continually changing patterns of adaptation to new circumstances?

Appiah's answer does not depend on a correspondence between African cultures – however similar or different from each other – and skin color. He argues that the notion of Africa does in fact have a meaning, and that meaning is historical. From the sixteenth century, European slave-traders began to treat various African ports as places to buy slave labor and the physical features of the slaves served as a marker of who, on one side of the Atlantic, could be bought and who, on the other side, could be presumed to be enslaved.

But if Africa was first defined by the most horrific aspect of its history, the meaning of "Africa" began to change in the African diaspora itself. Enslaved people and their descendants began to think of themselves as "African," not just other people's property; they were people who came from somewhere. In the United States, some Christians of slave descent began to call themselves "Ethiopians," not because their ancestors originated from that part of Africa, but because it evoked Biblical histories of King Solomon and the Queen of Sheba. "Ethiopia" or "Africa" marked their place in a universal history. Later, some African-American intellectuals began to claim that the ancient Egyptians were black Africans, and that, via Egypt, Africa had contributed centrally to Greece, Rome, and world civilization. Whether the evidence supports such a contention, and the very issue of what "heritage" or "descent" actually means, are not what is at stake here. The point is that "Africa" emerged as a diaspora asserted its place in the world. This book approaches Africa as defined by its history: its focus is on the African continent south of the Sahara Desert, but in the context of the connections, continental and overseas, that shaped that region's history.

Studying networks that crossed the Atlantic Ocean, the Indian Ocean, and the Sahara Desert, or which criss-crossed the African continent itself, gives a different picture of Africa from the stereotypes of African "tribes." Muslim scholars in Sahelian West Africa crossed the desert to North Africa or went to Egypt and Saudi Arabia as students and pilgrims; similar Islamic networks extended down the East African coast and inland to Lake Victoria and Lake Tanganyika. Within Africa, some kingdoms or empires incorporated culturally diverse populations, sometimes assimilating them, sometimes allowing considerable cultural autonomy while demanding obedience and collecting tribute. In some regions, kinship groups recognized affinity with relatives living hundreds of miles away.

That there was cultural diversity is true; that cultural specificity sometimes crystallized into a sense of being a distinct "people" is to an extent also true. But distinctiveness did not mean isolation, and it did not extinguish interconnection, relatedness, and mutual influence. The cultural map of Africa is marked by gradations of difference and lines of connection, not by a series of bounded spaces, each with "its" culture, "its" language, "its" sense of uniqueness. To be sure, a political entrepreneur trying to organize "his" people to fight for their interests had some shared group feeling to draw on, but so too did a political or religious organizer trying to bring together people across short or long distances. Which tendency would prevail was a matter of historical circumstances, not something determined by a supposed African nature of racial unity or cultural distinctiveness.

In the mid-twentieth century, the political meaning of Africa could be defined in different ways. To a Pan-Africanist, the diaspora was the relevant unit. For Frantz Fanon, politics were defined by imperialism, and he deprecated the idea of black nationality in favor of a conception of the unity of people oppressed by colonization. When Gamal Abdel Nasser, president of Egypt, challenged British, American, and Israeli power in the Middle East, he became a symbol for many Africans of a truly national leader. In the 1950s, the shared struggle against colonial powers, for the building up of national economies, and for national dignity, gave rise to a militant conception of the "Third World" – neither capitalist nor communist, uniting Asia, Latin America, and Africa against "the North" or "imperialist" powers. Still others sought a specifically African unity, limited to the continent. Other political leaders divided themselves into ideological blocks and formed alliances with power blocks led by the United States or the Soviet Union.

Long-distance connections were not just a matter for political activists. Africans – seeking education, developing careers in the UN and other international organizations, or migrating to European economies which now wanted their labor in their own territories – became a presence in

Europe, the Soviet Union, and the United States. They sometimes interacted with indigenous inhabitants, sometimes formed relatively self-contained communities of origin, and sometimes interacted more intensely with other migrants of African descent.

But it would be a mistake to substitute for the misleading notion of an Africa of isolated tribes a picture of an Africa immersed in an infinite web of movement and exchange. Internally, Africa's population was spread unevenly over a large space, meaning that movement was possible but transport expensive. It paid to exchange high-value commodities not found in certain regions, but less so to build dense networks of varied forms of exchange and connection. African leaders could find places for their people to prosper, but there were other places where people could flee and survive, making it difficult for power to be consolidated and exploitation to be intensified, in contrast to Europe in the seventeenth through nineteenth centuries. Overseas exchanges tended also to be quite focused, most horrifically in the case of the slave trade. Specific centers of production – of gold or palm products, for instance – or specific trade routes – the ivory traders who connected the interior of East Africa with the coast – functioned very well. But what they did was to forge specific, focused linkages from inside Africa to economies outside of Africa, not to develop a diverse and dense regional economy. Colonial economies, after the European conquest, built their railways and roads to bring out copper or cocoa and send in European manufactured goods, and they directed the movement of goods, people, and ideas to the metropole, not outward to the world in general. Colonial regimes based much of their power on their ability to control key nodal points, such as deep-water ports, in a relatively narrow system of transportation and communication. Africans tried to forge their own kinds of linkages – from trade routes within the continent to political relationships with other colonized peoples – with at least some success, but when the colonial empires fell apart, African leaders also faced the temptation to strengthen their control of narrow channels rather than widen and deepen forms of connections across space. This is a theme to which I will return.

## The many Africas: marking a time

African historians sometimes divide the continent's history into "pre-colonial," "colonial," and "post-colonial" eras. The first and the last, in such accounts, are marked by the autonomy of African societies. The first was a period of kingdoms, empires, chiefdoms, village councils, kinship systems, and the last a period of nation-states, each with its own flag, passport, stamps, currency and other symbols of sovereignty, and its seat in the United Nations, its claims to regulate and to tax production and commerce within its borders.

The Nigerian historian J. Ade Ajayi called the middle period the "colonial episode"; others refer to the "colonial parenthesis." Ajayi's argument came directly from a nationalist conception of political life: he wanted to emphasize the direct connection of "modern" African states to an "authentic" African past, allowing the new rulers of Nigeria, Kenya, or Dahomey to assume the legitimacy of the kings and elders of the past. More recently, disillusionment with independent African governments has led some scholars to make the opposite point: that "the state" is a western imposition, a direct determination of the post-colonial by the colonial and a complete effacement of the pre-colonial.

In such arguments, history is not a dead past, but a basis for making claims that are very much of the present. But both sides, in trying to use a particular version of the past, may miss much of the past's dynamics. It may be that the ballot box is a "European" institution, but that does not mean that the way it is used in Ghana has the same meaning and consequences as the way it is used in Switzerland. Even if one can demonstrate that "kinship" is as important to present-day Tanzanians as it was to people who lived within such a space in the early nineteenth century, that does not mean that kinship groups mobilize similar resources or that their members seek similar ends. To leapfrog backwards across time – to find in the 1780s or the 1930s the cause for something happening in the 1990s – is to risk missing the way change lurches in different directions.

This book bridges one of the classic divisions of African history, between the "colonial" and the "post-colonial." It does so in part so that we can ask just what difference the end of empire meant, as well as what kinds of processes continued even as governments changed hands. Some argue that the end of colonialism meant only that the occupants of government buildings changed, that colonialism gave way to neo-colonialism. It is indeed essential to ask just how much autonomy the governments of new states – many of them small, all of them poor – actually had, and whether states from the North (the United States as well as the former colonial powers) and institutions such as international banks and multinational corporations continued to exercise economic and political power even when formal sovereignty was passed on. But one should not substitute a hasty answer for a good question.

One needs to examine as well the extent to which African political leaders, ordinary villagers, and city-dwellers took some of the assertions of colonizing powers and turned them into claims and mobilizing ideologies of their own. In the 1940s and 1950s, colonial governments claimed that their scientific knowledge, experience in running modern states, and financial resources would enable them to "develop" backward countries. Such claims were quickly turned into counterclaims: by African trade unions asserting that if the African worker is to produce according to a European model, he should be paid on a European pay scale and benefit from adequate housing, water supplies, and transportation; and by political movements insisting that if African economies were to be developed in the interests of Africans, it was only Africans who could determine what those interests were. One can thus follow the development idea from colonial project to national project and can ask if the national project reproduced certain aspects of the colonial one – such as the belief that "experts" should make decisions for others – and if the national project contributed to the building of new kinds of economic possibilities.

## Static visions of dynamic societies: colonial Africa in the 1930s

One striking feature of colonial societies on the eve of World War II was the extent to which colonial ideologues and officials imposed a static conception on societies in the midst of considerable change. What is, after all, a colony? Rule by conquering outsiders was not unique in either Africa or Europe: African kingdoms often expanded at their neighbors' expense. In Europe the territorial struggles and brutalities of two world wars, the dictatorial and racist regimes of Hitler and Mussolini, and the survival of dictatorships in Spain and Portugal into the 1970s suggest that democracy and self-determination were not something that came with being European. Colonial empires differed from other forms of domination by their effort to reproduce social and cultural difference. At some level, conquest implied incorporation: the loser had to be taught who was the boss and to behave accordingly. But colonial conquest emphasized that the conquered remained distinct; he or she might try to learn and master the ways of the conqueror but would never quite get there.

How enthusiastic European publics were for colonies was also not so clear, despite large colonial lobbies that tried to make empire fashionable. Jacques Marseille argues that it was the weaker French firms that lobbied for treating colonies as a protected zone for their benefit, whereas the strong ones favored more open markets and sometimes thought of colonization as risky adventurism. In England, mission lobbies favored a form of empire that gave space to Christian conversion and to encouraging Africans to become self-reliant small-scale producers. In France, proponents of the "civilizing mission" helped to reconcile people who believed in a democratic, secular state to the practice of empire, although they were often embarrassed by the sordid actions of fellow imperialists.

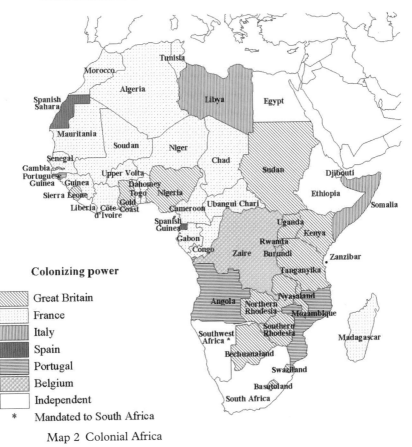

**Colonizing power**

- Great Britain
- France
- Italy
- Spain
- Portugal
- Belgium
- Independent

\*   Mandated to South Africa

Map 2  Colonial Africa

In both countries, proponents of conversion and civilization had to argue with their own countrymen, who looked at Africans as units of labor to exploit by whatever means possible. Although there were principled critics of empire from liberal and leftist camps, some people who saw themselves as progressive favored empire as a means to save indigenous peoples from their tyrannical rulers and backwardness, or even of bringing revolution and socialism to Africa.

Empire in early twentieth-century France and Britain was politically viable because some influential people wanted colonies very much and the others were not strongly convinced one way or the other. The two major colonizing powers insisted that each colony balance its books; they committed little in the way of metropolitan investment before the 1940s. In the 1920s, both rejected "development" plans that would have entailed the use of metropolitan funds, even though the plans promised more effective exploitation of colonial resources in the long run. Critics argued that money was best invested at home, but also that too much economic change in the colonies risked upsetting the state's unsure hold over African populations.

By the 1920s, the ambitious attempts of colonial rulers to remake African societies – by trying to turn peasants or slaves into wage laborers, for example – had petered out, as colonial governments realized the limits of their own power. Colonial officials were convincing themselves that their policy should not be to "civilize" Africans, but to conserve African societies in a colonizers' image of sanitized tradition, slowly and selectively being led toward evolution, while the empire profited from peasants' crop production or the output of mines and settler farms.

What was happening was far more complex than "timeless" African tradition. In the 1920s, West African cocoa and peanut farmers were migrating in order to open up new land, and Hausa and Dyula traders were covering long distances; Central African miners were moving back and forth between villages and mining centers; near cities like Nairobi, farmers were linking up to urban food markets as well as to markets in export crops. Yet European conceptions of Africa crystallized around the idea of "tribes," bounded and static. In part, this reflected the difficulties colonial regimes had in directing social change in ways they sought. In part, it was also a reaction to its opposite: many Africans, in the aftermath of World War I, in places like Senegal, Nigeria, and Kenya (and in a different way, South Africa) were acting like "citizens," insisting that their service in the war and their educational and economic achievements entitled them to a voice in their own affairs. The British conception of "indirect rule" and the French idea of "association", both emphasized in the 1920s, were attempts to put a positive light on colonial failure to remake African societies and to confine politics to tribal cages. Educated Africans and African workers became "detribalized natives," identifiable only by what they were not. During this period the expansion of ethnological research, and the increased interest colonial officials took in it, were part of this process of imagining an Africa of tribes and traditions.

During the world depression following 1929, the idea of tribal Africa carried all the more appeal, for the social consequences of economic decline could be sloughed off into the countryside. But with the beginnings of recovery in 1935, the edifice began to crack. That is where the next chapter will take up the story.

This was not the only way of imagining Africa in the 1930s. In Paris Léopold Sédar Senghor – born and raised in Senegal, educated in France in philosophy and literature, one of the best poets in the French language – met people of African descent from the Caribbean and acquired a new sense of what "Africa" meant within the French empire. Senghor, along with the West Indian writer Aimé Césaire, helped to found the "négritude" movement, which sought to capture and revalue a common cultural heritage, one which deserved a place in a broad conception of humanity. Senghor and Césaire used the French language for their own purposes and they fully participated in French institutions – when they saw their democratic potential. They refused the dualist conception of colonial ideology, which starkly opposed "civilized" and "primitive" people. But instead of reversing the dualism with a rejection of everything "European", they sought to reject dualistic thinking with a conception of cultural and political engagement that recognized the diverse heritages of humanity. Senghor's négritude, as critics within Africa pointed out, simplified, romanticized, and homogenized African cultural practices, and it only indirectly addressed issues of power and exploitation within colonized spaces. But it was one way of pointing towards a future that built on a painful past.

SUGGESTED READINGS

A full bibliography for this book may be found on the website of Cambridge University Press at http://uk.cambridge.org/resources/0521776007. It will be updated periodically.

General:
Freund, Bill. *The Making of Contemporary Africa: The Development of African Society Since 1800*. 2nd edn. Boulder: Rienner, 1998.
Mazrui, Ali, ed. *General History of Africa: Africa since 1935*. Berkeley: University of California Press for UNESCO, 1993.
Middleton, John, ed. *Encyclopedia of Africa South of the Sahara*. New York: Scribner's, 1997. 4 vols.

Rwanda:
Des Forges, Alison. *"Leave None to Tell the Story": Genocide in Rwanda*. New York: Human Rights Watch, 1999.
Newbury, Catherine. *The Cohesion of Oppression: Clientship and Ethnicity in Rwanda, 1860–1960*. New York: Columbia University Press, 1988.
Prunier, Gérard. *The Rwanda Crisis*. New York: Columbia University Press, 1996.

South Africa:
Evans, Ivan. *Bureaucracy and Race: Native Administration in South Africa*. Berkeley: University of California Press, 1997.
Lodge, Tom. *Black Politics in South Africa Since 1945*. Harlow, Essex: Longman, 1983.
Mandela, Nelson. *Long Walk to Freedom: The Autobiography of Nelson Mandela*. Boston: Little, Brown, 1994.
Posel, Deborah. *The Making of Apartheid, 1948–1961: Conflict and Compromise*. Oxford: Clarendon Press, 1991.
Seidman, Gay. *Manufacturing Militance: Workers' Movements in Brazil and South Africa, 1970–1985*. Berkeley: University of California Press, 1994.

# 2    Workers, peasants, and the crisis of colonialism

In the late 1930s and 1940s, colonial rule choked on the narrowness of the pathways it had created. Trying to confine Africans to tribal cages, seeking to extract from them what export products and labor it could without treating them as "workers," "farmers," "townsmen," or "citizens," colonial regimes discovered that Africans would not stay in the limited roles assigned to them. Instead, the constriction created the very sort of danger administrators feared. Urban unrest within a very rural continent challenged colonial governments; a small number of wage workers threatened colonial economies; a tiny educated elite undercut the ideological pretenses of colonialism; supposed "pagans" worshiping local gods and ancestors produced Christian and Muslim religious movements of wide scope and uncertain political significance; and commercial farmers – in a continent of "subsistence" producers – made demands for a political voice for themselves and opportunities for their children that colonial systems could not meet.

These problems came together in the years after World War II, a war which had exposed the hypocrisy of colonizing ideologies and the weakness underlying the apparent power of colonizing regimes. The conjuncture of diverse forms of African mobilization and the loss of imperial self-confidence produced a crisis in colonial policy and colonial thinking, a crisis that would lead governments, in something of a panic, to swing the pendulum toward an obtrusively reformist conception of their own role. But from the vantage point of the 1940s, it was not clear where all this ferment would end. To assume that diverse grievances, desires, and efforts at individual and collective advancement in the 1940s naturally converged on nationalist politics is to read history backwards from the triumph of African independence in the 1960s. This chapter looks at peasants, workers, and professionals, at husbands and wives, religious innovators and secular intellectuals during an uncertain, painful, but dynamic period of African history, to convey a sense of different possibilities and constraints and, above all, of different aspirations.

20

### The politics of the prosperous peasant

In parts of Africa, colonization drove rural dwellers into deepening poverty, sometimes as a deliberate policy to create "labor reserves" where people had little alternative to selling their labor cheaply, sometimes as a result of actions which made difficult ecosystems worse. Less familiar, but no less important, are the islands of peasant prosperity that grew up among cocoa producers in southern Ghana and western Nigeria, in the palm oil regions of coastal West Africa, in the peasant basin of Senegal, or in the coffee producing highlands near Mount Kilimanjaro in Tanganyika. In the case of cocoa, the colonial state deserved little credit, for the plantings came from missionaries and the initiative from Africans; but colonial governments were glad to have whatever export revenue they could get.

The cocoa farmers are revealing because they fit so poorly into the categories of agrarian society and agrarian politics deriving from European experience. They were not subsistence cultivators: they participated in markets for labor and for crops. But they weren't exactly capitalist farmers either. Starting in the late nineteenth century in southern Gold Coast and in the early twentieth century in southwestern Nigeria, cocoa production began among migrant farmers from the edge of the forest zone who negotiated access to good forest land from local land-possessing kinship groups. Planting cocoa bushes demands labor for years before any income comes in, and the migrant farmers used their kinship networks to survive. As cocoa took off, more distant migrants began to offer their labor services, and they were paid a mixture of wages and crop shares, but also established relations of clientage with the first generation of planters, who after a period of loyal service sometimes helped a worker become a planter himself.

So in its expansive phase, cocoa produced differentials of wealth; but this difference was not a line of class distinction. The wealthy planter cultivated supporters as well as crops, sponsored ceremonies, and otherwise strove to turn wealth into prestige. Rather than push agrarian capitalism to harsh extremes, the wealthiest planters were more likely to invest excess profits outside, in starting trading or transport companies or insuring their children's access to education and then to positions in the civil service. As good cocoa land became scarce in the late 1930s in the Gold Coast and in the 1950s in Nigeria, tensions developed: in the Gold Coast, older forms of association among young men sometimes challenged the combination of cocoa wealth and chiefly status. But nothing like a dichotomy of landlord versus landless developed, and cocoa wealth in fact deepened kinship and community, and the role of the "big man" in both regards.

3 Drying cocoa in Cameroon, 1970. Cocoa is the smallholder crop *par excellence* in forest regions of West Africa, planted first in the Gold Coast, then Nigeria, Côte d'Ivoire, and Cameroon.

The big man was, indeed, male. But the gender division of labor was not uniform. In some cash crop areas, males – by virtue of privileged linkages with missionaries, with colonial agricultural agents, or with traders – had privileged roles in the commercialization of agriculture, even if women were essential to food production and even if they relied on women's labor in export-crop production. But increased economic activity also enhanced possibilities for women. Among Yoruba cocoa growers, for instance, a complex division of labor within the household insured that women would get some of the earnings of cocoa production, and many used this to invest in marketing efforts. The West African "market woman" exercised considerable autonomy in her business and usually in her household; she often contributed to children's education. But men were much better positioned to use wealth to build up networks of clients and to enter the politics of the local chiefdom, and eventually regional and national politics.

Success did not mean acquiescence to a colonial order. African farmers had to do business with the big, monopolistic European import-export firms. In 1937–38 in the Gold Coast, wealthy cocoa planters organized a boycott of cocoa sales, using their considerable prestige and authority to enforce discipline over the smaller producers. They eventually forced the colonial government to intervene in cocoa marketing, replacing the European firms with a government marketing board and networks of African buying agents. The marketing board system (like a similar one in Nigeria) allowed, for a time, the government to appease concerns about the firms' price gouging, but African political leaders and colonial officials soon clashed over how the surplus should be used (see pp. 67–69).

In the coffee-growing zone of northern Tanganyika, relatively wealthy lineage heads and chiefs solidified their political control of the region, sometimes clashing with a colonial state that favored middlemen over producers. Among the Kikuyu of Central Kenya, peasant agriculture remained viable, despite land-grabbing by white settlers and extensive labor recruitment, and the region stood poised for bigger things when regulations forbidding Africans from growing coffee were ended in the early 1950s. Young men often worked for wages and saved enough to invest in agricultural improvements; chiefs used their connections with the colonial state to gain access to land and labor in the so-called reserves; women marketed beans and other crops in nearby Nairobi, where a growing working population needed foodstuffs. But in Central Kenya, the combination of accumulation of land by Africans with accumulation by white settlers produced a landless class, and this complex social system would explode in the late 1940s.

In Senegal, peanut cultivation since the mid-nineteenth century had been dominated by the leaders of Islamic brotherhoods. These leaders, called marabouts, pioneered new cultivation zones by settling with their student-followers (*talibé*), who benefitted from the protection of a collectivity and the knowledge, seeds, and organizational skill of the marabouts. After a period of working for a marabout, the *talibé* would go off on his own. The Mouride brotherhood in particular became wealthy and powerful, as a peanut-growing peasantry slowly emerged.

Colonial officials, when they added up their export figures, knew that African farmers – through a wide variety of social arrangements – were innovative and active producers. Yet in policy discussions such knowledge was eclipsed by a prior assumption of backwardness. In the 1930s, several governments set out to save the soil from bad African practices, and such clumsy interventions would lead to much rural opposition after the war. Later, colonial governments asserted the need for an "agricultural revolution" in Africa as if the evolution of the past century had not happened.

The widely uneven process of agricultural change in colonial Africa on the eve of World War II produced quite varied political consequences: the anger of the landless against both white land-grabbers and Africans who denied the implications of communal solidarity; the despair of the impoverished, who now needed cash to pay school fees and other "modern" expenses but who had less chance than ever of saving money; the grievances of the successful farmers against the low prices paid by middlemen or the authoritarianism of colonial agricultural agents; the patriarchal politics of chiefs who turned position into wealth and wealth into power; and the widening linkages that successful farmers developed via trade, investment, and the education of their children. Linkages put farmers in a position to act politically and also brought them into contact with the constricting arms of the colonial state. In the post-war era, rural political mobilization would come from several directions, from the moderately wealthy to the extremely poor.

## Intellectual linkages

One of the ironies of African political history is that the moment which seemed to open a new era in Pan-Africanist mobilization proved also to be its highest point. Politics would move in other directions.

Interwar Pan-Africanism had several elite versions. One was set out by African Americans and Caribbeans, who challenged imperialism for its racism on a world scale and argued that educated African Americans would be a vanguard leading Africa out of its wilderness; another was developed by Senghor and Césaire, whose idea of négritude posited a contribution of Africans to world civilization. Pan-Africanism also had its populist version, animated by Marcus Garvey, that spread via African and African-American sailors in African ports. There were London-based organizations, notably the International African Service Bureau, linked to Communist or Trotskyite anti-imperialist networks. All of these movements were angered when Italy invaded Ethiopia in 1935 and many tried to mobilize against this new imperialist conquest.

There were also regional linkages. Sierra Leone, where since the late 1700s the British government had sent "freed" Africans taken from captured slaving vessels and elsewhere, had been a dispersal point for African traders and missionaries, educated and Christian, who helped to build hybrid cultural forms along the West African coast from Gambia to Nigeria. Traders, artisans, lawyers, and doctors of Sierra Leonean origin lived in most port cities under British influence. In western Nigeria, many of these "returnees" – who had originally been taken from the region as slaves – pushed the diverse Yoruba peoples to see themselves as a "nation," while emphasizing that this nation needed the help of African missionaries to advance. Afro-Brazilians, also with western Nigerian roots, traded between Brazil and Nigeria and also helped to forge this diasporic "nation." Yoruba might be Christian or otherwise, wear English clothing or otherwise. Yoruba could be culturally self-aware, yet look outward, toward Africa as a whole and toward its diaspora, but to certain aspects of British culture as well. Just what practices were to be followed in, say, marriage, was very much in question.

In West African cities like Lagos, this self-conscious, professional, Christian class – linked by school ties, friendships, and business relations with similar people in other cities of British West Africa – was deeply affected by the exclusions of colonial rule. In the interwar years, the colonial government proclaimed that Christian Africans weren't the "real" Africans. It was out of this milieu, and the frustrations colonization imposed on it, that early political associations were built, notably the National Congress of British West Africa (NCBWA). The NCBWA was a regional organization of well-educated Africans who came together to write petitions, to publish journals and pamphlets, and to demand seats on the white-dominated advisory and legislative councils created by the British. The organization insisted that such people – not just the most seemingly "African" of chiefs – should have a voice in articulating affairs. Their political focus was not Nigeria, the Gold Coast, or Sierra Leone, but the cosmopolitan space that connected all of them.

In French West Africa, the equivalent population was much smaller; mission education was more limited. But in four cities in Senegal, colonized at an earlier date, inhabitants (called *originaires*) had most of the rights of French citizens. In 1914, a black African, Blaise Diagne, was elected to represent these cities in the legislature in Paris, breaking the political monopoly of mulatto and white citizens. During the war, Diagne realized how much France needed his help in recruiting soldiers, and he used this to entrench the citizenship rights of his constituents, to expand the voter rolls, and to build his own political machine. Later, the French administration tried to contain these gains by emphasizing the "traditional" nature of society outside the communes and the authority of chiefs within them; citizenship was proving to be too compelling an idea. But African representation had become an imaginable phenomenon, and even if most "subjects" stood no chance of becoming "citizens," they knew about the concept and could aspire to it. Later, politicians like Senghor would operate in a political milieu that emphasized both citizenship and négritude: the rights and obligations of the citizen of the French empire and the forms of expression and sensibilities of an African were not, according to Senghor, opposed or incompatible. Senghor summed it up with the expression, "to assimilate without being assimilated."

These were the politics of connections – regional and imperial. In the late 1930s, the people moving along these circuits moved in a more radical direction. It was partly a matter of generation, and younger men who saw their elders as stodgy; the West African Student Organization and the various "Youth Leagues" formed among African students and young city-dwellers made this point in the names they chose for themselves. It was partly the widening of the circuits: men like Kwame Nkrumah or Nnamdi Azikiwe were educated in historically black colleges in the United States, and they experienced at first hand the especially virulent forms of racism in the United States, as well as a variety of radicalisms among both leftist circles in England and African Americans in American cities. I. T. A. Wallace Johnson went from Sierra Leone to Moscow and took from that experience an internationalist concept of struggle against imperialism. Meanwhile, the increasing activism of a labor movement in African port cities and mines (see pp. 30–34) pushed a better educated stratum in a more militant direction.

These cosmopolitan, Pan-Africanist activists experienced the war in a cruelly contradictory manner. They were hearing constantly about the evils of Nazi racism and Nazi conquests and the virtues of "self-determination" for which Allies were fighting. The Italian invasion of Ethiopia had brought fascism to the African continent. Churchill's contention that the principle of self-determination applied to recent conquests in Europe but not older conquests in Africa was not convincing to many Africans. Some – Wallace Johnson for instance – experienced the war as repression, for they faced detention, censorship, and bans on political activity. All the while, great sacrifices were being made by colonized peoples in the name of the war effort.

So 1945, the moment of victory, took on a special meaning: political debts fell due, and the possibility that the anti-racist rhetoric of the Allies would take on a new meaning appeared open. It was a moment which Pan-Africanist leaders tried to seize, to formulate goals and strategy for confronting the entire edifice of colonialism across Africa and its diaspora. But it was also a moment in which the immediate issues of wages, housing, education, and crop prices were acute, all the more so because of the economic hardships of the war. The racism of colonial society was felt not only as the denigration of African culture and African life generally, but as hundreds of acts of discrimination felt day by day. And city by city, mining town by mining town, colony by colony, these issues were being pried open, both during the war and in the years immediately after it. The postwar moment presented opportunities to political and social movements to take on imperial administrations uncertain of their continued authority and aware of their need of Africans' contributions to rebuild imperial economies. A turning point had clearly arrived, but whether change would mean the reform of empire, the destruction of empire, or the forging of new kinds of political units was impossible to discern.

### Religion beyond the "tribe"

Intellectuals were not the only Africans who crossed frontiers. The image of "one tribe – one religion" that many westerners have of Africa never quite fit. Beliefs travelled somewhat different routes from people, so that networks of religious leaders or particular belief systems were often quite widespread. The influence of Islam and Christianity dates back before colonization, but colonial rule opened new spaces to Catholic and Protestant missionaries. Less obvious is the fact that colonization, despite the intentions of the colonizers, also resulted in a large-scale extension of Islam; something like a third of Sub-Saharan Africa's population are now Muslims. It is even less clear that the new religions have meant the eclipse of all elements of the old. Other forms of spirituality and other concepts of the supernatural are still capable of making sense of the world and articulating moral beliefs, and many of these coexist with the newer faiths.

The wide-ranging social changes that followed increases in communications and trade before colonization, as well as the increased mobility fostered by the colonial peace, labor migration, urban growth, and the commercialization of agriculture, brought people into contact with others whose beliefs were not necessarily the same. Robin Horton interprets the expansion of Islam and Christianity in the nineteenth and twentieth centuries as a consequence of people leaving the domain where "local" gods held sway. Monotheistic religion, he argues, travelled better and provided shared symbols, beliefs, and moral codes that permitted cooperation across distance. But indigenous religious practices could extend also in scale beyond ethnic borders, and prophets, healers, and spirit mediums were often regional, not local, figures.

Christianity brought the convert into relation with the colonizer's God. Some scholars argue that conversion to Christianity signified the colonization of the mind, that it went beyond changing a specific dimension of human behavior labeled "religion" to embrace the transformation of many personal practices, from mode of dress to design of houses to forms of initiation rites. Missionary practice focused on the individual, shunting aside kinship groups, councils of elders, age groups, and other collectivities basic to African social life. Missionaries often thought they were tearing down an entire complex of "savage" beliefs. What they accomplished is another question.

From early on, African converts refused to follow the missionary script. At times, African clerics took their flocks away from the heavy-handed control of white missionaries to build a church that was much like the one they had left. Autonomy movements also widened the range of doctrinal possibility by denying that being Christian meant acting like a

4 Rural Christian mission in the region of Ebolowa, Cameroon, 1949. Such missions not only added Christianity to the religious repertoire in much of Africa, but also provided education and an entrée into clerical and professional occupations. From the 1950s, government schools became more of a factor.

European. Polygamy was one source of contention, initiation rights another. Kikuyu converts and leaders who emerged among them in the late 1920s and 1930s, for example, founded schools and churches to enable them to maintain the Christian faith and educate their children, while rejecting what they saw as missionary efforts to destroy Kikuyu culture. They opened up a profound debate over what it meant to be Christian and to be Kikuyu. The "white man's religion" could serve instrumental purposes – acquiring literacy and other marketable skills at mission schools – or it could provide a mode of integration into a cosmopolitan world in a city like Lagos, a world linked to but not reducible to "colonial society." It could also give rise to movements, such as those in neighborhoods of Salisbury or along labor migration routes in Northern Rhodesia, that emphasized separation from the values and authority of colonizer, chief, and kinsmen. The diversity of the religious organizations that proliferated in Africa, and which proliferate to this day, suggests the many ways in which one could synthesize and combine different belief systems.

Many missionaries reduced African beliefs to "superstition," and while colonial era anthropologists were often more sympathetic, that field of inquiry tended to emphasize the holistic nature of beliefs and social organization within each "tribe." More recent thinking about religion in Africa emphasizes the flexibility, adaptability, and interactive nature of religious practices. Individuals juggled different belief systems and conflicting moral codes. The successful entrepreneur, for example, might be subject to pressure to distribute his wealth to kinsmen and neighbors, lest he be accused of having used occult forces to "eat" his competitors. Such an individual might in turn make use of his resources to acquire the services of diviners and other ritual specialists to bring the supernatural to his defense, or he might take up the practice of Islam to indicate his withdrawal from the moral domain of his demanding relatives and his entry into what he might see as a more inclusive moral universe. Ambiguity about collective norms was thus part of a tension over social relations: what did it mean for an individual to act within a kinship group or a village community, or to become involved in schools, wage labor, crop markets? What was the relationship between individual achievement and the social body? Accusations of violating community norms could be a leveling mechanism, directed against selfish accumulation, or it could be a distancing mechanism, marking marginal people as outside the circle of community.

These tensions were in turn linked to the uncertainty of life: people tried to understand why some children became sick and died while others survived; why some men had good jobs and bountiful crops while others suffered immiseration; why some women were at the center of strong family relations while others were not. A doctor might explain that malaria or bad water led to a high incidence of disease, or a union organizer might explain the devastating effects of colonial capitalism, but neither could explain why a particular individual suffered and another did not. In the late 1930s in Central Africa, a region facing agricultural degradation and disruptive forms of labor migration, witchfinding cults proliferated, crossing boundaries of language and culture to identify individuals who were transgressing social norms and whose fortune was seen to be based on their use of supernatural forces against others.

In the late 1930s and 1940s, in short, invention and innovation were characteristics of the religious field. The question of whether individuals would forge new sorts of connections across space and culture or seek to solidify the defenses of a perceived community against outside assaults affected much of Africa. But either position forced people to rethink the role of ritual specialists, to consider what they shared and where they differed with neighbors, and to ask what kinds of moral codes could govern their relationship with the familiar and unfamiliar people with whom they came in contact.

## Men and women, migrancy and militance

Between 1935 and 1950, numerous strikes enveloped ports, mines, railways, and commercial centers in Africa. The Northern Rhodesian copper mine strike of 1935 revealed that these were not routine industrial relations conflicts. Copper miners came from cruelly impoverished rural areas – deliberately bypassed by colonial transportation facilities – and they worked for periods of several months to several years. They were paid miserable wages, lived in inadequate housing, were disciplined arbitrarily, and had little chance to advance. Employers thought of mine workers as not really workers, but villagers temporarily earning money to meet fixed needs. They also thought of them as single males. In fact, many women came to mine towns to join husbands, and others, whether married or not, found in town the sort of autonomy their family members would not have allowed. Just as young men could use wage earnings to distance themselves from their fathers' control over the family resources they needed to marry, young women could find in town a partial escape from rural patriarchy. In the 1930s, lineage elders, chiefs, and colonial officials were trying to restrict women's movement to town, and extensive litigation in colonial courts over marriage produced a "customary law" more patriarchal and restrictive than what had been practiced before.

The 1935 strike in Northern Rhodesia spread from mine to mine and enveloped entire towns. Town workers struck alongside miners, and women were noticeably present at demonstrations. The strike was repressed and several miners were killed. A government investigatory commission – of the kind that would sit numerous times in the next decade – concluded that such events could best be forestalled by the more rigorous repatriation of miners whose contracts were up. The genii of African labor unrest had to be put back in the tribal bottle.

This was not an isolated event in the British empire. Between 1935 and 1938, a series of strikes, demonstrations, and riots in the British West Indies profoundly shook the government's sense of control. The strike wave washed ashore in much of British Africa as well, particularly in the form of general strikes that crossed lines of occupation and sometimes of gender: in Mombasa and Dar es Salaam in 1939; on the railway and mines in the Gold Coast in the late 1930s; on the Copperbelt once again in 1940. During World War II the strike wave continued, with major strikes, strike threats, and other menaces to economic continuity in Kenya, Nigeria, the Gold Coast, the Rhodesias, and South Africa.

The British government saw this for what it was – an empire-wide problem. The Colonial Office decided that further disorder could only be prevented if the colonial populations in Africa and the West Indies were provided with decent services and better job prospects. In the wake of the strikes – and only then – the Colonial Office got serious about a concept that had been occasionally debated: that a colonial government should undertake programs of "economic development" aimed at providing infrastructure to allow for larger and more efficient production. The Colonial Development and Welfare Act of 1940 was the first enactment by which Great Britain undertook to use metropolitan resources for programs aimed at raising the standard of living of colonized populations. Spending was to focus on housing, water, schools, and other social projects, mostly geared to wage workers, as well as on infrastructure and directly productive projects, with the idea that better services would produce a healthier and more efficient workforce, and above all a more predictable and less combative one.

The war, especially in British Africa, both increased the demand for African products – and hence the need for African labor – and reduced the availability of European manufactured goods Africans wanted to buy. It also delayed the implementation of the development act. And it led to escalating labor conflict, in Kenya, Nigeria, the Gold Coast, and South Africa most clearly. After the war, living conditions did not improve. There was a continued high demand for African labor, continued shortages of consumer goods and hence inflation, urban overcrowding, and poor services, all within a labor system that treated Africans as interchangeable units of labor power, whose desires to build a career or found a family did not need to be considered. There were more general strikes in Mombasa and Dar es Salaam in 1947, more strikes plus a serious urban riot in 1948 in the Gold Coast, a huge gold mine strike in South Africa in 1946, a railway strike in 1945 and a general strike in Southern Rhodesia in 1948, plus numerous other actions. These, as before, tended to spread throughout cities or even regions. Precisely because work forces were little differentiated, strikes tended to become mass actions. African workers, whether organized in trade unions (as in Nigeria or the Gold Coast) or not (as in Kenya or the Rhodesias), sensed that colonial regimes were economically and politically vulnerable. The strike wave was an embarassment to the ideological pretensions of colonial governments after the war, and a direct threat to the development drive.

In French Africa, with a weaker wage labor sector than in British Africa, the strike wave came late. The wartime experience was different as well, for the most economically advanced parts of it were blockaded by Britain and its allies after France fell to the Germans in 1940. The strike wave hit French West Africa in December 1945, when a two-month long strike movement began in Senegal. In 1947–48, the entire railway system of French Africa was shut down by a very well organized strike, and most of the system stayed out five months, until a settlement on terms relatively favorable to the African railwaymen was finally reached. The Belgian government gave no opening to any forms of labor (or political) organization, and with difficulty kept the lid on in urban areas, although it could not control rural ones. The Portuguese government relied extensively on forced labor, so that the reaction of angered workers was more likely to be desertion than strikes, and the Portuguese version of "development" relied heavily on white workers brought in from the metropole. Portugal avoided the strikes that beset French and British Africa in the late 1940s, but set the stage for a long and deadly struggle in the 1960s and 1970s.

South Africa, repressive as its government was, was also relatively industrialized, and urban workers were the vanguard of struggle for better living conditions for Africans in the war years and immediately thereafter. Its government for a time contemplated "stabilizing" its urban workers, but after the victory of the Afrikaner nationalists in 1948 the government opted instead for more rigorous policing of migration and massive expulsions of Africans from cities where they weren't properly registered as working. That nonsolution to the problem would also come home to roost at a later date.

The overwhelming majority of wage workers at this time were male. Scholars argue over why, in the early colonial period, wage labor was both short-term and masculine: men worked for limited periods in mines, railways, or cities, leaving their wives, children, and non-working relatives in villages. Some think of this as an effort on the part of colonial capital to lower labor costs, since a worker with a family in a rural setting could be paid less than the actual costs of keeping a family alive. But whatever the intention of employers, it is not at all clear that many Africans wanted to commit themselves to a life of wage labor, except where the extent of land grabbing undermined the ability of African agriculture even to produce a partial subsistence – most notably, in South Africa. Early colonial labor supplies depended on a mixture of pressures and incentives: the inadequacy (deliberate or otherwise) of marketing and transport facilities in rural areas, taxes that had to be paid in cash, and generational tensions within African societies that led young men to seek the autonomy of wage employment. Most zones of wage employment – the mines of Northern Rhodesia, for example – were surrounded by vast areas where food cultivation and periods of wage labor were both possible and necessary. But by the 1930s, the migratory labor system was criticized by officials and missionaries, for it seemed to produce stagnation in both town and countryside by both depriving agriculture of labor and initiative and leaving cities with a work force poorly trained and poorly socialized into industrial labor and little acculturated to city life.

In this situation, the chiefs and male elders in the labor recruitment areas of Central Africa tried to assert control over young women to insure that the "community" would not lose the labor and childbearing capacity of females and the money and labor of males. The migratory system required high levels of coercion to insure that males and females would be at work when needed and away from town when not wanted. In South Africa, the coercion was rigorously enforced; men (and women starting in the 1950s) were required to carry passes so that migration could be policed. In Southern Rhodesia, women were not legally permitted to be in cities unless they could prove they were legally married to a man who was entitled to be there (or, in some cases, were themselves employed and living in supervised settings). Kenya had a pass law, too. Such restrictions were a focus of outrage and political organization in the post-war years.

But even in the face of such harsh policing, African urban life in South Africa, the Rhodesias, and Kenya proved to be impossible to control, and women asserted their own place within that space; male migration created occupational niches for women, including cooking, beer-brewing, and prostitution. In West African cities, especially those like Lagos or Dakar which had older traditions of urban life, established populations able to defend their rights to urban property, Africans who played active roles in trade, and sometimes well-established African professional and artisanal classes, this kind of controlled system was out of the question. Officials still had to face the presence of "casual" laborers moving in and out of short-term jobs and of certain quarters of town where people could engage in all sorts of activities, legal or otherwise, without government control. By the 1940s, what colonial officials did not want to think about – an urban society, in which men and women, adults and children were trying to put together a life – had become a reality. Colonial policing and colonial neglect only made such a life harder – and potentially more explosive.

So when strikes swept from the Copperbelt to Accra and Mombasa, colonial officials wondered if the migrant labor system was really in the best interest of colonial economies, and if the the presence of a "mass" African population moving into and out of cities without being fully integrated into an urban social fabric was in the best interest of colonial societies. They could, as in the 1935 Copperbelt strike, pretend that the problem would go away, or they could try to shoehorn the labor question into the "development" question, and hope that a little capital investment and a little urban planning would solve it. A third colonial reaction was more complicated: a realization that how workers and their families lived would affect both how efficiently they produced and how orderly and predictable they were likely to be.

The social engineers coined a new word: stabilization. It was not exactly "proletarianization" as used in Europe, for officials still did not see wage labor enveloping all of Africa. Stabilization meant separation: creating an urban working class capable of living in the city and producing a new generation of workers in the city, independent of the "backward" countryside. It meant paying Africans more – "family wages" or "family allowances." In the British Copperbelt, the mining companies began to proclaim such a policy after the second major strike in 1940, but scholars now argue that the workers had begun to stabilize themselves even before. In the port of Mombasa, officials began to talk about stabilizing the dock labor force, on which the entire import-export economy of Kenya depended, after the 1939 strike, and between 1944 and 1954 they actually began to do it: thus turning daily ("casual") labor into steady, long-term work. These policies took colonial regimes into the daily intimacy of what work and urban life were all about: patterns of residence, conflict over work regimes, contentious issues about discipline, delicate relations between unions and managers.

I will return later to consider the actual effects of such policies. Suffice it to say for now that British and French labor policy did something to redirect labor militance, but not to tame it. The urban mass would become less of a factor, the labor union more. But the fact that colonial regimes were driven for the first time to take the labor question seriously is itself crucial.

Cities would be crucibles of social, cultural, and political change throughout the post-war era. It was not that they were intrinsically dynamic while rural villages were passively culture-bound. In cities, whatever happens in one street or neighborhood occurs in close proximity to everything else. Density has its consequences – and for a colonial regime, its dangers. The juxtaposition in cities of respectable mission converts with young male wage laborers, of established merchant families with women seeking autonomy, and of migrant workers with the offspring of urban households was becoming increasingly volatile. The mix changed not only as urban populations grew in the 1940s, but also as women became a larger part of the population. The growing differentiation and interaction among urban Africans took place in proximity to facilities intended for white residents and where the institutions and symbols of power stood, with all of their implications of possibilities and racial exclusions. Associational life – new "sociabilities", as a scholar noted at the time – was getting richer and more varied, built around occupational and residential affinities, around connections to common regions of origin, around churches or mosques or indigenous religious institutions, around mutual aid needs of various sorts, around the collective interests of traders or workers, around new forms of music and artistic creation. Most important was the mix of urban-born and migrant youth, a category marked, as Rémy Bazenguissa-Ganga puts it, by its "availability" – a vibrant, volatile force that could be channeled in different directions.

### Black men and women in a White man's war

World War II appears in the middle of a period of transformation for the African continent. Europe's war lasted from 1939 to 1945. Africa's struggle began earlier and lasted longer. The era of general strikes, starting first in British Africa, lasted from 1935 to about 1948. There was also conflict in rural areas over soil conservation and other heavy-handed interventionist policies. The world war weakened European powers for a short time militarily, and for a longer time economically. It fundamentally shook their self-confidence; and it destroyed the assumptions that gave colonial ideologies their fragile coherence.

At first, warring powers tried to use colonies as they normally did – as a resource. France was already stepping up pressure, above all through forced labor, on Africans before its short-lived participation in the shooting war began. When France fell in June 1940, its African empire split, a clear sign of the tenuousness of metropolitan control. The French administration in West Africa accepted the Vichy regime, which was collaborating with the Nazis, while French Equatorial Africa (not coincidentally administered by a black Governor-General, Félix Eboué, born in French Guyana) refused to take orders from Vichy and insisted that the London-based "Free French" of General Charles de Gaulle was still France. Both sets of colonies tried to mobilize colonial resources for their respective sides; neither was able to act very effectively, Equatorial Africa because the French had already stripped it of much of its assets (hardwood, rubber) and done little to develop others, West Africa because the Allies blockaded it. Later, the Allies' reconquest of French territories began in France's North African territories, and French West Africa, once its government realized who was winning the war, abandoned Vichy in favor of the Free French. De Gaulle recognized the African colonies' contribution to liberating France and that gratitude and self-interest required a re-examination of French colonial policy – a subject to which I will return.

Great Britain lost many of its Asian colonies, with the enormous exception of India, to Japan and relied more than ever on Africa for tropical products. It used African troops in Asia and needed African labor power still more. In Kenya and in the Rhodesias, it revived forced labor for crops which profited settlers and corporations, but which were held to be in the national interest. Even where work was voluntary, Great Britain tried as much as possible to restrict imports into colonies, even though it was intensifying export production.

One result was the accumulation of surpluses: the colonies' budgets were credited with revenue, derived from exports, which they were not allowed to spend. Funds accumulated in London banks and would become a source of contention after the war as African political leaders demanded that the surpluses be spent in the interest of those who had produced them. The war years offered some opportunities to African agricultural producers; at least they were receiving money for their exports, and they were not dependent on food imports. And the war economy was even more profitable for white farmers. But for urban workers these years were hard; imports were scarce, and nearby farmers could make more money producing export items than food for local markets. Hence the wartime strike wave described earlier in this chapter. The pattern continued after the war, for Great Britain's factories were so badly damaged by German bombing, its debt to the United States was so large, and its inability to meet the needs of its domestic population – which, unlike that of their African colonies, voted in elections – was so great that basic consumer goods like cloth remained in short supply in the colonies, and Britain's intention to undertake development projects was constrained by the scarcity of steel and concrete. Inflation continued, as did the strike wave.

Both Great Britain and France thought they would regain control through their new concept, "development". Post-war imperialism would be the imperialism of knowledge. The British Colonial Development and Welfare Act of 1940 was authorized at a higher spending level in 1945; the French passed their Investment Fund for Economic and Social Development (under the French acronym FIDES) in 1946. Both development programs, and the new thinking about African labor described above, entailed a re-imagining of African society and culture, and indeed of western knowledge itself.

Up to World War II, "scientific" theories of racial inequality, policies to curb the fertility of people whose genes were supposed inferior or unhealthy, and sharp cultural distinctions between the "primitive" and the "civilized" were controversial but within the norms of acceptable debate. Hitler gave racist ideologies and racist theories a bad name. And the widely publicized Atlantic Charter, an Anglo-American agreement that opposed the Allies' belief in "self-determination" to the Nazi and Fascist wars of conquest, left Africans wondering why it did not apply to them. Once the French and British publics had to think about why democratic states were worth defending, the kinds of questions previously raised by a colonized intelligentsia acquired a new pertinence.

Developmental colonialism was in part a response to the narrowing grounds on which a convincing case could be made for the exercise of state power over people who were "different." But developmental ideologies implied that difference would over time be eclipsed. When would the time come to declare that the backward were sufficiently developed to strike out on their own? Who was to judge whether the "tutorial" power was acting in the interest of its charges rather than for its own benefit? Such questions were not new, but they became much more immediate during the war.

European leaders would not get the chance quietly to think through their doubts. In this atmosphere of ideological uncertainty, they faced an escalation of demands coming out of the African continent itself. The demands were not, at first, focused on taking over the state. But they were focused on what states actually did: on education, on taxation, on investment in social services and productive resources, on judicial systems, and on the question of who was to participate in the making of vital decisions.

SUGGESTED READING

A full bibliography for this book may be found on the website of Cambridge University Press at http://uk.cambridge.org/resources/0521776007. It will be updated periodically.

Cooper, Frederick. *Decolonization and African Society: The Labor Question in French and British Africa*. Cambridge: Cambridge University Press, 1996.

Higginson, John. *A Working Class in the Making: Belgian Colonial Labor Policy, Private Enterprise, and the African Mineworker, 1907–1951*. Madison: University of Wisconsin Press, 1989.

Killingray, David and Richard Rathbone, eds. *Africa and the Second World War*. New York: St. Martin's Press, 1986.

Moodie, T. Dunbar. "The Political Economy of the Black Miners' Strike of 1946." *Journal of Southern African Studies* 13 (1986), 1–35.

Pearce, R.D. *The Turning Point in Africa: British Colonial Policy, 1938–1948*. London: Frank Cass and Co., 1982.

# 3 Citizenship, self-government, and development: the possibilities of the post-war moment

Looking backward from the 1960s, it is easy to see why the story of post-war politics is often told as if everything led to a single, inevitable outcome: national independence. It is more difficult to see what somebody in 1945 or 1947 – say, a young, politically-minded African returning from higher education abroad – aspired to and expected to attain. But what about a family who had just settled in a mining town after years of periodic separations, and who missed the familiar sociability of village life but perhaps not the constraints of their elders, and hoped that their children could obtain an education? Or a farmer, selling his cocoa in the booming world market, aware that colonial marketing boards were holding onto much of what his crops earned, and wondering if his children would continue to help with the harvest?

Africans faced the constraints and the humiliations of a colonial state, but they were, above all, human beings trying to survive, form relationships, find opportunities, and make sense of the world. They cannot be reduced to stick figures in a drama with two actors, colonizer and colonized, or a story with one plot line – the struggle for the nation. What is striking about the years after the war was how much seemed possible.

This chapter is about political imagination, constraint, and conflict in the post-war decade. It examines colonial imaginations, for the rulers of Great Britain and France most notably did not think in 1945 that their empires were about to end, but they did realize that they would have to think in new ways about their domains. Their illusion was that they thought they could control political evolution. In fact, the most reformist and flexible empires, those of France and Britain, collapsed the first; the most obdurate, Portugal's, survived the longest. The dynamics of reform and mobilization were crucial. In the late 1940s African political and labor movements saw that they had an opportunity, but what they saw as a goal in 1945 was not where they ended up twenty years later.

This chapter is built around three examples that illustrate the widening and narrowing of possibilities after the war. The first is French Africa. Officials believed that the slow admission of Africans into the category of citizen would preserve the unity of the French empire. In fact, the goal of "Greater France" turned into a trap, as African social and political movements used the language of imperial legitimacy to claim all the social and economic entitlements of metropolitan citizens.

The second example is that of the Gold Coast, where Great Britain, after the war, seemed to be pursuing an opposite strategy. British leaders claimed that their policy had long been to bring colonial subjects first into local government and then slowly, as they proved worthy, into territorial "self-government" within the Commonwealth. But the government was unable to define political change in such terms: urban youth and parts of organized labor joined a radical intelligentsia in quickly pushing for African self-government at the central, not the local, level, favoring street demonstrations, general strikes, and consumer boycotts over the orderly politics of petition. What in 1945 looked like Britain's model colony, moving towards development and self-government, became within a remarkably few years the place from which a rapid devolution of power to other colonies would spread.

Finally, there is South Africa. In its whites-only electoral system, a serious debate occurred over issues faced in colonial Africa as well, including whether Africans not actually living in isolated tribes had become a potentially useful part of a largely urban, partly industrial economy. But the decision that emerged was different: the 1948 election brought in a government that policed migration ever more vigorously, expelling millions of Africans from cities, clamping down on union and political activity, reinforcing urban residential segregation and the exclusion of Africans from agricultural land. By the 1950s, it was taking the watchword of self-consciously progressive colonial rulers – development – and turning it into a manifesto for maintaining distinct and grotesquely unequal destinies for South Africa's supposed races: "separate development."

These cases are illustrative; the variations are numerous. Each one, in different ways, shows how social movements pioneered different forms of collective mobilization and affinity, not just "nationalism." African politics did not develop in an autonomous world, but via interaction and conflict, and the struggle itself reshaped the kind of political projects that were or were not imaginable. The turning of the French and British toward a development-minded colonialism – the desire to expand empire resources while legitimizing colonial rule – became the basis for a profound engagement of African and European actors, which in turn changed the meanings of "development," of "citizenship," and of "self-government."

In the final sections, I will examine other kinds of collectivities whose political possibilities were pushed aside in the conjuncture of the late

5 Charles de Gaulle giving opening speech to the Brazzaville Conference, January 30, 1944. As World War II neared its end, colonial officials at the conference reaffirmed the unity of French territory while
promising economic, social and political progress to its inhabitants. Far
from averting dissent, this move opened the door to escalating claims to
equality within the French Union.

1940s and 1950s. And I will examine where colonial states tried to draw
the line and what forms of politics they could try to exclude. But one
should begin to study the post-war years by asking what African intellectuals, workers, traders, and farmers could imagine at the time and what
they did to turn imagination into action.

## Citizens of empire: French Africa, 1944–52

As German defeat became inevitable and the liberation of mainland
France a matter of time, Free French forces installed their government in
newly reconquered Algeria. The colonial establishment proclaimed that
the colonies had saved the metropole and that the significance of "Greater
France" would have to be rethought. In February 1944, in the presence
of General de Gaulle and in the absence of colonial subjects, leading officials met at Brazzaville to plan the future. They divided African society
into two categories, the *évolués* (western educated Africans, literally the
"evolved ones") and *paysans* (peasants). Workers, traders, and artisans

barely existed in the official mind, and the main labor issue on the agenda was forced labor, whose evils were fully acknowledged but which was seen as so essential, given Africans' supposed work habits, that the officials gave themselves five more years to phase it out. *Evolués* would be incorporated into French institutions; their numbers were too small to pose a threat. Peasants would benefit from lower taxes and the abolition of forced labor, and Africans growing crops within their own communities would make the empire more productive and raise the standard of living of its subjects. A new development initiative would reduce labor needs in transport. Industrialization would take place slowly and prudently. Although this program seemed to resemble the policy of indirect rule which British officials were then repudiating, officials accepted that within the small modern sector, Africans could participate like anyone else – as students, civil servants, workers, and voters. These officials were uncompromising on one point: the French empire would remain unified and permanent.

In the spirit of Brazzaville, France allowed a limited number of Africans to vote in elections in 1945, with separate voting and separate representatives for "subjects" and "citizens." About twenty Africans took their seats in the legislature in Paris; an absurdly low number in relation to the population of the colonies, but nonetheless a significant factor. They could say things about colonial policy that would otherwise be covered up; their votes could make a difference when metropolitan deputies were evenly divided (as they often were); and these deputies (like their foes representing white settlers) cared passionately about colonial issues, whereas most politicians were indifferent. Settlers had support on the legislature's right, the African deputies on the left, but often as well among a swing group of "social Catholics," centrists who sought to overcome conflict and combat communism by promoting good wages, family welfare, and social harmony. There have been endless debates over whether these constitutional reforms represented progress or hypocrisy. Both sides miss the point: the reforms meant no more and no less than how they were used.

In the spring of 1946, Léopold Senghor, Lamine Guèye, Félix Houphouët-Boigny, Aimé Césaire, and other deputies were instrumental in the passage of two crucial measures. The first, known as the Houphouët-Boigny law, definitively ended forced labor in all French colonies, three years ahead of the schedule advanced at Brazzaville. The deputies' initiative had its roots in rural Africa: Houphouët-Boigny's support in the Côte d'Ivoire came from both the people victimized by the forced labor recruitment imposed by government-sponsored chiefs to supply white farmers and the African cocoa farmers denied any such assistance. The second, the Lamine Guèye law, abolished the distinction between subject and citizen, and with it the demeaning judicial regime that gave French district administrators arbitrary power to punish non-citizens. The first measure was barely debated: merely reminding the world that a system akin to enslavement existed in French Africa rendered it indefensible. The second was a more complex measure, and its discussion was part of a wider debate on exactly how people in colonies would participate in affairs of the empire. It was a vivid affirmation that France was serious about treating the empire as a unity, while reserving to the Paris legislature – with its large metropolitan majority – the right to determine just what kinds of institutions would actually function at the level of each territory within Greater France. If Great Britain emphasized the specificity of each colonial territory, making it harder to reform the inequities of colonial societies, France insisted on centralized authority, in which Africans would be given a minority voice at the center, while institutions in each territory remained weak.

It was not the legal definition of citizenship which mattered so much as the language in which citizenship was discussed. Citizenship arguments carry particular power because officials hope that citizenship entails obligations as well as rights, that it gives rulers legitimacy at the same time as it gives people voice. And leading French officials hoped that their propaganda might really be true: that Africans, following French models, would prove to be orderly participants in politics and steady contributors to economic growth.

The dialogue across the colonial divide was not limited to the Paris legislature. In Dakar, Senegal, the labor movement – also in 1945 and 1946 – opened up an important space for making claims and reconfiguring politics. After the war, the demand for urban labor was high, but wartime and post-war inflation produced widespread misery. Unions suppressed by Vichy came back into operation under the less repressive post-war regime. In December 1945, laborers in the port of Dakar went on strike, and in January the strike spread throughout the city, embracing unskilled laborers, literate clerks in banks and businesses, skilled workers in the metal trade, and civil servants. For twelve days, Dakar was shut down by a well-organized general strike, and other cities were engulfed as well. The movement transcended the workplace: women participated and demonstrated; market sellers refused to supply food to whites; and daily mass meetings were held to keep the entire public involved.

French officials were unable to regain control. Finally, a new sort of expert came to Dakar, a specialist in labor issues, and he set about dealing with this unprecedented strike as if it were an ordinary industrial dispute, negotiating with each group of workers and making major concessions. Laborers got large wage increases, and civil servants won family allowances, a victory of particular symbolic importance, for it implied that the needs of African families were those of any French family. Throughout the strike, the slogan of the workers had been "equal pay for equal work"; they did not literally achieve equality, but they did much to show that, politically, African workers and their families would have to be considered in the same terms as French workers and families.

The 1946 strike revealed that the distinction between citizen and subject had broken down: both African "citizens" – from the old colonial cities on which citizenship rights had been bestowed – and African "subjects" – migrants from the interior – had participated side by side. The long railway strike of 1947–48 over all of French West Africa drove home the lesson that African workers would insist not only on equality, but on having a say about all dimensions and details of their working conditions.

From 1947, labor unions made the passage of a unified labor code, which made no distinction based on the race or origins of the worker, their prime political objective. The stakes of each provision were high and the debate dragged on. As it reached a climax, a solidly organized one-day general strike across all of French West Africa increased the pressure. African deputies in Paris played key roles in making sure that other deputies understood the dangers of compromising the principles of universal applicability and equality of wages and benefits.

If unions wanted a code to guarantee workers' rights, officials wanted it as a clear map of what was negotiable, what procedures would be, and what sanctions could be used against violators from either side. Both the government and the labor movement had before their eyes visions of a "modern" system of labor relations, with one party emphasizing stability and predictability, and the other workers' entitlements and the dignity of labor. When at long last the code became French law in 1952, it guaranteed all wage workers in the private sector a forty-hour work week, paid vacations, the right to organize and to strike, and other benefits. No sooner was this battle won than unions began fighting for family allowances for all private-sector wage workers (African public employees having already won equal benefits), and this was achieved in 1956.

Here was an argument conducted by an African labor movement and elected representatives, in the language of citizenship, universality, and entitlement – the conceptual apparatus of the modern state – and which put money into workers' pockets. Colonial officials' dream of the African as universal worker never did come to pass – workers on the job and in their homes had their own ideas about how to live and work – but this was, for unionized workers, a very useful fiction.

What this account leaves out is also important: the debate applied only to wage workers. It excluded "customary workers," those whose labor took place within the nuclear or extended family. It was ambiguous about the kind of relations which many agricultural laborers had with landowners, since much of their compensation came not in wages but as rights to land and crops as well as to the patronage of the landowner. It excluded the urban artisan, who gathered apprentices. Politicians, union leaders, and employers were content to leave them out of the 1952 code; such forms of work were too pervasive, too steeped in social relations that bureaucrats did not understand, and in some cases too vital to the patron-client relations that African politicians had with, for example, rural landowners. Few women were in wage employment, whereas numerous women were in unpaid and unregulated domains of the economy.

The reformed wage-labor sector stood in uneasy contrast to an un-known, unregulated, and unreformed area, where far more people lived and toiled. Officials wanted to "stabilize" the one and feared that the other would overwhelm whatever progress they made. This division between a protected wage-labor class and everybody else would come back to disturb the governments and societies of independent Africa.

The development program, using the tax revenues of France, aimed at reaching rural as well as urban Africa, and at bringing the range of services characteristic of a modern state, from schools to piped water, to the colonies. Complications soon developed. The old infrastructure was so bad that the equipment brought in for roads, buildings, dams, and other projects quickly clogged ports, railways, and storage facilities. Private investment did not come forth as expected, leaving many colonies with high-cost, poorly functioning facilities that were still not producing the expected growth in production.

Even in the midst of a large-scale expansion of agricultural and mineral exports driven by high prices in western markets, development investment as such was at best a partial success. Most important, colonial regimes set a largely unmeetable standard for the economic side of the development project: Europe had made itself the model for what a developed economy should be. Hence, one can see in the archival records from the 1950s the disappointment of officials with the development effort even when statistically the results, measured in exports, wages, and farmers' incomes, were not so bad. The problem was with the colonial development concept itself, particularly its detachment from what was happening in the countryside and cities of Africa.

Development, like labor, was a concept around which demands could and were being formulated. French officials could not simply dismiss such claims, for their own legitimacy depended on the concepts of citizenship and development. Most crucially for politics in the late 1940s and 1950s, the state's key role in access to resources encouraged participation in its institutions. African leaders would become deeply involved in the developmentalist state even before they acquired power.

One can distinguish different political situations. In Senegal, citizens of the four original colonial settlements had since 1914 been represented by a black African in the Paris legislature. Suppressed during the war, electoral politics re-emerged with renewed vigor afterward. There was now more at stake, notably seats in legislative bodies representing the territory, French West Africa, and France as a whole. A distinguished lawyer from one of the four communes, Lamine Guèye, and the brilliant scholar-politician Léopold Senghor, from an interior village, became Senegal's deputies in Paris.

Here the old citizenship, restricted to the four communes, burst its bounds. After May 1946, subjects became citizens and the voting rolls leapt from 45,000 to 130,000; they would steadily grow until universal suffrage was achieved in 1956. Senghor brought the former subjects into Senegalese politics. His entry into the elite was via his extraordinary achievements in education. Initially an ally of Lamine Guèye, he made his own move in 1948, founding the Bloc Démocratique Sénégalais (BDS). Although a Christian himself, Senghor slowly worked through the leaders of Islamic brotherhoods to forge a rural political machine. The marabouts were themselves masters of networks, and offered to their disciples both membership in a religious community and access to the resources of the entire network. This, not the blind obedience of *talibé* (follower) to marabout, was crucial. The brotherhoods crossed lines of region and ethnicity, which were in any case blurry in most of Senegal. Since the early days of Senghor, Senegal has had an exceptionally stable political life because the vertical relationship within the religious field meshed well with the role of political patronage in the secular world.

The Christian Senghor captured the Muslim countryside. He did the same with other constituencies, including to an extent with labor, whose leadership rather than its rank and file was the object of his attention. In 1951, his party soundly defeated Guèye's, and Senghor was in position to guide Senegal through the complex politics of the 1950s.

In the Côte d'Ivoire, Houphouët-Boigny also built a political machine early and came to be an undisputed father of the nation. He came from a chiefly family, earned a medical degree, and became a successful cocoa farmer. After the Vichy regime, which had been especially coercive in the Côte d'Ivoire, fell apart, he put together an organization of African cocoa farmers, the African Agricultural Society. This was part lobby group, part labor recruiting network (the government having refused to help African farmers although it supplied forced labor to whites). When the forced labor controversy heated up after 1944, the African Agricultural Society not only mobilized rural constituencies against it but also proved to the government that there were alternative ways to get work done. Its labor recruitment system, and the tenancy arrangements it used to attract people from the arid and populous north to work for African planters in the cocoa belt in the south, proved crucial. Over time, the white settlers were marginalized, while the Ivoirien cocoa planters would make this colony the wealthiest in French West Africa.

The Society was also the vehicle for Houphouët-Boigny's election to the French legislature in 1945, and he repaid his constituents by sponsoring the act which abolished forced labor. Political leaders from most French colonies met in 1946 in Bamako, in the French Soudan, and decided to found a political party for all of French Africa, the Rassemblement Démocratique Africain (RDA, or the African Democratic Assembly). The fledgling groups within each territory constituted themselves as branches of the RDA; the Ivoirien one was called the Parti Démocratique de la Côte d'Ivoire (PDCI). The branches exercised considerable autonomy, but the RDA maintained a degree of common action and publicity and acted as a unit in the Paris legislature, where it formed a marriage of convenience with the French Communist Party (despite the property-owning credentials of much of its leadership). In territories like Côte d'Ivoire and Guinea, the RDA became the dominant African party; in others, like Senegal, it attracted working-class support but could not match the machine put together by Senghor. RDA ideology, Siba Grovogui argues, was cosmopolitan, countering the French-centered model of citizenship in the "French Union" not with a "national" or "African" alternative, but with an attempt to work across territorial boundaries against international political inequality.

After 1947, when the French government lurched to the right, officials began to crack down on the Ivoirien RDA. The administration provoked a series of clashes with PDCI militants in rural areas. French security could not break the RDA, but they could harass it. Finally, in 1950 François Mitterand, Minister for Overseas France, negotiated with Houphouët-Boigny for the RDA to break with the Communist Party. In return Mitterand ordered the repression turned off. Houphouët-Boigny later took a seat in the French cabinet, and he insisted that the RDA steer clear of claims to independence from France. Ever since his early days campaigning against forced labor, Houphouët-Boigny had made use of French institutions and French rhetoric to make important demands. He only became interested in independence for the Côte d'Ivoire when it was practically a *fait accompli*.

The RDA in the Côte d'Ivoire sprang from strong rural roots; in Senegal, the RDA was largely urban and Senghor's BDS, working via rural power brokers, dominated politics in the countryside. In Guinea, Sékou Touré used the union movement as a springboard to building a

6 Voters depositing their ballots in the legislative elections in Dakar, Senegal, 1956. This election, the first under universal suffrage, devolved considerable power to the legislatures, eventually leading to full independence in 1960.

territorial political party linked to the RDA, but unlike other branches, his Parti Démocratique de la Guinée (PDG) was antagonistic to chiefs and other rural elites. He eventually found that expanding beyond his base meant dropping the trade union's way of seeing the world – its quest for equality with French workers – in favor of a language of politics that could appeal to peasants, for whom French life did not represent a meaningful form of comparison.

All these examples are illustrative of an important point: party organization did not spring automatically from any one social category or from the generalized grievances of the colonized. Some aspirations, such as those of the labor movement, focused on comparison with a French reference point. Others denied the French reference point, and looked toward connections that united Africans. A skillful politician like Senghor could weave together, for a time and in some circumstances, different forms of affiliation into a political machine that articulated the aspirations of people who called themselves "African." But Senghor was careful to avoid too sharp a break with the idea of citizenship in an empire, given his success in using French institutions and the French language to claim French rights and resources for his constituents.

Politics takes doing; it implies persuading people to think of link-ages they may not have perceived before. Parties, like Senghor's BDS or Houphouët-Boigny's PDCI, represented particular social experiences of living in a specific place, but covered over tensions among the people they were meant to represent. The RDA was really a coalition of diverse par-ties, but because it operated all over French Africa (Equatorial as well as West) it kept a focus on the inequities of Africa's relationship with France. Houphouët-Boigny's property-owning, export-producing constituency clashed with some of his RDA comrades' leftist, populist outlook, op-posed to accommodation with the French government. All of this meant for confusion and conflict, but it also constituted real politics: the effort to unite people with different interests and conceptions of themselves.

At another extreme, electoral institutions, as opposed to prior forms of affiliation, created their own defining logic. This was the case in much of French Equatorial Africa, a region first miserably exploited then miser-ably neglected, with a tiny wage-earning class, a tiny educated minority, and farming communities more detached, less well off, and less capa-ble of making the leap to acting collectively than those of Senegal or Côte d'Ivoire. But French centralization meant that they were part of the same post-war political institutions and held the same elections on the same day. Politicians tend to fill a vacuum, and they did in places like Gabon and French Congo. Florence Bernault argues that social constituencies grew out of politics rather than the reverse: the few people in a position to be candidates for office – because of education, civil service experience, and missionary connections – created rather than mobilized constituencies. Urban youth played a particularly important role in this process, for they were available, loosely attached to other urban institutions, and trying to find a way in a situation where following their fathers' model was not the only option. Youth did the door-to-door work of politics and at times something more muscular than that. The thin communications of this re-gion meant that chiefdoms, administrative units, and language-cultural groups were weakly cross-cut by trade union affiliation or by the cos-mopolitan experience of people with diverse migration patterns, wider religious affiliations, or long trading networks. Politics created its own logic, and that logic was largely ethnic, as inchoate cultural similarity was hammered into group identification by political organization itself.

That France gave particular play to the citizenship concept, and that its vision of rule was a centralizing one, gave certain social groups an opening to claim equality with an affluent European society. It was precisely the Frenchness of colonial society that was painful to other Africans – the pretense to representing civilization, the reduction of African society to either the "primitive" or the delightfully "exotic." France was irrelevant to still others – a periodically intrusive and oppressive, otherwise distant ruler whose claims to superiority did not apply. French colonial education and the increasing need for wage workers gave some Africans a chance to escape from patriarchal authority in their villages, but the city could be a humiliation as well as a liberation.

From the vantage point of the 1990s, the biggest danger in looking back on the 1940s is the assumption that people should have known that their future was the nation-state. Or that they should have seen through the nation-state and celebrated instead the authenticity of African culture. But in 1948 or 1949, the cracks in the colonial edifice were opportunities. French institutions and French ideology could be used against French power. In the early 1950s, the Senghors and the Houphouët-Boignys tried to turn French citizenship into something meaningful and useful to their constituents, rather than to claim another sort of sovereignty. It is hard to tell whether they – or the more radical critics of all that was French – knew that it was a logic whose time would be short.

## Self-government unbound: the Gold Coast, 1947–51

British officials did not try to relegitimize empire by making their colonial subjects into imperial citizens. The ruling fiction was "self-government": each territory would follow its own path; there would be no representation of Africans in the London parliament. Before the war, educated elites from different British colonies had sometimes acted together, in the National Congress of British West Africa. After the war, Great Britain carefully channeled electoral politics into individual territories. It thus avoided making the equivalence of voting rights or the social and economic benefits of inhabitants to those of British citizens such a salient issue, and it provided no venue in which an organization like the RDA could act.

The British Colonial Office in 1947 thought that the Gold Coast was "the territory where Africans are most advanced politically." It had great plans: new investment, improved education, agricultural improvement. The Labour government moved from the old policy of "indirect rule" towards "local government," in which regional councils and educated people from each region would play a strong role. But the Colonial Office was convinced that "internal self-government is unlikely to be achieved in much less than a generation."

If one looks beyond the pronouncements from the top to the secret correspondence of British officials, one sees that in official eyes farmers were backward subsistence cultivators, political leaders were all demagogues manipulating unthinking masses, and African participation in their own affairs was a kind of apprenticeship, practicing leadership rather than exercising it. Britain, in 1948, was a long way from having a plan to devolve power. By 1951, it had been backed into a situation where it did just that.

Since the nineteenth century, Gold Coast Africans had been self-consciously debating what kind of political institutions best suited their unique and complex world at the intersection of European and African cultures. Farmers had decades of experience with the cultivation and marketing of export crops like cocoa. Trade unions had years of experience representing the interests of diverse workers. Between 1939 and 1947, the population of the Gold Coast's major towns, Accra, Kumasi, Sekondi-Takoradi, and Cape Coast, increased 55 percent. Some 45,000 African soldiers ended their wartime service, having joined other subjects of the British empire in a war for freedom that was not truly theirs; on their return, many sought to live in cities, facing difficult urban labor markets, housing shortages, and inflation. All city dwellers confronted consumer goods shortages and price gouging by monopolistic European importing firms.

In the second half of 1947, the Gold Coast experienced a wave of strikes, which were strongest among the miners and railwaymen. Farmers, although benefitting from high cocoa prices, reacted against heavy-handed government attempts to cut out allegedly diseased cocoa trees. Then came a boycott of urban commerce, which focused on the sorest spot of all, the acute commodity shortage and galloping inflation. The boycott was organized by Nii Kwabena Bonne II, an Accra chief, a former worker and businessman, the kind of figure cutting across social categories who turns up in populist movements. Africans in Accra, Kumasi, and other cities boycotted European- and Syrian-owned businesses, arguing that their price gouging was responsible for the misery. Nearly a month later, the government engineered an agreement under which the firms in question cut their gross overall profit margins.

The boycott ended in February 1948, just when a group of ex-servicemen in Accra, encouraged by the United Gold Coast Convention (UGCC), were planning a protest march against the government's failure to help them find jobs. The undermanned and poorly led police contingent protecting the government headquarters panicked, fired into the marchers, and caused fatalities. As the news spread, a riot developed in downtown Accra, directed above all at European-owned shops. Women and men participated in the violence and looting, which spread to other towns. There were more casualties: a total of 29 deaths and 237 injuries.

The Gold Coast's old line political party, the UGCC, was moving gingerly toward a more militant direction, and it seized on the riot and the repression. Its second-in-command was now Kwame Nkrumah, whose education in the United States had exposed him to the racism faced by his African-American fellow students, and whose time in England had plunged him into leftist, anti-imperialist, and Pan-Africanist circles in London. The leader, the more elitist J. B. Danquah, also saw an opening in the situation. The UGCC offered to provide an "interim Government" to the Gold Coast, using the same rhetoric about mass disorder as officials and offering themselves as controlling intermediaries. The offer was not appreciated.

The UGCC leadership was using social tension to make self-government into an immediate issue, not a distant goal. It did not mobilize revolutionary action to effect such an end, nor, despite administration fears, did the hot-beds of trade unionism in the mines and railways capitalize on the aftermath of the Accra riots. But colonial issues were now generating international controversy: anti-imperialist groups issued statements, and Africans and West Indians organized a protest meeting in London. British officials took the threat very seriously: an Emergency was declared; troops were called in from other colonies; warships were sent to the area; and troops in nearby Nigeria patrolled the streets in case the movement spread.

Officials blamed the riots on disorderly masses and unscrupulous demagogues; they alleged "communist influence." Six leaders of the UGCC, including Danquah and Nkrumah, were detained without charges. In a radio broadcast Governor Creasy insisted that the arrests "are like the quarantine which is imposed on people who have caught a dangerous infectious disease." In London, the Colonial Secretary also worried about the dangers of "detribalised urban people." The government would seek "the sympathy and goodwill of responsible and educated elements."

Such dualisms would be heard again and again: the unruly, detribalized Africans, led by demagogues, versus the responsible leader and the respectable population. Officials did not yet realize that their brittle conception of Africa was opening a chance to leaders who could prove they were popular and claim they were moderate. Instead of a single mass threat, there was a differentiated society producing a range of political mobilizations. Unions were hesitant and divided on the issue of striking for "political" objectives; unemployed youth were angry; elite professionals were maneuvering for advantage.

The quest for the responsible African politician led colonial officials to convene a new constitutional commission, the Coussey Committee, which represented as wide a spectrum of moderate, educated African opinion as officials could tolerate. It included five of the UGCC Six, with the conspicuous exception of Nkrumah. The strategy insured two results: the Colonial Office would not be in a position to reject any consensus recommendation of the Coussey Committee and this, as one would expect from the modernizing Africans on the Committee, led to another step towards a system focusing on elections as the source of legitimacy. It also gave Nkrumah a position from which to criticize the incomplete nature of proposed reforms. Nkrumah used the opportunity brilliantly to forge his own support base among urban workers, young men with only a limited education, and other "popular" (and largely urban) elements, which eventually broke away from the UGCC and become the Convention People's Party (CPP). In official eyes, the UGCC turned from the demagogues of 1948 into the moderates of 1949, while the CPP took on the mantle of irresponsibility.

Another wave of strikes in 1949 was attributed to Nkrumah's effort to turn labor into "the spear-head of his attack on ordered government." Officials thought the colony was "on the edge of revolution." At the end of 1949, the unions were contemplating a general strike, and Nkrumah was building up support for a campaign of "Positive Action," civil disobedience intended to make it impossible for government to function.

In fact, officials underestimated the extent to which their policy of encouraging trade unions as autonomous bodies devoted to raising wages and other "industrial" issues had succeeded. The trade union movement was divided over "Positive Action." Nkrumah himself vacillated on the subject of a general strike, and the strike, when it came, proved less than general. Seeing its chance, the government arrested Nkrumah for fomenting an illegal strike.

Isolating the demagogues meant accepting the new steps toward devolving legislative and executive power recommended by the Coussey Commission. Otherwise, the British government concluded, "moderate opinion will be alienated and the extremists given an opportunity of gaining further and weightier support and of making serious trouble."

But London could not convince the people of the Gold Coast that its moderates were what they wanted. With Nkrumah in jail, the CPP won the election of February 1951. The CPP won the overwhelming majority of votes in the cities, where the enthusiasm of workers and of youth was high, but voter registration and turnout were still low; Nkrumah's majority translates into about 30 percent of the voting age population, not quite the mass mobilization of nationalist myth but enough to make him the only viable political option. Nkrumah went almost directly from jail to state house, as Leader of Government Business, a sort of junior prime minister. The next ideological task for the British bureaucracy was to reconstruct Nkrumah, the Apostle of Disorder, as the Man of Moderation and Modernity. By June, the Colonial Office was writing about the need "to keep on good terms with the more responsible political leaders such as Mr. Nkrumah."

If Great Britain had wanted to keep Nkrumah in jail, ban the CPP, and suppress all trade union activity, it could have. It had put down larger rebellions in Malaya in the late 1940s and Kenya in the early 1950s. But in those situations it was drawing limits, in the first case against an explicitly communist movement, in the second against an uprising of "primitives" – a misleading perception discussed in chapter 4. In the Gold Coast, the question was what would it have done after the agitation was put down? Great Britain's legitimacy in the age of self-determination depended on at least the illusion of orderly political progress. Betting on the moderates seemed more hopeful than shutting down all political activity, but officials could not impose their definition of the moderate. Meanwhile, plans to increase exports and build infrastructure were vulnerable to the actions of organized workers and farmers, and the evidence of their discontent undermined the ideological component of the development project. Perhaps the conservative colonialism of the 1930s could have survived an Nkrumah by ignoring or arresting him, but the developmentalist colonialism of the 1950s had less room to maneuver.

The British government thus felt constrained to accept Nkrumah as the most responsible and plausible politician it could work with. He became the head of an African-majority cabinet serving under a British governor. Officials had become trapped in their own theory of political change as a series of necessary steps and in their need to legitimize their role as teaching democracy. By 1951, the people of the Gold Coast had made it clear whom they wanted to lead them, and British officials had to adjust their political imaginations to the reality before them.

### South Africa: nationalism for Whites and struggle for Blacks

South Africa was not quite in a colonial situation – so much the worse for its black population. White South Africans were citizens of their own country, not people living "somewhere else." Many traced their ancestry to Dutch immigrants from the seventeenth century. Once farmers, cattle-owners, rural traders, many now worked in gold mines or industry; they called themselves Afrikaners. Other immigrants came from Great Britain or continental Europe, and new waves were attracted by the mineral revolution after the 1880s. In colonies, the state was something of an abstraction; the people who represented it came and went. The state in South Africa existed in a very human – and very inhumane – form. Most importantly, white South Africans voted.

South African capitalism also had a more down-to-earth existence than elsewhere on the continent. The bulk of South African land – some 87 percent – was designated for ownership by whites, and very few Africans had access to any commercially viable land whatsoever. From the 1890s, a proletariat was born, albeit one still linked to "reserves," where families stayed and eked out a below-subsistence living, while young men spent most of their lives in urban areas under the watchful eyes of white employers and white policemen, who enforced a strict control over migration.

Africans fought hard to find niches in the system and forged a more viable urban culture than most whites knew about. But the simultaneous presence of a strong state, powerful mining companies with draconian control over the "compounds" where single men lived, white bosses on farms, in shops, and in households who directly supervised black labor, and a system of ethnically structured "reserves" where government-backed chiefs exercised arbitrary authority, constituted an apparatus of control over African populations that went beyond anything found elsewhere in the continent. By the 1940s, this system, far from being a throwback to bygone notions of white supremacy, was fostering industrialization and urbanization.

But not without contradictions and opposition. In some urban neighborhoods, such as Sophiatown in Johannesburg, Africans became permanent residents, with access to property. Lively urban cultures developed, and because of back-and-forth migration urban culture increasingly influenced rural Africans. Meanwhile, strong mission education and the economy's need for literate African workers produced a segment of the population as aware as their West African counterparts of worldwide trends in political thought. The Garvey movement was influential in South Africa, as were African-American missionaries. This contributed to different political currents: a liberal view of politics oriented toward constitutional reform, a Christian vision of social justice, urban labor militance, and different forms of African nationalism.

The spurt in industrialization during the war augmented the demand for urban labor. Industrial capitalists generally supported expanding – selectively – the rights of Africans to live in cities, hoping for a more flexible labor market and less turnover. Gold magnates were content to preserve a migratory system of labor, including the balancing of recruitment within South Africa and controlled immigration from outside. Farmers opposed the loosening of control over migration, fearing that many Africans would rather take their chances in cities than face the predictable misery of agricultural labor. White workers feared competition. Meanwhile, there was widespread cultural and intellectual uncertainty in white South Africa. Afrikaner ideologues, firmly anchored in a fraternal order, the Broederbond, as well as the Dutch Reformed Church, observed their group's increasing success in an industrial society, but feared that Afrikaners were losing their moral vision. The National Party (NP), which garnered most Afrikaners' votes, was pragmatic in its thinking about race. It was doing its best to reconcile the various demands of its constituents, and it was not inhibited by the agonized reflection about self-determination and egalitarian values that beset certain other wartime and post-war empires; some leading Afrikaners were, on the contrary, sympathetic to Nazi racial thinking.

All of this came to a head in the 1948 election. The United Party (UP), although close to big capital and English-speakers, was led by an Afrikaner, Jan Smuts. The UP was aware of political ferment elsewhere in the continent and favored a more flexible policy of urban migration and residence and a "native" policy that was paternalist, pragmatic, and no real compromise from principles of white supremacy. The National Party articulated a strong defense of Afrikaner culture and a restrictive vision of African participation in the economy, more favorable to the interests of farmers and small businessmen, less so to big business. The Nationalists and their allies narrowly won the 1948 election, and over the ensuing years tightened their grip on an African population that was increasingly restive politically.

The basic tools of what the Nationalists called apartheid ("separate-ness") had long ago been put in place, and not particularly by Afrikaners. But they were now used more rigorously. Massive expulsions from urban areas occurred, although a divide-and-rule strategy implied important distinctions between those Africans entitled to live in cities and those officially consigned to miserable rural reserves, who in practice moved illegally between reserve and urban jobs, with frequent stops in prison.

Until the 1950s, women were not covered by the pass laws, and their ability to establish themselves in cities constituted what some scholars called the "weak joints and soft spots of the structures of urban control." Their presence helped make urban life and family formation possible for men as well. Controlling women was thus one of the central preoccupa-tions of apartheid planners, and the attempts to apply pass laws to women led in turn to widespread mobilizations, boycotts, and marches of women throughout the 1950s. The state eventually got its way, and the "endors-ing out" of many women from cities, combined with the policing of their efforts to return to separated families, rendered women in impoverished rural areas increasingly vulnerable. But many women persisted in finding niches within the illegal urban economy and others remained activists in the townships, both trying to bring a measure of stability to township life and fighting apartheid.

The state's repressive action nonetheless criminalized much of urban family life; being jailed for violation of pass and residency laws was an or-dinary experience. The state inadvertently contributed to the emergence within cities of an alienated and often violent youth culture, as well as organized gang systems that both preyed upon and drew support from young men caught between the vitality of urban life and the increasing impossibility of providing for a family.

Social and political mobilization among black South Africans reveals important parallel developments to the rest of the continent as well as an awareness of events elsewhere in Africa. The wave of strikes that hit much of Africa in the 1940s was particularly powerful in South Africa, notably with numerous strikes in the city of Durban and a giant gold mine strike in 1946. In the Johannesburg area, "squatter invasions" were frequent, and between 1944 and 1950 somewhere between 60,000 and 90,000 South Africans organized themselves into bands, seized a piece of vacant land somewhere in the periurban sprawl, built their shacks as quickly as possible, and defended themselves against police raids. Their actions went against the efforts of the state to build planned, segregated cities and gave rise to a combative political culture within certain encampments. The state's efforts to build fenced-in African townships at some distance from cities – the most notorious being Soweto (for South Western Townships) outside Johannesburg – reflected as much a response to African collective action as a grand design of apartheid.

Elsewhere, relatively settled working-class communities in cities expanded in the 1940s, and in some of them the Communist Party of South Africa (CPSA) made headway by concentrating on immediate issues: residential rights, transportation, and housing. The CPSA was banned in 1950 and many of its activists committed themselves to the African National Congress (ANC), but in a certain moment it brought together African trade unionists, white radicals, and activists in the African locations, helping to push the ANC into greater concern with working-class Africans. Politics moved beyond the petitions and constitutional claims characteristic of the pre-war ANC and toward strikes, boycotts, "stayaways," and other forms of collective action that ultimately depended on getting a large number of people to act together and at considerable risk. Political coherence was affected by tensions between those people strongly rooted in urban culture and those more closely connected to rural areas. Yet migration brought the effects of urban radicalism to rural districts too, catalyzing, for example, the Sekhukhuneland revolt of 1958 against oppressive government land and agricultural schemes and those chiefs who cooperated with them.

The trend toward urban and industrial life remained strong in the 1950s, and the long-term effect of apartheid regulations restricting migration was to degrade rural conditions and encourage new waves of urban migration. The state was constantly trying to disrupt community building among Africans, and from the 1950s to the 1980s ruthlessly "re-moved" people from some places, especially city locations, and put them in others, especially state-run townships or barren settlements in rural "homelands."

A new tendency, typical of the generational transitions in Africa in these years, emerged from the 1940s among better educated South Africans. This became known as "Africanism," associated with leaders like Anton Lembede. It emphasized the integrity and value of African culture and above all the militance that lay within it – if only it could be mobilized. Africans were not just victims of injustice; they were agents of a na-tional future. This Africanist tendency emerged within the ANC's Youth League. Nelson Mandela himself came out of the Youth League into the main part of the ANC. In the late 1940s, Africanism did more to give a shot in the arm to the ANC than to create a separate movement.

Both the communist tendency and the Africanist tendency drew on and contributed to an increasingly politicized urban culture. The ANC's "programme of action" in 1949 emphasized demonstrations and civil disobedience. This was pushed further in the "defiance campaign" of 1950–52, in which ANC supporters massively violated segregation laws and courted arrest. Boycotts and stay-aways were organized. Women's groups also became active, drawing on the vital roles women played in townships and locations and in certain professions.

Militance invigorated the ANC, whose membership jumped from 4,000 to 100,000 in the early 1950s. The ANC's increasingly militant style went along with its continued emphasis on multiracialism, demo-cratic participation, and the rule of law, to which a socialist vision of eco-nomic and social justice and equality was increasingly added. The 1955 Freedom Charter embodied these principles. The South African govern-ment counterattacked in 1956 by indicting 156 Congress members and their allies for treason, a prosecution which tied up the movement for years before ultimately failing. And in 1958, the "Africanist" tendency that had influenced the ANC in the 1940s now split off to form the Pan-African Congress (PAC), with Robert Sobukwe and others criticizing the ANC for cooperating with non-Africans, and finding in the success of African nationalism elsewhere on the continent a model for a movement for a South Africa that would be truly African.

The main difference between South Africa and the colonial empires to its north was the ruling fiction of each power. By the late 1940s, Britain and France – and the other empires, to a notably lesser degree – were pre-tending that Africans could be made into "modern" men and women, that they should no longer be kept in their tribal cages. The post-1948 South African government, however, carried to an extreme the idea that

Africans existed in their peculiar cultures, that these differences were essential and unbreachable, and that a regime could be organized to keep them that way. South Africa excluded blacks from citizenship and pretended that their lives should remain centered on tribal homelands, not in the national space which their labor was enriching.

South African industry and its white population prospered as did no other industry or population group in Africa. Whether this was because of or in spite of apartheid has been much debated. The devastating effects of apartheid on African family life are without question, as is the vehemence with which individuals and collective organizations struggled both against the system and to find ways to survive within it. For a long time, the apartheid state was strong enough to contain opposition. But the seeds of apartheid's unraveling were already present in the 1950s, in an African urban culture that could not be tamed, and a political leadership and organization able to demonstrate to the rest of the continent and the world that they – not the white rulers – represented the values of democracy and the rule of law which the "west" thought it stood for.

### Militance in different keys: Pan-Africanists and prophets

Let us stand back from these tales of specific territories to look at a possibility that got shunted aside in the immediate post-war years. One might have thought, at this moment, that Pan-Africanism's time had come: the war against Nazi racism gave plausibility to a critique of imperialism based on the principles of imperial governments themselves. Pan-Africanist leaders did not fail to seek public attention. That they failed to seize the moment has much to do with the processes described previously in the cases of the Gold Coast and French West Africa. The political imagination of leaders in each colonial territory was captured by a process that seemed to be going somewhere, which bit by bit conceded to Africans the possibility of entering institutions capable of exercising real authority over the territories in which they lived. Pan-Africanism had opened a much wider dialogue about the meaning of race and oppression, and of liberation and solidarity, but it had never had a clear vision of what sort of institutions it wished to create in order to supplant the colonial states.

At the end of the war, George Padmore took the lead in organizing a new Pan-African Congress in 1945, with the involvement of past and future leaders like W. E. B. Du Bois, Nkrumah, and others in Africa, the Caribbean, and North America. The congress, held in Manchester, aimed to make the elimination of imperialism and the reconstruction of Africa part of the post-war agenda. The Manchester resolutions condemned the oppressiveness of colonial institutions, the "regression" induced by economic and social policies, the inadequacy of the "pretentious constitutional reforms" of Britain and France, and indirect rule's "encroachment on the right of the West African natural rulers." They affirmed the principles of the Four Freedoms and the Atlantic Charter and called for an end to racial discrimination, educational and economic reforms, and elections with universal suffrage. But they were not specific about what sort of political units would govern themselves, what the role of "natural" leaders would be in an electoral process, and least of all how Africans could get from here to there.

Nonetheless, this was a basis on which to build. The trouble was that other edifices were being built more rapidly – less visionary, more compromised – but offering African politicians concrete benefits. To win an election to a territorial or imperial legislative body was to obtain a platform from which to speak and possibly dispense patronage, hence the opportunity of enlisting supporters.

Pan-Africanism was one of several ways in which African organizations looked beyond individual territories. African unions, meanwhile, worked with in international trade union organizations, notably the leftist World Federation of Trade Unions, to link their demands for equal wages, for the end of oppressive colonialist legislation, and for fuller recognition of collective bargaining to a world-wide movement. Anti-communist trade unionists in the United States and Great Britain felt obliged to counter this form of labor internationalism by promoting their own trade union organizations in Africa and elsewhere, the International Confederation of Free Trade Unions, and African activists found this organization, too, would support them in clashes with colonial administrations.

In rural areas, a variety of mobilizations were being made, from attempts to solidify the power of chiefs who could represent people in large regional groupings to efforts by farmers to demand fairer prices for their crops. Often, the first or second generation of western-educated people attempted to weave together – in local publications, mission journals, and other forums – their knowledge of "traditional" myths and local histories with their command of written language to foster coherence and self-consciousness within a given area, strengthening ethnic solidarities, which in turn could be used by political parties to mobilize.

Developmentalist colonialism was confronted with a variety of forms of rural mobilization. When colonial agricultural agents in the 1940s cajoled and coerced African farmers into following what officials regarded as proper techniques for cultivating the soil – disregarding the social and spiritual implications of entering a domain of land, rain, and people – tensions mounted. In a hilly region of Tanganyika, Steven Feierman's research has revealed, the post-war agricultural development regime clumsily intruded into the way people conceived of their relationship to the environment. The Shambaa people linked the idea of spiritual health to the well-being of the land. Religious figures were concerned with rainmaking and above all else with balance and harmony: good relations among people were indicative of good relations with nature, and vice versa.

The peasant movement that countered the agricultural agents stressed the harm that was being done to the land, meaning that social relations as well as food production were being damaged. Chiefs who collaborated with the British were criticized for failing as rainmakers, for their inability to intervene with the supernatural to assure the welfare of the community. Feierman argues that the movement was led by "peasant intellectuals," men with a little primary education but who remained farmers and were firmly entrenched in their local communities.

This is an instance of a discourse focused within an ethnic group and using a local idiom. But not entirely. Some peasant leaders constituted themselves as the Ushambaa Citizens Union after comparing notes with a citizens' union formed in another locality, and some years later the movement began to work with the Tanganyika African National Union, the leading nationalist formation that began among city-dwellers and teachers. TANU, like other parties, expanded by convincing people in many localities, rural as well as urban, with many causes that the colonial state was the common denominator of their grievances. It would, for a time at least, suggest that politics perceived through a local prism did not have to remain that way.

Religious affinity in Africa, as I argued in chapter 2, often crossed lines of ethnicity and so, whether Islamic, Christian, or otherwise, created the potential of extending bonds. It is tempting to see religious movements in rural and urban Africa in the late 1940s and early 1950s through the lens of nationalist hindsight, and conclude that religious autonomy, assertion, and organization created both networks that had political implications and a feeling of solidarity that was a precedent for political assertiveness. But does such a conception do justice to the history of religious movements in the 1940s and 1950s?

In the Belgian Congo, a Christian messianic movement, partly repressed since the 1920s, took on a new vigor after 1947. Simon Kimbangu, educated by Protestant missionaries, had proclaimed himself a healer and acquired a large following among Bakongo around 1920. Arrested in 1921, he spent the next thirty years in prison, until his death in jail. One of his sons and some of his followers, literate and educated, acquired positions close to important officials in the civil service. Secretly, they helped to keep Kimbanguism alive, especially after the leader himself died in 1951. Meanwhile, another set of cults loosely associated with

Kimbangu sprang up in the same region. Kimbanguism, with its stress on healing, its melding of Christianity with a sense of Bakongo uniqueness, and its sense that the importance of the cult exceeded that of the state or the officially-sanctioned Catholic Church was perceived by officials as a threat.

Elsewhere in the Congo, especially in the copper mining area that overlapped with British Northern Rhodesia, a movement called Kitawala flourished. This, too, had earlier roots and it spread throughout this zone of intense labor migration and back and forth, cross-ethnic, cross-border movement in Central Africa. It was an offshoot of the Jehovah's Witnesses, carrying with it a Christian messianic vision while adapting to varied religious practices in the area, including the identification of evil with the workings of witches. Adherents believed that the triumph of good over evil would come from the outside, sometimes in the form of African Americans sweeping into Africa in airplanes and driving out whites, a belief no doubt reflecting the influence of the Garvey movement. Belgian authorities, like the British, detested the Witnesses and Kitawala not because they espoused rebellion against the state, but because they proclaimed the irrelevance both of the ideologies of chiefdom and tradition on which colonial authority depended and of the state's developmentalist vision. Such religious movements, despite the repression, appealed to many Africans in the cities and the countryside, and as movement back and forth accelerated after the war, they kept open, for people living between different cultural and moral orders, an inclusive form of belief and a fervid vision of a future devoid of the tensions of the present.

In the post-war years, Luise White notes, rumors of vampirism spread across wide stretches of East and Central Africa. Firemen, ambulance drivers, forest rangers and other Africans – usually skilled men, working with Europeans and working with vehicles or other kinds of technologies, but sometimes female prostitutes – were accused of kidnapping people, hiding them in vehicles, taking their blood, and leaving them dead. Unlike witchcraft accusations, usually found within the tense intimacy of kin and villagers, vampire stories were boundary-crossing. Blood-sucking was more than a crude metaphor for colonial extraction. The spread of these stories reflects efforts to come to grips with both the power of new objects and the fact that Africans were now associated with activities, objects, wealth, and power acquired from Europe.

Other religious leaders focused on healing. Just outside Salisbury, Rhodesia, a woman named Mai Chaza built a community of believers in her healing powers and in a mixture of indigenous and Christian conceptions of morality and collectivity. In rural Rhodesia, shrines and cults spread widely in the countryside. The networks of spirit mediums would one day help guerrilla leaders mobilize support, but in the 1950s they provided people in a harshly oppressive regime with a means of expressing a social and spiritual affinity among themselves. In rural Central Kenya, independent Christian churches flourished, while certain Kikuyu prophets were revered as pointing the way to a new order, combining messianic visions with a specifically Kikuyu sensibility.

In West African cities where migrants from northern parts of West Africa became increasingly numerous in the post-war era, spirit possession cults became increasingly important. By seeing themselves as possessed by spirits specific to the modern city, rural migrants with limited experience of urban life (unlike their well-established neighbors) created spaces to imagine new forms of participation in social life. In other parts of Africa, women could make demands in the name of a spirit which possessed them, thus gaining influence within the household without overtly challenging patriarchal assumptions.

This interplay of religious organization and secular politics was intimate: it could take a radical form (as it eventually did in Central Kenya) or a quite moderate one, as in Senegal. It could focus on particular municipalities (Salisbury) or entire regions (the Copperbelt). It could provide solace or channel anger. Religious movements deserve to be analyzed in their own terms, as spiritual communities, as attempts to give moral anchorage to people crossing cultural and moral boundaries, and as innovative syntheses of a range of doctrinal and ritual practices. The older interpretations that see autonomous religious organizations as a substitute for or precursor of political parties have a point, but these miss the multiple dynamics that play out over time. What is above all important to grasp is the ferment and sense of possibility of the post-war decade.

## The limits of modernizing imperialism

The multiple forms of political and social mobilization in post-war Africa were not confronting a static colonialism but a moving target. France and Great Britain were trying to relegitimize colonial rule, to increase African political participation in a controlled way, and to give Africans a stake in expanding production within the imperial economy. South Africa, expanding economically as it escalated repression in the 1950s, marked another vision of "progress" in the post-war era.

Post-war change could appear in even more stunted forms. Economically weak Portugal built its own repressive version of the developmentalist colonial state in Mozambique, Angola, and Guinea-Bissau. Portugal had depended on foreign capital, especially British, to develop plantations and factories in its territories, and much of the post-war effort depended on bringing in whites from Portugal to make up the middle and lower middle levels of enterprises. Africans were largely excluded from whatever benefits economic growth bestowed. Portugal's white citizens, let alone its African subjects, had little political voice – it was ruled by the dictators Salazar and Caetano from 1926 until 1974 – and its leaders did not worry about how to justify ruling over others. That Africans should organize themselves, in trade unions or political parties, was unthinkable.

In Belgium's vast colony, the Congo, a mining corporation forged what seemed the epitome of capitalist order and progress. The copper mining complex was huge and tightly run, and from the 1920s the company managers accepted that Africans were coming to the mine towns to stay. Its version of stabilization predated the British and French ones, although it flagged during the depression of the 1930s. After the war, the Belgian Congo experienced economic growth and urbanization, and its government actively sought to control urban space, improving health and other social services. But it would not tolerate trade unions or political organization. The Belgian government had never had the resources to develop its vast domain, and it had granted "concessions" to corporations to exercise governmental as well as economic functions in large areas. The Congo was a hodgepodge of zones of mineral and agricultural exploitation and zones of neglect, except for labor recruitment. Even by colonial standards, it was highly disarticulated. In some domains, Belgium was the most socially interventionist of colonizers: it established childbirth centers, midwife training, and orphanages, and tried to shape how Congolese women took care of their children. But there was no effort to provide post-primary education or to give Africans entrée into professional activities, the civil service, or local politics.

France and Great Britain, for all their interest in economic and political change, made clear the limits of their reformative effort. Even when the African standard of living became the goal of development policy, European commercial and mining enterprises remained an important, and privileged, part of the picture. If, as in the Côte d'Ivoire, white farmers sometimes faded from view behind the success of African counterparts, in other instances, as in Kenya or especially the Rhodesias, white settlers tried to place their own role at the center of regional economic development. They also invoked the concepts of citizenship and self-determination to claim for themselves a role, even a dominant one, in the political process, and used it to keep African claims to citizenship and self-determination at bay. In British Rhodesia and, most notoriously, in French Algeria, colonial governments lacked the will to counter such moves, with disastrous results (see chapter 6 on the Rhodesian case).

French leaders nevertheless thought that the citizenship law of 1946 epitomized their enlightened outlook, but when the unfairness of having

each colonial deputy represent vastly more citizens than each metropolitan deputy was pointed out in the Paris legislature, a deputy replied that
it had to be this way, or else France would become the "colony of its
colonies." Senghor, also a deputy, replied that such an argument was
racist. It was important that an African deputy could be in a position to
say this and that an accusation of racism in an imperial institution carried
weight. But there never really was a question of equal representation, for
exactly the reason advanced.

British leaders, from near the end of the war, talked a great deal about
bringing responsible politicians into positions where they would learn
their craft. Yet in the Gold Coast, Nigeria, Kenya, and elsewhere, it
seemed to them as if all the political activists were irresponsible demagogues. Trade unionism was, from the 1940s, officially encouraged; trade
unionists were almost invariably found to be flawed. Officials most often expressed their view of African progress in the language of tutelage:
Africans were all young men who needed to be taken under the wing of
kindly but firm schoolmasters.

Such limits of citizenship, self-government, and development were,
however, not the prerogative of French or British rulers to set. No one
exposed this more clearly than Nkrumah, the epitome of the dangerous
demagogue, who put together a movement sufficiently strong that there
was no real alternative to its claim to govern. The British reinvention
of Nkrumah as a responsible leader reveals the importance of political
imagination in the decolonization process. It had to be imaginable to the
British that a Nkrumah could preside over a self-governing colony, just as
it had to be imaginable to the people of the Gold Coast that the colonial
territory was the unit on which they could focus their political efforts and
get something in return.

The other side of the limit-setting process was the way in which certain groups, individuals, and political tendencies were excluded from the
politically imaginable. Even if colonial governments were constrained,
they in the end drew lines; and in some cases, they made them stick. In
Madagascar in 1947 – a year after the French citizenship law, and the
year in which a vast railway strike in West Africa was handled cautiously
by French authorities – a rebellion broke out. The government insisted
that demagogues had stirred up the primitive masses. Settler farms were
burned and settlers killed; officials lost control of parts of the island. It
was also true that political activists were trying to dynamize the – now
legal – electoral politics. To the government, it was not a question of over-
lapping forms of collective action, but of elected politicians conspiring to
set off an insurrection. The self-consciously reformist colonial minister
and governor general orchestrated a brutal repression of the rebellion. Up

to 100,000 Malagasy died; agriculture was disrupted; and the trauma of 1947 is still in the minds of Malagasy today.

Some years later, the French government would also draw the line against a political movement in Cameroon that was too leftist and spoke too early about independence, while the British government would banish from the political scene a movement that rejected the modernizing framework of post-colonialism, dragging along with that movement other radical and moderate political forces – but only for a time. As with Nkrumah, the image of Kenyan leader Jomo Kenyatta would have to be transformed from a force of "darkness" into a spokesman for moderation and British-African economic cooperation. These are themes to which I will return.

A Senghor, a Houphouët-Boigny, or an Nkrumah could make use of the very terms in which colonial regimes defined danger – African primitiveness, the specter of communism – to widen a space of "moderation." Colonial rulers, in the post-war decade, knew they needed to associate themselves with Africans' own aspirations for progress if they were to make their exercise of power in Africa legitimate, efficient, and progressive. In the end, leaders such as Nkrumah and others showed that they were indispensable to help France and Great Britain find a way out of their imperial engagements.

SUGGESTED READING

A full bibliography for this book may be found on the website of Cambridge University Press at http://uk.cambridge.org/resources/0521776007. It will be updated periodically.

Austin, Dennis. *Politics in Ghana, 1946–1960*. London: Oxford University Press, 1964.

Bonner, Philip, Peter Delius, and Deborah Posel, eds. *Apartheid's Genesis, 1935–1962*. Johannesburg: Ravan, 1993.

Feierman, Steven. *Peasant Intellectuals: Anthropology and History in Tanzania*. Madison: University of Wisconsin Press, 1990.

Manning, Patrick. *Francophone Sub-Saharan Africa 1880–1995*. 2nd edn. Cambridge: Cambridge University Press, 1999.

Morgenthau, Ruth Schachter. *Political Parties in French-Speaking West Africa*. Oxford: Clarendon, 1964.

Sorum, Paul Clay. *Intellectuals and Decolonization in France*. Chapel Hill: University of North Carolina Press, 1977.

Vaillant, Janet. *Black, French, and African: A Life of Léopold Sédar Senghor*. Cambridge: Harvard University Press, 1990.

White, Luise. *Speaking with Vampires: Rumor and History in Colonial Africa*. Berkeley: University of California Press, 2000.

# 4    Ending empire and imagining the future

French and British rule in Africa collapsed not because of an all-out assault from a clearly defined colonized people, but because the imperial system broke apart at its internal cracks, as Africans selectively incorporated into political structures based on citizenship or self-determination seized the initiative and escalated their demands for power. Meanwhile, in the mid-1950s Portuguese and Belgian rulers, and the whites who dominated South Africa, were vigorously holding on to political power and appropriating economic gains for a tiny fraction of the population. However, they were slowly moving from being ordinary members of an international club where colonialism was the norm to being outliers in a new world where legitimacy was measured in terms of progress toward self-government and economic development (chapter 6). In the long run, neither Portugal, Belgium, nor South Africa could contain the pressures coming from neighboring territories or from the transformation of international norms, but it was the colonialism that identified itself with political reform and economic development that first proved unsustainable.

By 1956 or 1958 French and British governments knew that the colonial endgame had begun. But where could colonial governments set the limits on the kinds of politics allowed in the ambiguous space between colonial domination and territorial autonomy? What could the first generation of African political leaders allowed a measure of power do with their opportunities? In this period, French and British governments on the one hand and African movements and leaders on the other struggled with and occasionally fought each other, and ended up defining a certain kind of decolonization, one which opened up some political possibilities and shut down others. Supra-national possibilities – federations of more than one territory, and Pan-Africanist imaginings – were excluded from the political map. And as British and French governments came to realize that hanging on to power would be too painful and costly, they made clear that the responsibility for the consequences of these decolonizations would fall on African shoulders.

## Redefining political space

By the early 1950s, citizenship in French Africa was proving to be an immensely powerful construct, seized by African social and political movements to claim all of the equivalence that being French implied. Self-government in British West Africa was exploding out of the confines in which the Colonial Office had hoped to keep it. But how wide was the opening, and how did Nkrumah's generation wish to fill and expand it?

The core of the agenda for the new political class owed something to the post-war agenda of British and French colonial rule, but it was given a new twist. The development project, to colonial administrators, implied that the possessors of knowledge and capital would slowly but generously disperse these critical resources to those less well endowed. But to African political parties, development meant resources to build constituencies and opportunities to make the nation-state a meaningful part of people's lives. In the Gold Coast and Nigeria the politics of development began with marketing boards, particularly in cocoa. As noted earlier, British governments in West Africa had put these institutions in place as the sole purchasers of export crops from African farmers, first to placate African opposition to the European businesses that had monopolized such trade, then to use as a source of development funds, to be doled out (or accumulated) as British officials thought wise. The CPP or the Action Group in Western Nigeria (the cocoa-producing region) quite accurately saw the surpluses held by these boards by the late 1940s as a source of development funding, and British arguments that too rapid spending of the surpluses would cause inflation were seen, with reason, as self-serving.

As Leader of Government Business from 1951, Nkrumah was in a position to manage development in a new way. But he did not choose to change a crucial element of British policy: maintaining government control of marketing board surpluses. The farmer continued to get only a fraction of the world price; the government now used it more actively than had the British to promote government development initiatives. These took the forms of schools and roads – highly visible to a voting constituency – and industrialization, increasingly in the 1950s seen as the answer to economic dependence. The biggest industrial project backed by Nkrumah was originally a British one: building a dam on the Volta River to supply electricity to a hopefully industrializing economy and to power the smelting of the territory's bauxite into aluminum, making it a more valuable export and reducing dependence on cocoa.

Kwame Nkrumah told his followers, "Seek ye first the political kingdom." He captured the imagination of a wide range of followers, who now saw in the idea of building an African nation a means to combine their personal ambition and idealistic goals, free of the constraints of colonial authority and an inward-looking traditional elite.

Nkrumah thus gave another inflection to the centralizing character of post-war imperialism. But his national focus quickly led to Nkrumah's first serious political conflict, and it came from advocates of regional autonomy and a weaker, federal state. People in the Asante region were not only conscious of the former power of the Asante kingdom, but they were among the leading cocoa growers and hence the most affected by the state's confiscatory policies toward cocoa wealth. Such revenue was vital to Nkrumah's national ambitions and, equally important, wealth in Asante hands constituted a danger to his ambitions, for such people were not dependent on the state for resources and were capable of financing political movements.

Asante nationalism, organized into a political party, the National Liberation Movement (NLM), was itself torn between a conservative elite – close to the leading chiefs who had exercised administrative power under the British system of indirect rule – and younger men who saw themselves as nationalists and modernizers, but identified "the nation" with the Asante people. Some NLM leaders, such as Joseph Appiah, had been early supporters of Nkrumah, but had come to fear that his centralizing thrust was the harbinger of a dictatorial one, and that the Asante were likely to be its victims. The movement oscillated between violence and constitutionalist opposition.

The British government pretended to referee the contest, but protecting minority rights was not their priority. The NLM, for its part, was both divided and unable to convince people from other regions that it represented something other than Asante privilege. The CPP won elections in 1954 and 1956.

Nkrumah's effort to preclude alternatives to his power went beyond Asante. Chiefs throughout the country were stripped of effective power, replaced by CPP loyalists, or co-opted into the CPP fold. Labor leaders, critical to Nkrumah's rise to power, were co-opted into a CPP-controlled union federation or else marginalized; the militant railway and mining unions were kept in check. Cocoa farmers, outside as well as inside the Asante region, were given little alternative but to market crops through state agencies and participate in CPP-dominated farmers' associations.

But except for many Asante, Nkrumah captured the imagination of a wide range of Africans; he understood their dislike of colonial rule, their sense that Africa's time had come, and their belief that a new, African state could improve the lives of its citizens. In 1957, the Gold Coast became independent and Nkrumah renamed it Ghana, after an old African empire that had been located to the north of the present territory. The festivities were exuberant; the joy palpable. And one of Nkrumah's first acts as the head of an independent state was to ban all political parties organized on a regional basis – including the NLM.

In Nigeria, Africa's most populous country, the quest for state resources had important consequences for regional conflict from the early 1950s. The British had divided Nigeria into three regions, Eastern, Western, and Northern, and their vision of the future was of a Nigerian federation presiding over three regional governments with legislative power. This structure had the perverse effect of encouraging first a winner-takes-all quest for electoral power *within* each of the three regions, and then competition *between* the regions for power at the federal level. The civil service was regionalized in 1953: each region would control its bureaucracy and hence its patronage resources. But the three regions were not equivalent. The north was the most populous, but had the weakest educational system and was firmly ruled by a traditionalist, Muslim elite. The west, thanks to cocoa, was the wealthiest, and the capital city of Lagos was within its borders. The east had the best educated population, many of whom held clerical or skilled labor jobs in Lagos or in northern cities.

In each region, a party dominated by members of the majority ethnic group obtained office and used it to provide services and patronage within its bailiwick: the Igbo-led National Council of Nigeria and the Cameroons (NCNC) in the east; the largely Yoruba Action Group (AG) in the west; and the Hausa–Fulani-led Northern People's Congress (NPC) in the north. In the early 1950s, British control of marketing board surpluses was a sore point, and a target of the regional governments elected in 1952. The regional governments soon competed with each other to show who could deliver the most to constituents, and what voters wanted above all was schools. Universal primary education became the goal in the eastern and western regions.

In each region, oppositions developed, to some extent (notably in the north) as populist challenges to governing elites, but most importantly among regional minorities. Each majority party had its patronage system and occasionally used thuggery to keep its control. The instability was greatest in the west, partly because of the ambiguous position of the federal capital Lagos, in and not of its region, and partly because of intense rivalries between Yoruba factions. The system encouraged corruption in each region, but Nigeria's agricultural exports in the 1950s were sufficient to allow politicians to play their patronage games while real progress was made in building educational institutions within each region. The NCNC was the most nationally focused of the parties (in part because easterners lived in all of the regions) and the NPC the most conservative, because of its domination by a traditionalist hierarchy.

Instead of allowing a wide variety of interest-groups to make claims on the Nigerian state, the federal system focused power on the three regions, each governed by a party dominated by a single ethnic group and with the budgetary means to solidify its regional constituency. This structure fostered an unhealthy mix of ethnicity and regional patronage. The center remained important, for in an economy dependent on exporting primary materials and importing manufactured goods, ports, customs, and transportation – all "federal" jurisdictions – were lucrative. Easterners and westerners both wanted to use an active federal government to accomplish their developmental goals, but feared that the NPC would ally with one or the other to dominate the minority region. The disaster that was to envelope Nigeria was brewing by the early 1950s.

In French Africa, leaders such as Houphouët-Boigny and Senghor were very reluctant to step outside the framework they had used to build solid political machines in Côte d'Ivoire and Senegal and which they were using to make effective demands on the government of France. The nonracial labor code of 1952, guaranteeing important rights and benefits to all wage workers, was a good example of the powerful effects of a logic of citizenship combined with active campaigns to turn it into something concrete. In Senegal in particular a more radical opposition emerged in the mid-1950s, led by intellectuals like Abdoulaye Ly, who tried to move the BDS in a left direction and eventually split with it. Labor unions constituted a potential node of opposition, but Senghor was able to co-opt a considerable range of opinions into his fold, and his relationship with the Muslim brotherhoods gave him a base that was hard for anyone to crack. Houphouët-Boigny's control was even tighter, and his status within the RDA had a dampening effect on anti-imperialist radicalism in other territories as well.

The strongest effort to develop a decisively anti-colonial movement came from Sékou Touré in Guinea. He got his start in the trade union movement, first as a government clerk and organizer within the civil service, then as leader of the Guinean branch of the Confédération Générale du Travail (CGT), the communist trade union federation. He became a hero for leading a general strike in Guinea in 1950, for playing a crucial role in the CGT's campaign throughout French West Africa for the enactment of the labor code in 1952, and in 1953 for leading a long strike in Guinea over the implementation of the labor code. He made astute use of French assimilationist language to insist that African workers deserved the same pay and benefits as workers born in France, and he looked to allies – white, black, brown, and yellow – throughout the internationalist labor left.

Sékou Touré used his union base and his militant reputation to enter politics, running first for the territorial assembly, then for the French legislature, and eventually for the leadership of the Guinean legislature. In order to succeed, he had to broaden his appeal beyond the wage workers who could directly compare themselves to French workers, and to do so he invoked his own illustrious ancestry while fashioning a rhetoric that increasingly contrasted French colonialism with African unity. Within the union movement, he repudiated by 1955–56 the alliance with the French left and insisted that African unions be strictly African. He and his collaborators wanted to drop "class struggle" from the language of African unionism, insisting that African workers should set aside their particular grievances and strive alongside peasants and others for the good of Africa as a whole. Within Guinea, he assembled a populist coalition of considerable breadth, drawing on tensions between commoners and chiefs in some regions and on the support of women shaking loose from patriarchal control.

Trade unionists, political leaders, and others had seized the openings of the post-war moment and made a variety of claims: for access to material resources, for their voices to be heard, for the exercise of power. The African leaders who were beginning to govern their territories did what political elites usually do: tried to eliminate certain kinds of demands and certain forms of organization from the realm of the possible. Amidst one of the great political openings of the twentieth century, the closures of a particular decolonization were becoming visible.

## The reinvention of savagery and the boundaries of decolonization

By 1951, the British government in the Gold Coast had grudgingly admitted that it could neither hold African political aspirations within the confines of "local government" nor decide which leaders claiming a national role were acceptable. Elsewhere, the struggles over limits and possibilities continued.

In Kenya, British officials attempted to draw the line against a movement they called "Mau Mau", which they saw as a primitive, violent rebellion against order and progress. Before the war, officials tended to think of Africans as quaintly backward, but with the developmentalist ideology of the post-war era, any militant rejection of the "modern" world became an affront. The story of Mau Mau does not fit the British view – expressed by officials and the British press – of backward-looking rebellion, but neither was it just another modern mass nationalist movement. The ideology of the forest fighters, who eventually called themselves the Land and Freedom Army, was indeed anti-modern, rejecting more about developmentalist colonialism than the fact that it was colonial.

The root causes of rural anger were, above all, the entrapment of Kikuyu in the development initiatives of the post-war colonial state. In some districts, the issue was heavy-handed conservation policies which forced Africans, especially women, to do anti-erosion work that did not increase yields. Most starkly affected were women and men who, for some decades before, had left crowded areas to move to white settler farms in the Rift Valley. There they became "squatters" and were allowed to grow some crops and keep some animals in exchange for providing family labor to the settler farms. After the war, the booming world market for agricultural goods encouraged settlers to farm more intensely, to mechanize, and to bring more land under export crops. They increasingly expelled squatters and employed wage laborers as needed.

The Labour Government of Great Britain was not pro-settler, but it was pro-development and convinced that settler agriculture provided needed revenues and an example of modernizing agriculture. It also eased restrictions on Africans growing some of the most lucrative export crops, including coffee. But this opening to African rural capitalism compounded the problem: expelled squatters, returning to Kikuyu settlements where they thought they had ancestral rights, were not welcomed by the Kikuyu elite, who were intent on using the land themselves. Meanwhile, the Nairobi labor market – reflecting British stabilization policy – was providing some Africans with more secure and better paying jobs, but leaving less place for those on the margins. Ex-squatters were caught between different forms of exclusion and marginality, whether in country or city. Development, for them, was catastrophic.

Many Kikuyu had eagerly entered mission schools in the 1920s and 1930s, but the missionaries' efforts to get their converts to abandon a range of Kikuyu social practices (clitoridectomy most notorious among them) led to vigorous defense on the part of Kikuyu male elders of Kikuyu culture and a more quiet defense of their own role in cultural reproduction by female elders. In the 1930s, a strong movement among the Kikuyu to found independent schools and independent churches made it clear that it was possible to be Christian, western-educated, and Kikuyu at the same time.

The post-war crisis cut to the heart of social life. To ex-squatters, their inability to gain access to resources – including land in villages they saw as theirs – was a denial of a chance to marry, in other words to attain full adulthood. But the older, better-off, Christian Kikuyu who opposed the rebellion also had their moral ideas, a point emphasized by the Kenyan historian B. A. Ogot. They were profoundly offended by the young men who went against their elders. They thought that their long effort to build African churches and African schools gave them legitimacy as defenders of Kikuyu integrity, and they resented being told they were stooges. The constitutionalist political party led by Jomo Kenyatta, the Kenya African Union (KAU), was dismissive of the aspirations of the marginal working class of Nairobi and the increasingly radical labor leaders who were speaking for it.

It was among the excluded that a wave of agitation began in the popular districts of Nairobi, spearheaded by an organization of Kikuyu who were supposed to have passed the rituals of male initiation in 1940 and who faced the denial of masculine adulthood. They called themselves the 40 Age Group. They invigorated an earlier pattern of oath-taking: to swear loyalty to the Kikuyu ancestors, a classic tactic in ambiguous situations to get people to commit to one side. After the failure of the 1950 general strike in Nairobi, urban disorders, including assassinations of conservative African politicians, began. This spread to rural areas, and when an important Kikuyu chief was assassinated in 1952, in the midst of escalating raids on settler farms and government posts by guerillas based in the forests of central Kenya, the government declared an emergency.

The victims of post-war development confronted a moral and ideological edifice which defined them as primitive and their exploiters as progressive. The squatters were increasingly attracted to an ideology which harked back to a mystic sense of Kikuyu integrity, unsullied by the ambiguities of the past hundred years, evoked in the oath and in the songs and rituals of the forest fighters.

Mau Mau cost the lives of 95 Europeans and nearly 2,000 "loyal" Africans, plus – in official figures – 11,503 rebels. Around 30,000 Kikuyu were arrested or captured, with many placed in detention camps and put through psychologized rituals to cleanse them of their collective "insanity," accustom them to healthy labor, and reinsert them into a purified Kikuyu society.

It is hard to understand the excess of government repression without appreciating the seriousness with which the post-war British governments took their self-definition as progressive, set off against African backwardness, reactionary settlers, and even the past record of the Colonial Office. In 1945 Phillip Mitchell, governor of Kenya, saw the issue in these terms: "the African has the choice of remaining a savage or of adopting our civilization, culture, religion and language, and is doing the latter as fast as he can."

White settlers saw the rebellion as proof that the African could only be kept down by the sustained use of force – a position that offered London no hope for the future. The emergency hardened the conviction of top officials that the crisis of transition could only be solved if the Kikuyu were pushed through the dangerous middle ground, between their supposedly primitive political behavior and a modern electoral system, and to the other side. By the mid-1950s, the Kenyan colonial government was seeking in earnest to work with allegedly moderate politicians. Tom

Mboya, a young man from western Kenya who started out as a labor leader and became party leader while Kenyatta remained in jail, skill-fully wove the specter of disorder before officials to make claims for more active social and economic policies and an increased share of power. Colonial officials, as Mau Mau was finally contained, fantasized about property-owning Africans sharing cities with stable, respectable workers, and sturdy farmers in rural areas giving employment to reliable agricultural workers. Class would replace race as the organizing principle of society. As late as 1959, officials could not predict when they could allow Kenya to become independent; the answer turned out to be 1963.

The costs of managing a developmentalist empire had become clear. In the Gold Coast and Nigeria, a combined fear of disorder and hope that "modern" Africans could contain the conflicts of their rapidly changing societies led officials to allow the move towards self-government to accel-erate. In Kenya, protecting developmental colonialism meant abandoning white settlers and eventually abandoning colonialism in favor of develop-mentalism. In Central Africa, another version of developmentalist impe-rial policy came unstuck. In 1953, the British government had proclaimed the Central African Federation, uniting its three colonies of Southern Rhodesia, Northern Rhodesia, and Nyasaland, hoping that this larger unit would foster economic planning and stave off South African ambi-tions to bring the region's white settlers into its white-supremacist orbit. African political leaders saw the danger that the British policy of self-government would be captured by white settlers, most of whom lived in Southern Rhodesia, and used to dominate the entire region. The British promised "safeguards" for the indigenous majority which predictably proved inadequate. The regional economic strategy mainly benefitted Southern Rhodesia, where most industry was located, and agricultural expansion there meant encroachment on African lands and regulations on African herds. In Nyasaland and Northern Rhodesia, educated Africans saw their opportunities constricted by white dominance of federal institu-tions. In the Northern Rhodesian copper mines, the African Mineworkers Union had to fight not only for better pay, but also to get Africans into the supervisory and skilled positions zealously guarded by the union of white mineworkers. Meanwhile, white settler politics swung in an increasingly racist direction. The region seethed with tension. African political parties in all three territories became more militant and focused on breaking up the federation. In 1959, a state of emergency was declared in Southern Rhodesia and riots broke out in Nyasaland. African political parties were banned and leaders arrested.

Once again, repression only underscored the untenable nature of the situation. Regional development for all races was an illusion, and main-taining the federation would be a very expensive illusion. Britain accepted the end of its Central African dream, allowed Nyasaland and Northern Rhodesia to move toward independence as distinct countries (Malawi and Zambia) and temporized with the white leaders of Southern Rhodesia until the latter, unable any more to defend racial privilege within British colonialism, defended it by declaring their own version of independence in 1965, dragging out the story of this ugly decolonization for another fifteen years at the cost of much human life (see chapter 6).

France committed its share of violent and repressive acts; the Madagascar revolt of 1947 (chapter 3) brought out a repressive excess comparable to that witnessed in Kenya. The Cameroons witnessed a later attempt to exclude a political party deemed too radical. The Union des Populations du Cameroun (UPC) had started out much like any other party in this colony (once a German possession) which France ran under a mandate from the United Nations. Cameroon had given much less space to *évolué* politics, to trade unions, or to the development of an associative life than had Senegal, and when the same electoral law was applied to it, politicians had less to draw on. As in French Equatorial Africa (chapter 3), electoral politics created its own logic: politicians used what cultural capital they had – ethnic associations, ties to the Catholic church, and above all positions within the colonial bureaucracy – and successful ones immediately turned office into a basis for mobilizing supporters.

In the late 1940s, one party tried to get away from this form of politics – the UPC. It had a regional base in the Bassa region near the southern coast, but tried to make itself national. It was close to the left-wing trade union movement, and it tried to articulate a clear program of social reform and assertiveness at the national level. At first it hesitated to take a clear position against the French Union and for independence. The UPC did poorly in the elections of the late 1940s, and without anything concrete to offer its supporters it moved toward increasingly radical positions on social and political questions. The French government disliked the UPC from the start and worked against it. What officials could not abide was its call for independence for Cameroon; they did not know that within a decade, French policy itself would be moving in that direction.

The government did what it could to disrupt campaigns and rig election results. The UPC was pushed further into marking its distinctiveness. At home, it set itself apart by its increasingly radical positions, and overseas, it embarrassed France by its criticisms before the UN, the supervisor of France's mandate. In 1955, the UPC's public meetings became increasingly militant, its trade union allies launched a series of strikes, and police repression escalated too, culminating in urban riots. The French government then banned the UPC. The RDA, then cooperating with France, disassociated itself from its one-time affiliate. After trying to regain legal status, the UPC under Ruben Um Nyobé went underground and began a guerilla struggle in southern Cameroon. This was harshly repressed and Um Nyobé was killed. That left the field to the more ordinary political parties, each balancing its ethnic base, its access to government resources, and its efforts to find just the right degree of militance and collaboration with the government to keep its supporters engaged and anticipating results. The party of Ahmadu Ahidjo prevailed; its conservative policy of co-operation with the French complemented the conservativism of Ahidjo's regional base in the hierarchical Islamic societies of North Cameroon.

Colonial officials could not often draw the line where they wished but they could try, and in Cameroon and Kenya they showed that movements which were too radical or too anti-modern could be destroyed. Still, Kenyatta had once been identified with the forces of darkness and Nkrumah dismissed as a demagogue. Both forced colonial regimes to move the boundaries of the permissible; they, too, helped to define a certain kind of decolonization.

## The end of empire and the refusal of responsibility

In Eastern Nigeria, the government of Nnamdi Azikiwe had made social development the cornerstone of its program. But by 1955, British officials were convinced not only that the ministers were corrupt, but that the key social program, Universal Primary Education, exceeded the region's ability to pay. Given its policy of devolving power to self-governing regions, it could neither kick out the politicians nor alter their policies – unless it suspended the painfully negotiated constitution. The governor told London, "Inevitably the people are going to be disillusioned, but it is better that they should be disillusioned as a result of the failure of their own people than that they should be disillusioned as a result of our actions." Here we have a frank statement of British thinking on the eve of decolonization: defining the structures in which the move toward self-government would take place, while preparing to place the blame for the failures of the process squarely on African shoulders.

In 1957 Prime Minister Harold Macmillan asked his officials to give him "something like a profit and loss account for each of our Colonial possessions." The Colonial Office had not dared to ask such questions before. The answers that came back revealed a cold calculation that the benefits and costs of continuing colonial rule had to be set against the economic and political advantages of good relations with ex-colonial states. If defending colonial rule would be prohibitively expensive, the key to policy was managing the transition: "during the period when we can still exercise control in any territory, it is most important to take every step open to us to ensure, as far as we can, that British standards and methods of business and administration permeate the whole life of the territory."

Officials' best hope was thus that ex-colonies would become western-style nations. But country-by-country analyses were not optimistic. In Nigeria, "Barbarism and cruelty are still near the surface . . . [w]e are unlikely to have long enough to complete our civilising and unifying mission." The Colonial Office did not see "any prospect in the foreseeable future of . . . relinquishing control" in all three East African countries.

In France, similar issues were debated in public. In 1956 a popular journal published an article on French Africa which insisted that one must ask about each colony, "What is it worth? What does it cost? What does it bring in? What hopes does it allow? What sacrifices does it merit?" Aware that France had just lost a colonial war in Indochina and was fighting another in Algeria, the author argued that African demands for self-government were growing and could not be blocked: "It is necessary to transfer as fast as possible as much responsibility to Africans. At their risk and peril." In private, officials were assessing their decade-long development drive and finding that labor costs had shot upward, that backward infrastructure had choked on the new material coming in, and that the private sector had failed to invest where the public sector had pioneered. In the post-war context, colonialism on the cheap was no longer possible: the investments of the development years were not rapidly paying off, and the social costs were escalating. The Africa that colonial officials had fantasized creating was not to be. They faced the difficulties of ruling Africa as it was.

For British officials, self-government presented a way out: each colony would be led step by step along a path that increased the power of the elected legislature and eventually resulted in the appointment of elected members to cabinet positions, including eventually a prime minister. Meanwhile, officials realized how little had been done to Africanize the bureaucracy, and programs were hastily put in place.

It was not so apparent how France could devolve power without abandoning the centralizing and assimilating structure of the French Union. The union consisted of federations – French West Africa and French Equatorial Africa most importantly – with all citizens electing a legislature in Paris; French policies since the war had tilted away from treating Africans as "different" and toward defining everyone as equivalent in social and political terms. So devolution would imply repudiating an old policy. In 1956 the French government did precisely that.

Confidential files of the government make clear how much officials felt trapped by the ever-escalating demands made within the framework of French citizenship. Discussion of education, health, wages, and urban services invoked metropolitan France as a reference point. By 1956, confronted with the war in Algeria and the dangers of social equivalence with the metropole, French officials came up with a new concept:

"territorialization." Each territory – Dahomey, Chad, Senegal, Côte d'Ivoire – would be given the power to set its budget, under French overview, and to administer much of its domestic affairs. France would maintain responsibility for defense and foreign affairs. If African leaders still wanted to push the logic of equivalence, regarding civil service salaries or health facilities, the costs would fall not on "France," but on the taxpayers of each territory, to whom the politicians looked for votes.

Pierre-Henri Teitgen, who had helped to draft the new law, asserted that Africans had taken assimilation to mean "well, give us immediately equality in wages, equality in labor legislation, in social security benefits, equality in family allowances, in brief, equality in standard of living." And that, Teitgen said, demanded a sacrifice that French people would not accept. This enactment – known as the framework law (loi cadre) of 1956 – was a big step towards decolonization, if not in so many words.

The loi cadre was passed in Paris at a time when the language of autonomy and of the nation was increasingly spoken in Africa. Even the trade union movement was falling into this in 1956, despite the gains that had been made by referring to the wages and benefits of French workers. The shift did not come from the rank and file; it was the union leadership that spoke in the name of "autonomy," of finding means of expressing African cultural distinctiveness, of speaking with solidarity in the name of the nation.

Intellectuals, Senghor foremost among them, had long spoken of African cultural integrity, but had argued that this contributed to the larger entity that was the French Union. Senghor could carefully conjugate the interplay of cultural assertiveness and the language of rights and equality within the Union. But the language of equivalence meant less and less to an expanding electorate; in 1956, for the first time, elections were conducted with universal suffrage. A railway worker on the Dakar–Niger line might compare his benefits to that of someone working the Paris–Marseille line. But such a comparison would make little sense to a peasant living five miles from the track. As political leaders – even those whose springboard came from the labor movement – looked toward stitching together broad constituencies, they had to look beyond the language of equivalence within imperial citizenship.

It was in this context that a rhetoric of "autonomy" and of "African unity" was increasingly heard. By the time of the loi cadre, Sékou Touré had already abandoned the quest for equality with French standards and was calling for a radical break with French imperialism and the unity of all Africans in the struggle. He, too, had to build his political movement step by step, and he did so effectively. In the first elections after the loi cadre, Sékou Touré became the head of the council and so, in effect, prime minister of Guinea. African party leaders in the other territories of West and Equatorial Africa similarly stepped into positions of authority.

In the case of Guinea, Sékou Touré's insistence that all Africans, from the peasant to the skilled worker, should unite turned from an appeal to something like a compulsion. As he told his former allies in the labor movement in 1958, a strike against colonial employers was progressive, but against an African government it was "historically unthinkable . . . The trade union movement is obligated to reconvert itself to remain in the same line of emancipation." As Guinea became independent, strike movements were suppressed, the trade union movement was subordinated to the political party, and union leaders who advocated different positions were arrested.

At one level, the French government's calculation had worked: the semi-sovereign African governments installed after the 1956 elections resisted the escalating demands for social and economic parity that had been the hallmark of politics since 1946. But with Sékou Touré, officials badly miscalculated. His anti-European rhetoric was not a mere political stratagem. He meant it, and he meant what he said about African unity, even if he imposed his vision on other Guineans.

The French government thought it could make its system of semi-self governance, with each territorial administration having authority over the budget, endure. In 1958 Charles de Gaulle, newly installed as the French president, preoccupied with the war in Algeria and eager to insure stability in Sub-Saharan Africa, tried to firm up this position. He offered each African territory a choice in a referendum between autonomy within the French Union or immediate and absolute independence. He calculated that the political leaders were deeply enough entrenched in the current system – with possibilities of French aid, of privileged entry of export commodities into French markets, of access to French systems of higher education – so that continued participation in "Greater France" would be attractive. For the most part he was right. But the campaign was open and the debate serious. The strongest voice for voting no on the referendum was that of Sékou Touré, who was convinced that African territories had to make a decisive break and become independent nation-states. In the end, only Guinea voted for immediate independence.

The French government responded vindictively; Guinea was cut off from aid, and departing French officials reputedly removed equipment needed for a functioning bureaucracy. Guinea was left to its fate. Yet only two years later, France would itself decide that the cord needed to be cut to all of its Sub-Saharan colonies.

Everywhere, elected African leaders welcomed their power within the territories, and the parties that won the elections of 1956 and 1957 moved quickly to establish their authority. But some, notably the civil service unions and leaders like Senghor, realized the costs. The French government was devolving power to individual territories and weakening the federations of French West Africa and French Equatorial Africa. Dahomey, Niger, Senegal, Gabon, and so on were becoming the units in which decisions were made, in which politicians built constituencies, and on which demands were focused. Whereas in 1946 the RDA had looked beyond individual territories towards a wider confrontation and engagement with France, juxtaposing a language of equality with a critique of imperialism, now everything was focusing on the territory. The irony was that a language of "African unity" was becoming abstract at the very moment it seemed to be triumphant. Senghor warned in 1956 against the "balkanization" of Africa, a division of the Franco-African federations into units too small to be economically viable, too weak politically to challenge former imperial powers. Indeed, the French strategy of divide-and-cease-to-rule was separating a leader like Houphouët-Boigny, who presided over a rich territory and could use its resources for the people whose votes he depended on, from the leaders of the arid, landlocked countries in the West African interior, such as Upper Volta, French Soudan (Mali), and Niger, and from Senghor, whose country stood to lose by the diminished importance of the headquarters of French West Africa in Dakar.

Even Senghor was trapped in the "balkanization" against which he warned. Each African government had come to power through the mobilization of its own set of followers. Senghor had worked through the leadership of Islamic brotherhoods in Senegal even as he had appealed to intellectuals, trade unionists, and other constituencies. On the eve of independence, he tried to negotiate a smaller-scale federation with neighboring French Soudan, soon to be renamed Mali. But both he and Mali's Modibo Keita had to face the fact that they had built their constituencies in their own ways. They feared that in a single unit, each would make inroads against the other, Keita using a unified party structure and Marxist social policies to undercut Senghor from the left, and Senghor using his affiliations with Islamic networks and his good relations with France to offer pragmatic policies to Mali's citizens. The brief attempt at a new federation failed, and the territories of once-centralized French Africa went their separate ways.

The French government was not only devolving power, but also disavowing the central tenets of its post-war policy and imperial ideology. It was pulling back from the implicit offer that incorporation into the French Union would mean that all imperial citizens could aspire to French standards of living, French levels of social services, and French education. It was conceding something to claims – as much those of Senghor as Sékou Touré – for forms of cultural expression distinct from those of France, but most important it was abdicating responsibility for the material welfare of Africans. This move was softened by the continued provision of aid, but this was now foreign aid, a gift rather than an imperial obligation; and it would be hardened by French political intrigue and military support for Africans it deemed friendly against those it believed acting contrary to its interests. But sovereignty would have its consequences.

In British Africa, meanwhile, the flag had come down first in Ghana in 1957. Nkrumah's coming to power marked for colonized peoples all over an event of great symbolic importance, and this was one of the main reasons why France had to look beyond its regime of semi-autonomy after 1956. In 1958, Nkrumah held his All African People's Congress in Accra, and this became the occasion for making Ghana's independence into an assertion of a universal right to self-government and sovereignty for all African nations. Even South Africa's oppressed political organizations were present, and the occasion allowed them to associate their struggle with the successes of African nationalism. Nkrumah was trying to oversee the rebirth of Pan-Africanism, forgotten for a time in the preoccupation of political leaders with institutions that were giving them a measure of power. But it was becoming a Pan-Africanism of independent states, and it would prove to be an elusive goal. In any case, within English-speaking Africa, the events of 1957 symbolized that devolution had been established and would become inevitable. No matter what the concerns among officials might be about the "readiness" of particular territories for independence, independent they would become.

That leaves Belgian and Portuguese Africa, and, of course, South Africa. The latter two would try to prevent the winds of change from blowing their way, but they too would soon be caught up in the fact that independence was happening all around them. I will return to this theme later on. In the Belgian Congo, independence came via a stunning reversal, and it was so ill-prepared that its failure was immediate and tragic. Only in the 1950s did Belgium begin to send Congolese to higher education, and only after 1954 did it allow parties to act openly. Belgian scholars in 1955 proclaimed that independence was at least thirty years away.

Up to then, the most important associations permitted were those formed along ethnic lines, so that when the stakes of politics suddenly rose, ethnic difference was accentuated. The Bakongo party, Abako, centered in the capital of Leopoldville, emerged in 1954. It represented above all the urban évolué outlook of the Bakongo population of the city. In the copper-mining province of Katanga, a new party, Conakat, focused on regional autonomy and on the ethnic tensions in a region where high

Map 3 Decolonizing Africa

labor immigration seemed about to swamp long-term inhabitants. Abako and Conakat would provide the platforms for two of the important political actors of the early 1960s debacle, Joseph Kasavubu and Moïse Tshombe; the latter was the closest Congolese ally of European interests. It was Patrice Lumumba, from the eastern side of the country, who attempted to put together a party that was truly national, and the others regarded him as dangerous to their power bases for just that reason. His Mouvement National Congolais articulated a radical critique of Belgian colonialism and looked toward the forging of a Congolese nation.

The Belgian government saw Lumumba as the most threatening of Congolese politicians. But it realized how difficult it was to control the situation when the rest of Africa was rapidly moving toward decolonization. When riots broke out in Leopoldville in 1959 – in a context where no one had experience in orderly political processes and where religious, ethnic, and other tensions were ripe – the government panicked. Perhaps it cynically calculated that an ill-prepared independence would result in continual dependence on Belgium, but if that were the case, officials misread the eagerness of other international actors to meddle, too. The ensuing "Congo Crisis" that began in 1960 at virtually the moment of independence (see chapter 7) would reveal that decolonization was more complicated than tearing down the flag of an oppressor and raising the flag of a new nation. Belgian's abdication of responsibility for its brutal colonization and inept decolonization opened the way to the United States, the Soviet Union, France, and the United Nations to inject their own interests, while allegedly trying to bring order to a land whose people had never been allowed to enjoy the riches their country possessed.

Alongside the extreme irresponsibility of Belgium, decolonization French and British style mixed a certain political cynicism with a different kind of political imagination. At the end of World War II, the idea that independent nation-states would rule in Africa was to European officials conceivable only in a hazily defined future, detached from their views of actual African leaders as apprentices in need of training or demagogues who had to be restrained. Ordinary Africans needed to learn how to behave in cities, or how to run simple organizations and local governments, or else they could participate in small numbers but in institutions where they would represent but not decide.

By the early or mid-1950s in both British and French Africa, the "modern African" – in the workplace, in an urban neighborhood, or in a government office – was an imaginable being. Officials might ignore the connectedness of such individuals to the rest of Africa. The very idea of "stabilization" in labor policy, for example, emphasized that the urban worker must be separated from village life. But the repeated emphasis on the modern quality of city life, on the imperatives of the modern bureaucracy, on the need for modern enterprises and modern forms of labor administration, opened up to Africans a set of possibilities which many were able to seize. Colonial officials now defined those Africans who followed the script as if they were a-cultural, a-social beings, embodiments of modernization, and they now saw Africans who refused to enter such roles as dangerously recalcitrant, as stubbornly primitive. As for the vast majority of people who did not live such a dichotomous life – their place in the colonial vision was unclear.

This imaginative leap, with the enormous reality that it obscured, allowed French and British officials to think of an Africa which they did not rule. They could still think that the modern Africans that they had created would willingly and even eagerly embrace the modern institutions open to them, that they would continue relations with the Europe that had taught them so much about science, technology, literature, and statecraft, and that they would maintain their integration into world markets. France and Britain transformed their colonial development apparatus into a foreign aid system, with the crucial difference that it reaffirmed generous superority while denying responsibility for the social and political consequences of economic change. Other figures on the world scene, including the US and the USSR, began to look at the disintegrating colonial empires as spaces that were being internationalized, still at the bottom of a developmental hierarchy, but now the object of concern of all "advanced" nations. Africa would become the world's project for uplift, and also a magnet for power politics and exploitative interest.

SUGGESTED READING

A full bibliography for this book may be found on the website of Cambridge University Press at http://uk.cambridge.org/resources/0521776007. It will be updated periodically.

Allman, Jean Marie. *The Quills of the Porcupine: Asante Nationalism in an Emergent Ghana*. Madison: University of Wisconsin Press, 1993.

Beckman, Bjorn. *Organizing the Farmers: Cocoa Politics and National Development in Ghana*. Uppsala: Scandinavian Institute of African Studies, 1976.

Berman, Bruce and John Lonsdale. *Unhappy Valley: Conflict in Kenya and Africa. Book Two: Violence and Ethnicity*. London: James Currey, 1992. 2 vols.

Coleman, James S. *Nigeria: Background to Nationalism*. Berkeley: University of California Press, 1958.

Gifford, Prosser and Wm. Roger Louis, eds. *The Transfer of Power in Africa: Decolonization, 1940–1960*. New Haven: Yale University Press, 1982.

Hodgkin, Thomas. *Nationalism in Colonial Africa*. New York: New York University Press, 1957.

Iliffe, John. *A Modern History of Tanganyika*. Cambridge: Cambridge University Press, 1979.

Kanogo, Tabitha. *Squatters and the Roots of Mau Mau, 1905–63*. London: James Currey, 1987.

Rathbone, Richard. *Nkrumah and the Chiefs: The Politics of Chieftaincy in Ghana, 1951–1960*. Athens: Ohio University Press, 1999.

Tignor, Robert. *Capitalism and Nationalism at the End of Empire: State and Business in Decolonizing Egypt, Nigeria, and Kenya, 1945–1963*. Princeton: Princeton University Press, 1998.

Zolberg, Aristide. *One-party Government in the Ivory Coast*. Revised edn. Princeton: Princeton University Press, 1969.

*Interlude: rhythms of change*
*in the post-war world*

Let us pause for a moment to think about ways to grasp the timing of change during the half-century after World War II. A narrative of "triumph and failure," of "hope and disillusionment" captures something of the time. It calls attention to the struggle for independence, the joy of seeing colonial rule end, and the subsequent despair at the inability of independent African states to sustain peace, democracy, and economic and social progress. The crisis that hit the Congo within weeks of independence in 1960, the coup that overthrew the pioneer of nationalism, Kwame Nkrumah, in 1966, and the Biafran war of 1967–70 mark political turning points.

By the late 1960s Africa's leading intellectuals were calling attention to moral corruption and political passivity in the wake of earlier hopes. Some scholars began to argue that independence was an illusion: the new states of Africa were "neo-colonial," politically sovereign, but economically dependent and culturally submissive. If the neo-colonial interpretation located power and blame in the west, others argued that the years after 1960 revealed a weakness in Africa itself, habits rooted in either African culture or the still-powerful mental grip of colonialism. The delayed freedom of Portuguese Africa in 1975 or Zimbabwe in 1979 suggested repeat performances: even intense mobilization for protracted armed struggle in these regions offered no better preparation for independence than the largely peaceful decolonizations of the 1960s. And some warn that the freedom of South Africa in 1994 may lead to similar disillusionment.

But this rise-and-fall story is too simple. Let's look first at economic change, a process subject not only to rhythms generated in the African continent itself, but to the shifting tendencies of the world economy. These patterns do not fit a break point coinciding with political independence. Rather, they suggest a break a decade later, in the mid-1970s, when modest progress turned into prolonged crisis. The period 1940–73 can be dubbed the development era. The initiative, as noted earlier, began with colonial regimes, first Britain and then France, trying to make conflict-ridden colonies both productive and legitimate. Portugal and

Belgium, and even more so South Africa and Rhodesia, gave little thought to the standard of living of most Africans, but in their own ways used state authority to foster production. Colonial development, in the end, produced more conflict than it resolved, but the development idea had immense appeal to many Africans. Colonial and nationalist versions of development shared a belief that government planning and government investment – not just the "natural" operations of the market – would help African economies emerge from backwardness.

A nationalist vision of development shaped the policies of African governments and received outside support. Its results were mixed and, to many, disappointing. But they should not be slighted. As shown in chapter 5, growth rates were uneven but for the most part positive in the early post-independence years. Exports grew, often dramatically, in the 1950s and 1960s. In Kenya or the Côte d'Ivoire, where a small group of white settlers had once received most of the attention and most of the wealth, small and medium-sized African-owned farms became the leading edge of growing economies, and such farmers took a larger share of the wealth. The labor mobilizations of the 1940s often paid off in the 1950s, with better wages although not necessarily with the growth in employment that planners anticipated. Most important (chapter 5), literacy rates improved greatly in the 1950s through the 1970s, life expectancies grew, and infant mortality fell. Africa's population surged upward in the postwar decades. These are all strong indicators that life was improving for ordinary people in Africa.

Economic growth became much more problematic after the 1970s. This can be interpreted as the result of failure to make deep changes in the structure of African economies; whatever the record of growth, the goal of many leaders to achieve economic independence had not been met. Many economists argue that unwise economic policies were catching up with African countries. But the immediate shift in Africa's fortunes came from outside. In 1973, oil prices skyrocketed, as war in the Middle East had widespread consequences, including efforts by oil producers to restrict supplies. This had a double effect on the externally-oriented African economies: it increased their bills for fuel at a time when transport, agricultural machinery, and fledgling industries were becoming more energy-intensive; and they fostered a recession in the industrialized countries of Europe and North America, lowering demand and prices for African agricultural and mineral products. It was at this point that a modestly positive economic picture turned decisively negative.

African governments were ill-prepared to cope with the oil shocks which continued throughout the 1970s, and their indebtedness shot upward, fostered by unwise lending from financial institutions in the Middle

East and Europe and by the rising interest rates through which the United States tried to solve its own economic problems. When the world economy remained sour for years, many countries were trapped, and paying off the debt consumed the capital needed to make economic improvements. Social as well as economic development began to be reversed: school systems declined, there was a growing lack of medical facilities and supplies. Many African governments turned to international financial institutions for help when they could not meet debt payments or find the foreign exchange they needed for even the most vital imports. Those institutions imposed conditions – "structural adjustment" – on anybody who received their help. Whether the continued economic malaise, including declining per capita income in the worst affected states, was the result of the disease (bad market conditions or bad government policies) or the medicine (imposed austerity, lowered wages) is much debated. So, too, is the question of whether an expanding world economy at the turn of the new century is bringing about modest improvement or continued malaise in Africa's economies.

In economic terms, then, the break points occur not so much in relation to political independence, but in relation to the rise of the developmentalist state, 1940–73, and then its crisis, 1973–90, with an ambiguous period following. The social effects of this sequence were powerful: drawing men and women into towns and export production, giving them access to new ways to earn an income and new forms of social relations, and then pulling the rug out from many of them as unemployment rose, social services and pension funds collapsed, and modern health facilities and schools deteriorated. If the expansive phase gave men new resources through wage labor and civil service positions, it accentuated female dependence on husbands' wages and benefits. But as the contracting phase undercut men's jobs and wages and jeopardized the security of families, it made the "informal" income earned by women ever more important to the survival of urban households. In both phases, gender roles were rendered uncertain and often conflictual.

Assessing the key dates in political change also poses difficulties. There is no question that the decolonizations of the 1950s and 1960s mattered. It is unwise to see the post-colonial state as a mere reproduction of the colonial state with African personnel – if only because the Africanization of personnel tied leadership into social networks within the African continent itself, whereas colonial personnel were more rooted in England or France than in Africa. The extent of democracy in African states, however, is very much in question.

We need a broader context. The colonial state of the 1950s, especially in French and British Africa, was already much transformed. This was the era of the activist state, eager to obtain knowledge about all dimensions of life within its territory and to intervene in many of them, from labor policy to health. In the 1920s, the model colonial official was a man who "knew his natives" – that is, who understood the politics of the many little communities into which Africa was thought to be divided. In the 1950s, the model colonial official was a technical expert, who knew how to eradicate malaria, organize a school system, teach new cultivation techniques, or manage labor disputes. The 1960s African state sought to take over the interventionist aspect of the colonial state, and indeed to intensify it, in the name of the national interest and (for a time) to demonstrate to voters that the state was improving their lives.

But could the new, independent state be simultaneously developmentalist-interventionist and populist-clientalist, insuring support by providing services with general appeal and rewarding personal followers with state resources? By the early 1970s, the answer appeared to be negative. In some places and in some ways, the activist state ceased to be so – in any interest except the venal ones of its leading agents – long before international agencies began to talk of the alleged need to "shrink" the state. By the early 1980s, some years after the economic steam had been taken out of the development drive, international financial organizations and some African governments were claiming that the activist state should be banished from the realm of the possible. Had the African state gone full circle, presiding in the 1990s over a feeble infrastructure and a country divided into regional and ethnic bastions of power, rather like the politics of indirect rule in the 1930s?

Just as important as the capabilities of states is the question of how much voice people within them had in selecting their leaders. Taking the case of French- and English-speaking Africa, one can note distinct phases in the degree and form of popular political participation. The period 1945–1960 featured externally sanctioned and limited electoral competition. In their final years, colonial regimes expanded eligibility to vote and the power of elected legislators. They also tried to keep certain political movements, like the UPC in Cameroon, out of the realm of the permissible, but learned to live with others, including the CPP in the Gold Coast, the PDCI in the Côte d'Ivoire, and KANU (Kenya African National Union, the party of Mboya and Kenyatta) in Kenya. After independence, there was no external power insisting that elections be held. Once on the receiving end of the demands of citizens and independent organizations, African regimes rapidly became distrustful of the kind of political process which they had ridden to power. This closing down of political space was true in essentially all of the new African states, but the degree of closure varied greatly, from dictatorship to guided democracy. The 1960s thus constitute the period of developmentalist authoritarianism. By the late 1970s and 1980s, only the authoritarianism was left, for rarely was the state actually delivering on its developmental promises. With the export and debt crises, state leaders could no longer pass out resources – jobs, a share of bribes, privileged access to markets – to clients, so that even the patron-client system was failing. This was a highly unstable situation, giving rise to numerous coups and regional conflicts.

By the 1990s, many African leaders were unable to resist demands from below or outside to reform, so that the 1990s represent a tentative – very tentative – move toward a kind of guided democracy rather different from that of the 1950s, as this time internal leaders tried to manage democratic openings and to keep them from opening too far. The results remain to be seen.

This chronology applies mainly to formerly British and French Africa, which accounts for a good deal of the continent. The timing does not fit Portuguese Africa (independent in 1975) or Zimbabwe (1979) or South Africa (1994), but there may be parallel processes at work; I shall return to this subject.

Finally, culture and religion fit the economic and political chronologies to an extent, but not neatly. The mood of the 1950s and 1960s, directed by the last colonial rulers and the first African ones, shifted towards opening a European conception of social order to people of all races. The first rulers of independent Africa had often been educated in Europe; they had come of age at a time when missionaries and other teachers presented a clear cultural blueprint for the ambitious to follow. This had never been uncontested or unmediated; cultural forms in Africa had long been adaptive and creative. But the political elite of the 1950s was particularly affected by the possibility of using the state to direct the "modernization" of a society it perceived as backward.

By the 1960s, this elite was trying to blend its own modernizing tendencies with a political move seemingly in the opposite direction: to give culture a distinctly national character, to make it "Senegalese" or "Kenyan" or "Zairois." This entailed a blending of symbols that were not national at all and separating them from their local logic, to dilute the power embodied in forms of dress or music or art that were "Igbo" or "Kongo" into something that could be considered "Nigerian" or "Zairois." This project, too, came undone in the 1980s, in the face of diverse and unruly forms of particularistic expression, not necessarily the "tribes" of old, but forms of symbolic affinity that left the state and the nation out. These forms were sometimes religious, as in the Islamic brotherhoods or even more strikingly in the mushrooming of evangelical Protestant churches in Africa in the 1980s, with their focus on individual salvation and their distancing themselves from social and political action. They could take the form of a volatile popular culture, especially among young men and women in cities, often with a sharp hostility to the powers that be, sometimes shaping their own world of musical, artistic, and religious expression, sometimes falling into drugs and criminality. What these forms of cultural expression signified politically within African states is hard to judge, but some of them had an effect outside. African music, above all, has had a great influence in Europe and the United States – it is at the core of "world music" – and visual artists like Cheri Samba have been shown in prestigious museums in Europe. Whereas in the 1960s, it was the creation of new nations and the development of an articulate cultural expression of politically independent peoples which captured the world's imagination, in the 2000s it is fragments of oppositional culture that are most readily transmitted abroad.

# 5    Development and disappointment: social and economic change in an unequal world, 1945–2000

No word captures the hopes and ambitions of Africa's leaders, its educated populations, and many of its farmers and workers in the postwar decades better than "development." Yet it is a protean word, subject to conflicting interpretations. Its simplest meaning conveys a down-to-earth aspiration: to have clean water, decent schools and health facilities; to produce larger harvests and more manufactured goods; to have access to the consumer goods which people elsewhere consider a normal part of life. To colonial elites after the war, bringing European capital and knowledge to Africa reconciled continued rule with calls for universal progress. To nationalists, a development that would serve African interests required African rule. After independence, new rulers could claim a place for themselves as intermediaries between external resources and national aspirations. But African rulers were in turn subject to criticism for sacrificing development for the people to personal greed.

The development concept, some have argued, allowed for an internationalization of colonialism, as the one-to-one relationship of metropole to colony was transformed into a generalized economic subordination of South to North, of Africa and Asia to Europe and North America. New actors entered into trade relationships and provided capital and foreign aid: the US, the USSR, and Scandinavian countries, as well as international agencies like the United Nations, the International Monetary Fund, and the World Bank. Development became international in the most literal sense, as a process negotiated between sovereign nation-states, legally equal but in fact distinguished into those who gave and those who received.

The idea that human populations could evolve and progress was a very old one – that states should intervene to shape such a process much less so. Colonizers' assertions of the benefits of "opening" Africa to commerce through railway construction and health campaigns were precedents for the state project of development. The colonial initiative of the 1940s (chapter 2) was still new, particularly in its stated goal of improving the standard of living of Africans and its insistence that states should do what markets could not.

By the late 1940s, the field of economics was in general becoming more activist – advising governments how to stimulate as well as regulate economic growth – and it spawned the subdiscipline of "development economics." Early theorists argued that poor economies needed a "big push" to give them the infrastructure, the quality of workforce, and concentration of capital to compete in world markets. Development economists were sought after by African governments and aid agencies. The field gave intellectual sustenance to the idea that poor regions could look to their future without overthrowing the international order. But even before the new development economists had consolidated their place in the establishment, they were challenged by economists who used similar scholarly tools to make an opposite argument: that the world economy, far from being a source of progress for all who participated in it, made the rich richer and the poor poorer.

At their most radical (the "dependency school" prominent in Latin America in the 1960s and in Africa from the 1970s), these arguments called for poor countries to distance themselves from world markets. Radical and orthodox versions overlapped to the extent that both agreed on the importance of using resources to build *national* economies. Many agreed that new industries needed protection from outside competition so that the national economy would develop mutually supporting sectors, avoiding a situation where foreign companies picked off the best niches and left everything else to stagnate.

Development economics provided an effective language with which African governments and nongovernmental organizations could appeal to rich nations and international organizations for aid in the form of grants and low-interest loans. The stress on state planning coincided with many politicians' distrust of groups within their countries that could provide a base for counter-organization, farmers' associations and labor unions in particular. The developmentalist state, in its post-colonial as much as its colonial manifestation, was thus a peculiar entity: it exercised initiative, yet it suppressed initiative too, and it above all encouraged citizens to *think* of the state as the prime mover for raising the standard of living.

The irony of the period 1960–73 is that post-colonial regimes, intent on establishing the autonomy of the nation, reinforced the externally dependent economy of the colonial era. Africa's small-scale farmers of the 1940s and 1950s were a model of modest expansion, adapting kinship and clientage and other forms of social relations within indigenous societies to channel labor and other resources into export agriculture. In the best endowed regions, a class of moderately wealthy farmers became a force for further investment in transport, marketing, and banking, and they used their political influence to obtain spending on education and other services for their regions. Like Nkrumah, many rulers of the 1960s feared that such farmers would be the nucleus of conservative opposition to their populist, state-centered visions of the future, and they wondered if small-scale agriculture would really get the country over the economic hump that decades of colonialism had created. They had a point, both because of the limitations within agriculture and because of blockages in national and global economic structures. Let us first consider agriculture.

### The promise and limits of peasant production

Peasants had a big place in the major rise in per capita GNP through 1975 (figures 1a–1c). In Kenya, the lifting of the ban on Africans growing coffee in 1951 led to a spurt of growth that changed the nature of the colonial economy. Peasant output rose at an average of 7.3 percent per year between 1954 and 1964, and the smallholder became the backbone of an economy once dominated by white settlers. This economy for a time proved dynamic: GNP per capita rose almost 30 percent in the decade after independence in 1963, even as population soared. African planters similarly displaced white settlers in the coffee and cocoa sectors of the Côte d'Ivoire, and this colony became

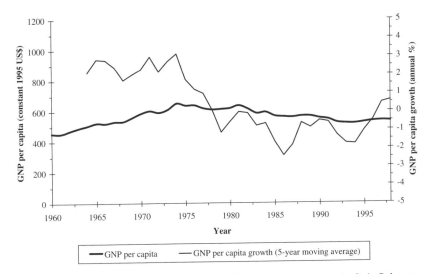

Figure 1a  GNP per capita and GNP per capita growth in Sub-Saharan Africa, 1960–1998.

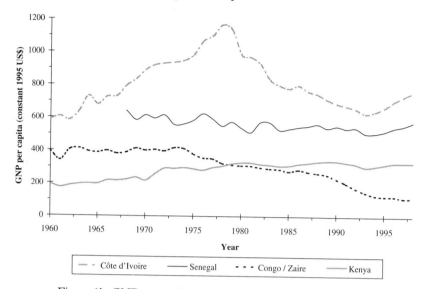

Figure 1b GNP per capita in selected African countries, 1960–1998

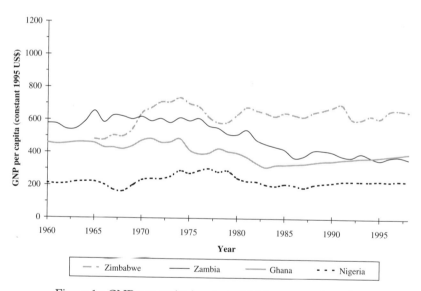

Figure 1c GNP per capita in selected African countries, 1960–1998.
*Sources* (for figures 1a–1c): World Bank, *World Development Indicators* (Washington, DC: World Bank, 2000).

the economic star of French West Africa; after independence in 1960, it doubled its real per capita GNP in twenty years. When Zimbabwe finally rid itself of white rule in 1979, marketed output from peasants went in a decade from 10 percent of total production to over 50 percent. The stalwarts of earlier peasant agriculture – Yoruba cocoa farmers in Nigeria and Chagga coffee planters in Tanganyika – increased their output, income, and political influence in the 1950s.

Such success stories, nonetheless, were based on crops that were produced in many parts of the world. The favorable prices of the post-war years weakened by the late 1950s and early 1960s and badly hurt the economy of Ghana; the more drastic fall in the 1980s cut the Côte d'Ivoire's GNP per capita in half, erasing the impressive gains of the two previous decades. Overall, Africa's coffee and cocoa farmers were producing three times as much in 1998 as in 1958, but their share of the world market remained about the same (figures 2.a and 2.b).

One of the virtues of peasant agriculture was its flexibility. Using family labor, producers could increase or decrease export crop output while insuring their own food supply. African peasants were able to survive low world prices because they engaged in "self-exploitation," making use of the unpaid labor of women and children to maintain production even when sales prices could not have justified paying hired labor a market wage. In the relatively prosperous zones, farmers – and their wives and children – kept their options open: members engaged in food production, export crop production, off-farm wage labor, off-farm enterprises. Many used earnings not just to reinvest in the agricultural enterprise but also

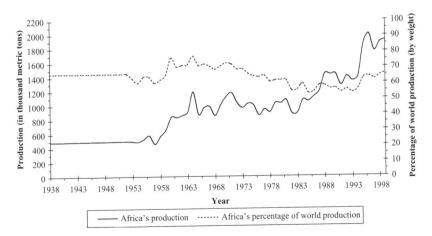

Figure 2a Africa's cocoa production, 1938–1999

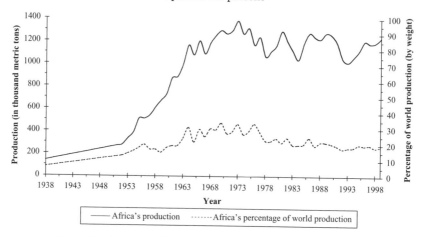

Figure 2b  Africa's coffee production, 1938–1999. *Sources* (for figures 2a and 2b): Food and Agricultural Organization, *FAOSTAT*; UNESCO, *General History of Africa VII* (London: Heinemann, 1993), pp. 348–49.

to pay children's school fees or to participate actively in local politics, in the hope that more career options would open up.

In much of the world, agricultural expansion has been a brutal process, dependent on the dispossession of rural people by an elite capable of managing land and labor to maximize profits. In much of Africa, however, agricultural relations entailed what Sara Berry calls "exploitation without dispossession." In cocoa production, for instance, family labor was indeed exploited, as was the labor of immigrants seeking to move into the cocoa zone, but there was no rigid line between a planter class and an agricultural laborer class. Berry argues that employers in such circumstances found labor hard to discipline and hence lacked the coordination to make full use of productivity-enhancing inputs like fertilizer and irrigation. Claims to land could only be sustained with community support, making it harder for a distinct planter class to emerge. None of this was an obstacle to productive agriculture, or indeed to considerable inequality in the resources for agriculture and pastoralism, but it did stop short of transformation into the kind of ruthless capital accumulation and continuous pressure to enhance productivity characteristic of capitalist agriculture in Europe, North America, and parts of Asia and Latin America.

It is easier for a scholar to say that incremental improvements in small-scale farming may be the best that can be done in African circumstances than it is for a new state to accept such limitations. African leaders wanted a farming sector that was economically strong and politically weak and feared they would get exactly the reverse: that cocoa or coffee producers, well networked among themselves, would constitute a political challenge without delivering the "modern" agriculture that the leadership sought. This helps to explain some of the apparently self-destructive tendencies of both the colonial and post-colonial eras. Colonial states in the 1940s and 1950s spent vast sums of money on centrally-directed agricultural schemes, such as the cotton and rice systems of the Niger valley in what is now Mali or the "ground nut scheme" to grow peanuts on a vast tract of land in Tanganyika, using wage labor and heavy war surplus equipment. Later, Kwame Nkrumah and Sékou Touré tried to create state-run collective farms, which – like the colonial ventures – failed. So, too, did schemes like the Tanzanian government's "villagization" which made farmers live in clusters and devote time to collective fields, where they could both provide services and be observed, all under the pretense that this represented the essentially cooperative nature of African society.

Colonial governments after the war used marketing boards to take much of the earnings of the commodities boom out of farmers' hands, creating stabilization funds to support farmers in case prices declined. Nationalist parties in the Gold Coast, Nigeria, and elsewhere fought the marketing boards, but once in power kept them in place, this time emphasizing the importance of using agricultural income in an activist fashion rather than as a hedge against market fluctuations. Schools were at the heart of many governments' programs. From Nkrumah onward, rulers not only emphasized social services, but industrialization as well: to use cocoa revenue to find alternatives to cocoa. Nkrumah took over the colonial project to build a huge dam over the Volta River which would produce the electricity to transform Ghana's abundant bauxite into aluminum. That thousands of Ghanaians lost their land to the lake behind the dam was to be offset by a claim that they would be relocated into areas where they could begin "modern" farming.

Such state-run projects soaked up vast amounts of capital and required continued intervention from foreign experts and skilled workers, as well as inputs of foreign goods, while producing a disappointing revenue stream. For a time in countries like Ghana, Nigeria, and the Côte d'Ivoire, cocoa or coffee revenues remained buoyant enough to make possible a measure of state-centered growth in a variety of industries, the rapid Africanization of the bureaucracy, the expansion of the educational system, and the provision of other services. State-centered development perpetuated a tendency of colonial states: to appear as distant, extractive, and imposing. And the centrality of tariffs, as opposed to other kinds of taxes, to state revenue perpetuated the quality of the colonial state as a gatekeeper, policing the intersection of internal and external economies. This is a point to which I will return.

So far, I have been writing about countries with strong cash crop sectors. Some regions which should fit this picture – good land not too far from ports – do not: Liberia, Guinea, parts of Congo/Zaire. In areas of marginal rainfall or other environmental difficulties, adding new crops to old ones, feeding a growing population, and maintaining larger cattle herds could severely strain resources. Deforestation, accelerated by the use of wood fuel in the face of the scarcity and high cost of alternatives, had particularly deleterious ecological effects. In the 1970s, the prolonged drought in the Sahel, the large region south of the Sahara, was a warning of ecological danger, and wide droughts have been repeated in parts of eastern and southern Africa as well. Ecological problems are rarely purely "natural"; the confining of growing populations of Africans to "reserves", in parts of southern Africa where white settlers had appropriated extensive land, caused profound degradation in many areas. Worst of all were war zones, where insecurity compounded environmental vulnerability and produced devastating famines. A million people may have died in Ethiopia in 1984–85 in a famine induced by government oppression and civil strife. The food supply in the war zones of southern Sudan has been dangerously meager since the 1970s.

The late colonial era witnessed often heavy-handed efforts of agricultural experts to counter allegedly neglectful African practices with scientific conservation practices. Such interventions have produced as much conflict and uncertainty as "improvement." Ecological history reveals evidence of thoughtful adaptation by African farmers to environmental stress, and scholars debate the relative merits of different approaches – indigenous, foreign or cooperative – to insuring "sustainable" agriculture.

Parts of the countryside witnessed large-scale labor migration (discussed later in this chapter). The loss of labor power from migration can disrupt the farming cycle, particularly in regard to clearing land, but the money sent back by migrants is critical both to survival in the worst areas and to breaking out of low-intensity agriculture in zones of more potential. In colonial and post-colonial Kenya, urban wage labor was a crucial source of capital for agricultural improvements, since banks and other sources of credit did not supply the majority of farmers. Since young men were the most likely to migrate, the effect on women was above all to increase not only their work load but also their vulnerability, for their fate depended on remittances a man chose to send back, on his not finding a "city wife," and on his staying healthy. In some arid areas near the Senegal River, remittances make up to 20–50 percent of family budgets. A newly endowed mosque or an expanded herd tended by relatives could be the sign of a successful migrant laborer in France; the unsuccessful one leaves only misery. In South Africa, the dependence of rural women on the insecure urban earnings of men worsened in the 1950s and again in

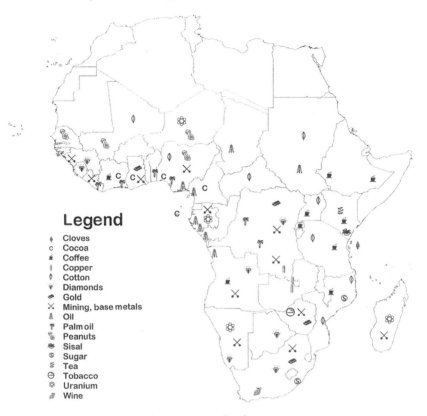

**Legend**

- ♠ Cloves
- c Cocoa
- ☕ Coffee
- ∥ Copper
- ◊ Cotton
- ▽ Diamonds
- ◗ Gold
- × Mining, base metals
- ⋀ Oil
- ⋔ Palm oil
- ⅋ Peanuts
- ❧ Sisal
- ⓢ Sugar
- ☲ Tea
- ⊖ Tobacco
- ⚛ Uranium
- ℐ Wine

Map 4 Resources for export production

the 1970s as expulsions of women from cities under apartheid regulations exacerbated the pressure on land. Such areas were no longer regions for the social reproduction of a workforce; they were dumping grounds.

### The industrialization that never was

The cure for a colonial economy dependent on sales of a narrow range of agricultural or mineral products and on purchase from outside of manufactured goods seemed – to economists and political leaders in the 1950s and 1960s – to be industrialization. It didn't work out so simply.

Africa has long had great difficulty in attracting capital, given its spread-out population divided by colonial and post-colonial borders, the continent's generally low income levels, and the uncertainties of labor force development among people whose long and bitter experience encouraged them to avoid subordination to an employer by keeping other options open. The mining industry – in gold, copper, and other minerals – has been the biggest exception, but only in South Africa and, to an extent, in Southern Rhodesia did it spawn broad regional industrial development. Even in the early 1950s, French and British officials were noticing that private overseas investment was not following in the wake of their public development investments. African political leaders thought that independence would make a decisive difference; they could build their own industries.

And to an extent they did. States used tariff barriers, taxing imported finished products heavily and inputs lightly, to get investors to manufacture products within their borders. Much investment in the 1960s was import substitution industrialization (ISI), relying on transnational corporations headquartered in the United States, Europe, and Japan. States also founded parastatal corporations in sectors that they hoped would stimulate a wide range of private activity or else built industries that they hoped would constitute the core of a socialist economy. But in either case, the constraints were severe: industry demands technical knowledge as well as finance, and that is highly concentrated in the world economy. Transnational companies often bargained to keep competitors out, and state-owned industries were given protected markets, so that ISI usually meant that producers were sheltered and inefficient, and that citizens were stuck with products more expensive and of lower quality than available on the world market. Continual importation of machinery and supplies was necessary for industry to function. The economics of industrialization in countries with small markets and little infrastructure were bad enough; the politics were worse, for politicians were tempted to use protected industries to enrich themselves and their clients and to distribute relatively well paying jobs.

Industrialization nonetheless had its moment: between 1965 and 1973, industry expanded twice as fast as GDP. Much of this was in mining, but manufacturing, albeit from a low base, grew at nearly 7 percent per year between 1960 and 1980. This was concentrated in food processing and textiles. Except for South Africa, where industrialization stretched back to the nineteenth century, it was concentrated around a few centers: in Zimbabwe and in Kenya, near Nairobi. But after the oil shocks, growth declined, and by 1980 it was negative: Africa was slowly de-industrializing. Only Mauritius, a tiny country, imitated the South East Asian pattern of the 1980s, producing textiles for export markets. Nigeria, Botswana, Kenya, and for a time Zambia could build industry to service a significant mining or agricultural economy, but they were vulnerable to the loss of demand for their usual exports. By the 1970s, world manufacturing capacity was excessive; Africa was in a bad position to make

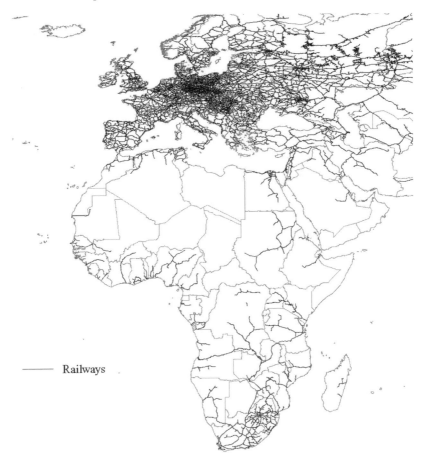

Map 5  Railways

either ISI or export industrialization competitive. South Africa, even after apartheid, had difficulty exporting manufactured goods and becoming a pole of regional economic activity, and it remains vulnerable to declining prices for gold. Building an industrial center requires more than cheap labor or even natural resources. Good communications, reliable electricity and water, linkages among firms, skilled labor, and management capacity are all factors which tend to encourage industrialization where it is already advanced and where states are capable of delivering consistent services. Even a glance at a railway map of Europe and Africa (map 5) suggests the enormity of the gap between a densely networked region and a zone (with the single exception of South Africa) of limited connections, mostly directed toward evacuation of products rather than regional interaction.

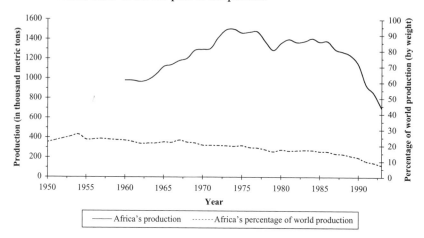

Figure 2c Africa's copper production, 1950–1993. *Sources*: Economic Commission for Africa, *Economic Bulletin for Africa* (New York: United Nations, 1961), pp. 53, xiv; UNCTAD, *Yearbook of International Commodity Statistics* (New York: United Nations, 1984, 1995).

So investment outside of agriculture has focused above all on mining. A copper boom brought wealth to Northern Rhodesia and Zaire in the post-war decade and at times thereafter; gold enriched South Africa over many decades, and boomed in the late 1970s. Other minerals have had their moments: iron ore in Liberia; bauxite in Guinea and Ghana; uranium in Niger and Gabon. These moments have only rarely been sustained and even more rarely have they had effects beyond the mining enclaves and the labor reservoirs which supplied them. Multinational mining corporations play off the diverse locations of supplies around the world and sometimes the substitutability of products; mining enclaves in Africa are vulnerable to state incapacity and disorder. Even gold has been an unreliable source of export income, and two of the world's leading copper producers, Zambia and Zaire, experienced, from the 1970s, plunging prices, declining output, and growing unemployment (see figure 2c). The hopes of mineworkers, once the vanguard of labor stabilization, for a new sort of life fell along with the copper prices and national policies built on mine revenue.

Industrial investors have many options worldwide, and Africa is risky. The degradation of infrastructure since 1980 has made those obstacles higher: deteriorating roads; unreliable electricity; few telephones; workers with inadequate education and health protection; and arbitrary regulatory and judicial systems. Outside of South Africa, investment per capita in Africa dropped from $80 in 1970 to $73 in 1997. Meanwhile, the idea of a more self-reliant industrialization, using "appropriate technology" and concentrating on product lines based on domestic supplies of raw materials, has been more hope than strategy.

## Economics beyond borders

Another solution for Africa's economic ills that has repeatedly been proposed is unification: increasing the size of markets. Colonial borders reshaped the varied spatial linkages that African trading groups forged long ago. Official and unofficial appropriations take place at borders. The most ambitious experiment to transcend this problem was the common market and common services arrangements among Kenya, Tanzania, and Uganda, begun under the British and continuing in altered forms until 1977. This experiment had its accomplishments, but it couldn't overcome the rigidities of the state system, including leadership rivalries (especially after the eccentric and repressive Idi Amin became dictator of Uganda in 1971) and differing ideologies (self-reliance and socialism in Tanzania and Africanized capitalism in Kenya). Given the unevenness of physical and human resources in the region, the common markets produced conflict: the tendency of industries to locate in Nairobi, the best equipped city, was unacceptable to Kenya's partners, and issues of favoritism in transport services proved equally divisive. The East African Community broke up amidst acrimony.

The more modest goals of the Economic Community of West African States (ECOWAS) have led to common action particularly in banking and remains promising for the future. But the most concrete results have come from a more compromised sort of cooperation, that is cooperation between the former French colonies and their former master. The common currency (the CFA franc) has been pegged to French currency and supported by France. This injected external discipline into financial policy in the region, since printing more money when the till ran empty has not been an option, and these states have been less troubled by inflation than others. Yet the CFA franc gives considerable power to France, and its decision to devalue the franc by half in 1994, although regarded as overdue by most economists, brought home the fact that crucial decisions were being made in Paris. Meanwhile, former French colonies have since independence tried to generalize their relationship with France into one with the European common market (now the European Union) that gives their goods privileged access to European markets.

As Senghor predicted in 1956, the form of decolonization chosen by France – devolving power to individual territories and weakening supraterritorial federations – left each territory with limited resources and created a vested interest among political elites in keeping countries separate (chapter 4). African economies are at least as likely to compete as to complement each other's strengths; all are trying to get narrow ranges of goods into the same "developed world" markets; all want to buy the same manufactured goods from Asia or Europe. Intraregional trade in Africa as a percentage of total trade is much less important than in Europe.

Unofficial cross-border trading networks (smuggling) may well be doing more to create regional trading relations than official efforts, albeit with high transaction costs. Smuggling is not necessarily incongruent with state interests, since officials sometimes take the lead in undercutting, for a price, their own trade regulations.

African leaders have not been insensitive to these problems. The UN-associated Economic Commission for Africa (ECA) conducted studies and issued reports that provided alternative ways of thinking from those coming from the World Bank or the International Monetary Fund (IMF). Leaders met in Lagos in 1980 and in Khartoum in 1988 to work toward an African Economic Community, with concrete steps along the way to promote regional integration and cooperation toward basic goals, including the alleviation of poverty and the providing of critical needs. In the midst of anti-apartheid struggles, South Africa's free neighbors created the Southern African Development Coordination Conference (SADCC) to provide an alternative to doing business with South Africa. However, international cooperation assumes that state leaders are disinterested advocates of African or at least national interests, and many are anything but.

Difficult economic conditions sharpened interstate rivalries. There have been numerous border closures and expulsions of aliens – Ghanaians from Nigeria, Burkinabé from Côte d'Ivoire, Mozambicans from South Africa. Those expelled were often following the paths of migrant labor and regional trade that their fathers took during the colonial era. Most notorious was Ghana's expulsion of 100,000 aliens, mostly from Nigeria or Burkina Faso, in 1968. In the 1990s, the Côte d'Ivoire government's campaign for "ivoirité" aimed at excluding from full participation in national life people who came, sometimes generations back, from Burkina Faso or Mali. Anxieties about unemployment and trade competition – and the propagation of xenophobic images – have been behind this exclusionary version of citizenship.

If the Africa of sovereign nations has become uneasy with its own history of migration and regional trade, the internal conflicts of some states have spilled across the borders of others. World news has become saturated with pictures of refugees streaming from Rwanda, the eastern part of Congo/Zaire, the southern Sudan, Liberia, or Sierra Leone. There is a grim reality behind these images. The UN estimates that 6.3 million Africans have fled their countries and taken refuge elsewhere in Africa (with smaller numbers in Europe); another 10 million have been displaced by conflict within their country's borders.

Africa's place in the wider world is paradoxical, particularly when journalists and scholars write – often glibly – of global interconnection as the hallmark of our age. Africa's interconnections are old, but in some ways its linkages with the rest of the world have been diminishing. Its share of world trade fell from over 3 percent in the 1950s to less than 2 percent in the 1990s, 1.2 percent if one excludes South Africa. Africans have the use of one telephone line per 100 people (one per 200 outside of South Africa), compared to 50 in the world as a whole. Foreign aid has declined to a minuscule .23 percent of donor country GNP, but in Africa this still represents over 13 percent of GNP, vastly higher than in any other "developing" region; governments like Tanzania and Mozambique would close down overnight without donor support.

### Modest accomplishment and devastating failure

Africa's economic disasters have been very disastrous, and they have befallen the best as well as the worst endowed of its territories, such as mineral-rich Zaire, victimized by predatory governments and the looting of diamonds and gold by networks organized by its neighbors, allies as well as rivals. Then there are the oil-producing states, which in some ways became caricatures of state-centered development. They were spigot economies. Nigerians, Gabonais, or Angolans turned on the tap, their governments collected massive rents, and the oil companies collected massive profits; few indigenous workers were employed. With so few linkages to the domestic economy, oil production represented the extreme of what troubled African economies anyway: extroversion, a relationship between outside corporations and a state elite that guarded the interface between national resources and world markets. The revenue could of course have been used to diversify productive resources, but it was more likely used in symbolically important projects, as oil-fed officials built roads and schools in home villages or prestige projects in capital cities. Indeed, states did little to encourage development that might have produced a business class autonomous from it. In Nigeria oil ruined cocoa – a product which had the virtue of involving thousands of Nigerians in production and marketing – and over time Nigeria became more dependent, not less, on oil exports for government revenue and foreign exchange (figure 3).

But it would be misleading to dismiss the development era as without accomplishment, even if not a single African state achieved the often-stated goal of autonomy and economic security for the mass of the population. Statistics reveal that for the most part African states were able to achieve modest growth in per capita income in the period 1950 to

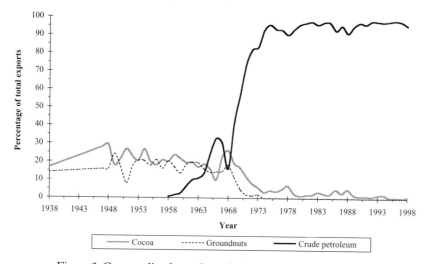

Figure 3  Commodity dependence in the Nigerian economy, 1938–1998. *Sources*: Food and Agricultural Organization, *FAOSTAT*; Economic Commission for Africa, *African Statistics* (New York: United Nations, 1962), p. 70; UN, *Yearbook of International Trade Statistics* (New York: United Nations, 1951); International Monetary Fund, *International Financial Statistics Yearbook* (Washington, DC: International Monetary Fund, 1979, 1999).

1975, albeit at rates lower than in the already wealthy regions of the world. Between 1950 and 1975, per capita GNP in Africa as a whole grew by an average of 2.4 percent a year, Sub-Saharan Africa trailing North Africa somewhat (see figures 1a–1c). Agricultural output grew in absolute terms in the 1960s, but only kept pace with population growth. The variation within Africa, however, is notable. Ghana's GNP per capita grew at 1.9 percent per year in the 1950s, but turned negative (−0.7 percent) in the 1960s, as the cocoa sector all but collapsed. Kenya grew slowly in the 1950s, then at an impressive rate of 3.2 percent in the 1960s. Zambia's mineral economy did well in both decades – 2.7 percent annual growth in the 1950s, 3.2 percent in the 1960s. Botswana, Cameroon, and a number of other countries – unlike Senegal and Ghana – grew quite modestly in the last decade of colonial rule and quite rapidly in the first decade of independence. Rwanda and some other countries failed to grow in either decade.

Then came the 1970s. The oil price peaks of 1973 and 1976, the subsequent downturn in demand for tropical products, and the rise of world interest rates sent Africa into a tailspin. Whereas in the decade before 1976, GNP per capita from Sub-Saharan Africa as a whole grew nearly 20 percent, in the next decade it fell 20 percent, and as of 1996 was only a little ahead of 1966. In Zambia, where the copper market collapsed (see figure 2c), GNP per capita fell 36 percent in ten years and stagnated for another ten. It was a terrible decade for Tanzania, for Ghana, and for Senegal. Oil producers moved, although far from steadily, in the opposite direction. The malaise would prove to be long-lasting. All low-income countries in the world suffered after 1973, but East and South East Asia recovered substantially in the 1980s (until their own short-lived crisis in the late 1990s). It has only been in the late 1990s that African exports have picked up and then to modest and varied growth rates (figure 1a). Roughly half of Africans live in what experts consider absolute poverty.

GNP figures tells us only so much. National income could go to a wealthy elite or big corporations, and much of what people consume may be grown and even exchanged outside of visible and measurable market transactions. Indeed, if the official figures for production in a country like Zaire were valid, it isn't clear how so many people, particularly in urban areas, could have remained alive. The versatility of small-scale farmers and traders remains an unacknowledged and uncounted fact of African life, just as the obstacles they have had to overcome remain unappreciated.

But other statistics reveal that something important happened in the late colonial and early independence years: major improvements in health and education. In the early colonial years, Africa lost population. The taming of epidemic diseases (but not endemic ones like malaria or sleeping sickness) as well as lowered infant mortality and higher birthrates turned the post-war decades into years of burgeoning population growth, as rates of population growth moved from about 1 percent at war's end to 3 percent in the 1960s (figures 4a and 4b). The modernization project required better networks of health facilities, and some independent African governments, like Tanzania's, made a strong effort to bring clinics to rural areas. In Sub-Saharan Africa as a whole, life expectancy rose from 40 to nearly 52 years between 1960 and 1990, and infant mortality fell from 284 per 1,000 live births to 175 (figures 5a–5c). Whereas 27 percent of Africans had access to safe water in 1975, 40 percent did so in 1990.

Once considered underpopulated, Africa is now seen as the opposite. The issue is in fact complex, and high population growth reflects not just the accomplishments of modern medicine, but their limitations: childhood mortality is still so high that families needing assurance that a young generation will survive have more children than experts consider optimum, and the importance of diversifying options – given the risks of farming, wage labor, or any other survival strategy – also encourages larger families. Improved health care would, in the long run, lower population growth, as would increased schooling and job opportunities for young women; all areas where early independent governments made considerable, but insufficient and unsustained progress.

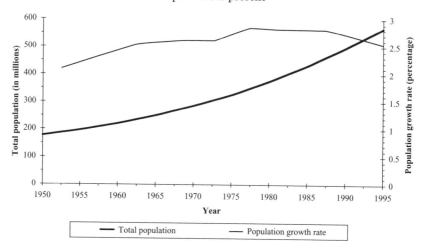

Figure 4a  Total population and population growth rate in Sub-Saharan Africa, 1950–1995

The economic crisis of the 1970s and 1980s had powerful effects on welfare beyond the stagnation of GNP. Efforts to build health and sanitation facilities in many countries lost ground. In some countries, there are fewer physicians per capita now than in the 1970s. Preventable

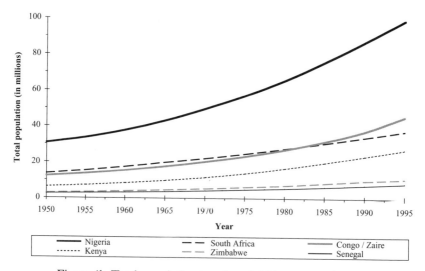

Figure 4b  Total population in selected African countries, 1950–1995. *Sources* (for figures 4a and 4b): Population Division, Department of Economic and Social Affairs, *World Population Prospects: The 1998 Revision* (New York: United Nations, 1999), pp. 18, 448–49.

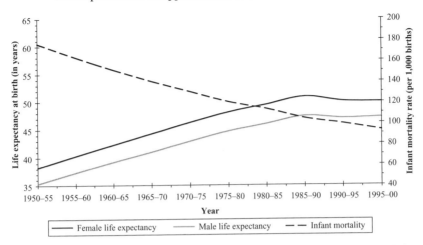

Figure 5a Life expectancy at birth and infant mortality rate in Sub-Saharan Africa, 1950–2000

and curable diseases are still killing people, particularly children. Nearly 3,000 children a day die of malaria, and large numbers die of diarrhea.

The inability of African health systems to cope with their challenges became strikingly clear with the emergence of the AIDS epidemic in the

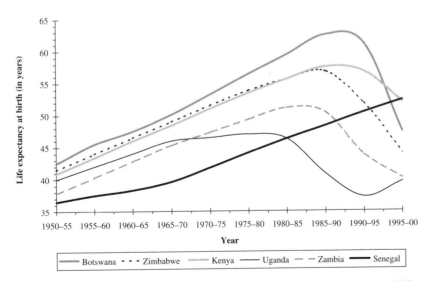

Figure 5b Life expectancy at birth in selected African countries, 1950–2000

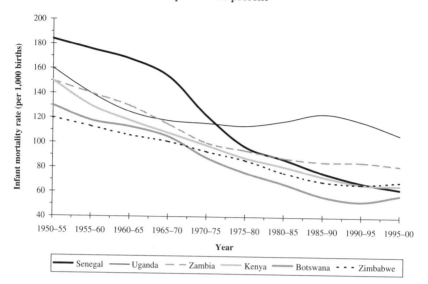

Figure 5c Infant mortality rate in selected African countries, 1950–2000. *Sources* (for figures 5a–5c): Population Division, Department of Economic and Social Affairs, *World Population Prospects: The 1998 Revision* (New York: United Nations, 1999), pp. 18, 552–59, 580–81.

1980s. AIDS is not a uniquely African scourge, but its extent and its particular pattern reflect post-1970s African conditions. Of all the deaths from AIDS worldwide, 83 percent have occurred in Africa. South Africa has the largest number of people living with AIDS in the world, over 4 million, and in the southern region generally one adult in five is infected. From the mid-1970s to 1999, it claimed nearly 14 million African lives – a holocaust equal in magnitude (but over fewer years) to the slave trade. An estimated 12 million children have been orphaned; skilled work forces have been particularly affected; and every worker who becomes sick has children, brothers, wives, and other relatives who also suffer. In Kenya, Botswana, Zimbabwe, Zambia, Uganda, and Malawi, life expectancy has been in steep decline since 1985, falling from the fifties to as low as forty, wiping out much of the gains since the 1960s (figure 5b).

The incidence of AIDS in Africa follows a distinctive pattern: most cases appear to be transmitted by heterosexual contact rather than by homosexual contact or shared needles. Around 55 percent of HIV-infected Africans are women, whereas in the United States and Europe, women account for 20 percent of infections. Heterosexual transmission has something to do with the importance of migration – especially male labor migration – across much of the continent, and the high rates of HIV infection (25 percent) in a relatively prosperous country like

Botswana suggest that a more active exchange economy can produce more infections. But the pattern of the epidemic also reveals the failure of governments to provide routine health care and adequate nutrition. HIV infection is rendered more likely by poor basic health: inadequate nutrition, endemic diseases, and lack of treatment for curable venereal infections. Now, a panicked international medical establishment intervenes in Africa to try to contain AIDS, but part of the cause of this pattern of infection lay earlier in the shortfalls and reversal of an effort to provide basic medical care and nutrition.

Education was arguably the most important priority of new African governments. In the 1950s, before formal independence, transitional governments in Nigeria made "universal primary education" a key element of their platform. Fifty years later the promise remains unfulfilled, but the effort was impressive, as it was in most African countries, where it often was the largest item in the state budget (as high as 20 percent). When Kenya became independent, for example, 900,000 students were in primary school; thirty years later, there were 5.5 million. In Africa as a whole, primary enrollments went from 43 percent of the population in 1960 to 77 percent in 1997, secondary from 3 percent to 26 percent, university from practically nil to 4 percent (table 1 and figures 6a–6d). Adult literacy rose from 27 percent in 1970 to 45 percent in 1990 (table 2). Universities entered the colonial imagination quite late: after World War II British and French officials thought they could get away with one university each (Ibadan, founded in 1948 and Dakar, in 1957) for their West African colonies. But universities quickly became a national project. Most African states have at least one; Nigeria has many. Nevertheless, Africa's educational attainments remain among the world's lowest, an honor shared with South Asia. In both areas, women's access to education lags behind that of men.

Table 1 *Education: Gross enrollment rates in Sub-Saharan Africa, 1960–1997 (percent)*

| Year | Primary | | | Secondary | | | Tertiary | | |
|------|------|--------|-------|------|--------|-------|------|--------|-------|
|      | Male | Female | Total | Male | Female | Total | Male | Female | Total |
| 1960 | 54.4 | 32.0 | 43.2 | 4.2 | 2.0 | 3.1 | 0.4 | 0.1 | 0.2 |
| 1970 | 62.3 | 42.8 | 52.5 | 9.6 | 4.6 | 7.1 | 1.3 | 0.3 | 0.8 |
| 1980 | 88.7 | 70.2 | 79.5 | 22.2 | 12.8 | 17.5 | 2.7 | 0.7 | 1.7 |
| 1990 | 81.9 | 67.6 | 74.8 | 25.5 | 19.2 | 22.4 | 4.1 | 1.9 | 3.0 |
| 1997 | 84.1 | 69.4 | 76.8 | 29.1 | 23.3 | 26.2 | 5.1 | 2.8 | 3.9 |

*Source:* World Bank, *Can Africa Claim the 21$^{st}$ Century?* (Washington, DC: World Bank, 2000), p. 106.

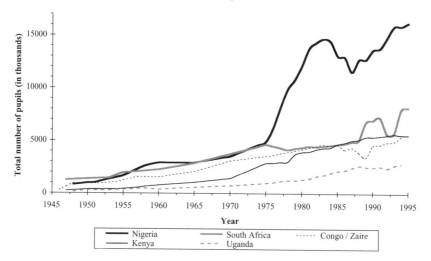

Figure 6a Primary education: total number of pupils in selected African countries, 1946–1995

Again, the budget crisis of the 1980s affected schools. Government spending per pupil has declined around 20 percent since then. Primary enrollments often stagnated after 1980, but show signs of recovery. Teachers' plummeting salaries force them to do other work; sometimes

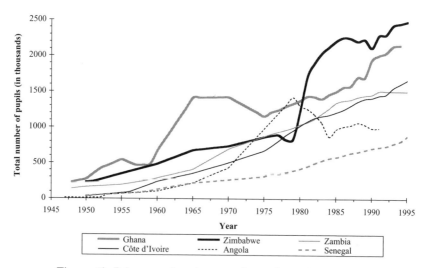

Figure 6b Primary education: total number of pupils in selected African countries, 1946–1995

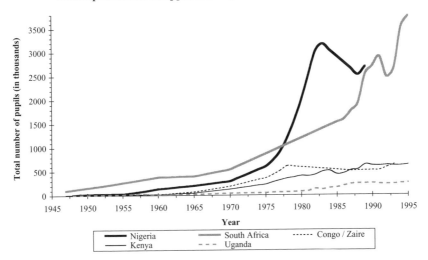

Figure 6c Secondary education: total number of pupils in selected African countries, 1946–1995

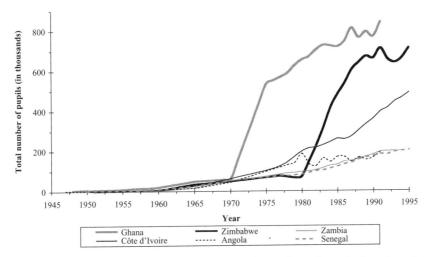

Figure 6d Secondary education: total number of pupils in selected African countries, 1946–1995. *Sources* (for figures 6a–6d): United Nations, *Statistical Yearbook* (New York: United Nations, 1949–50, 1952, 1954, 1955, 1957, 1960); Economic Commission for Africa, *A Survey of Economic Conditions in Africa* (New York: United Nations, 1968); World Bank, *World Development Indicators* (Washington, DC: World Bank, 1998); United Nations Educational, Scientific and Cultural Organization (UNESCO), *Statistical Yearbook* (Paris: UNESCO Publishing, 1999).

Table 2 *Literacy rates in selected African countries, c.1960–1998 (percentage of males and females aged 15 and above)*

| Country | c.1960[a] | | 1970 | | 1980 | | 1990 | | 1998 | |
|---|---|---|---|---|---|---|---|---|---|---|
| | Male | Female | Male | Female | Male | Female | Male | Female | Male | Female |
| Congo/Zaire | 49 | 14 | 35 | 11 | 48 | 21 | 62 | 34 | 71 | 47 |
| Côte d'Ivoire | 8 | 2 | 25 | 6 | 34 | 13 | 44 | 24 | 53 | 36 |
| Ghana | | | 43 | 17 | 58 | 31 | 70 | 47 | 79 | 60 |
| Kenya | 30 | 10 | 56 | 26 | 70 | 43 | 81 | 61 | 88 | 74 |
| Nigeria | 25 | 6 | 31 | 10 | 45 | 22 | 60 | 38 | 70 | 53 |
| Senegal | 10 | 1 | 23 | 6 | 31 | 12 | 38 | 19 | 45 | 26 |
| South Africa | 41 | 40 | 72 | 68 | 78 | 75 | 82 | 80 | 85 | 84 |
| Uganda | 44 | 26 | 51 | 22 | 61 | 31 | 69 | 43 | 76 | 54 |
| Zambia | 53 | 30 | 64 | 32 | 72 | 47 | 79 | 59 | 84 | 69 |
| Zimbabwe | 48 | 31 | 66 | 49 | 78 | 62 | 87 | 75 | 92 | 83 |

[a] All are 1962 except Senegal 1961, South Africa 1960, Zambia 1963.

*Sources:* World Bank, *World Development Indicators* (Washington, DC: World Bank, 2000); United Nations, *Demographic Yearbook* (New York: United Nations, 1960, 1963, 1964, 1970); United Nations Educational, Scientific and Cultural Organization (UNESCO), *Statistical Yearbook* (Paris: UNESCO Publishing, 1980), pp. 44–46.

they go unpaid. Class sizes have increased – to 75 in Dakar, for instance – and facilities have become degraded. Many schools don't have black-boards and most lack books. Studies of schooling in rural Mali and Togo reveal the discouragement of students and parents and declining enrollments: too many primary school graduates cannot get jobs, and families can no longer put so much faith in education. Nevertheless, self-help efforts are organized at the village level to promote schooling, some-times with results that credit the effort more than the accomplishment.

The sudden effort to promote secondary and university education in the 1950s and 1960s gave Africa a substantial class of people conver-sant in literature, science, and technology, and with ambitions to know more. Many of them came from very modest backgrounds. In the early twenty-first century, education of sufficient quality to lead to professional opportunities has increasingly become a privilege for the children of those already in such a position.

The economic crisis of the 1970s and 1980s has thus had powerful effects. In the 1940s, the leading colonial regimes had decided that de-velopment required a healthy, skilled, and educated workforce, capable of sustaining itself without the resources of "backward" villages. African governments backed education for other reasons, above all as the sub-stance and symbol of national progress. Rural and urban citizens devoted enormous effort to insuring that at least some would get schooling. The reversals of the 1980s are a step away from development goals – putting in place a workforce capable of attracting investors and making production efficient and predictable – and they have undermined the hope for a better future that sustained Africans through the humiliations of colonization and the sacrifices of freedom.

The crises of the 1970s and 1980s also left Africa with a burden that makes the new situation more difficult to escape: debt. Most African regimes tried as long as they could to reduce expenses while continuing politically necessary expenditures, such as paying off clients and providing visible services to political constituencies, and carrying out a measure of productive investment. It didn't work. By 1980, many countries faced huge and mounting indebtedness to international banks (which had been all too willing to lend in an earlier era) and to organizations like the IMF. They were having to devote an increasing percentage of export revenues to debt repayment, leaving little for necessary imports, let alone for investment. Uganda devoted 5 percent of its exports to debt service in 1980, and 66 percent around 1990; Kenya's debt service went from 16 percent of exports to 34 percent, and Côte d'Ivoire's from 25 percent to 60 percent. Facing bankruptcy, many countries appealed to the IMF for further loans to enable them to stretch out payments. The IMF imposed stern conditions, known as structural adjustment.

IMF economists blame the crisis on bad policies of African governments. African leaders stand accused of technical mistakes – for example, of overvaluing their currencies, which discourages exports and encourages imports – and of misguided social policies. Above all, they were accused of creating too many sinecures in the civil service and state-owned businesses, paying urban wage workers too much, and setting agricultural prices too low. Officials are accused, sometimes accurately, of "rent-seeking" behavior: establishing restrictions on doing business, then collecting bribes for exceptions or allocating monopolies to friends and relatives. The remedy for this is held to be the market: shrink government; remove regulations; lower trade barriers; and let the market work its magic, especially by stimulating agricultural production and exports.

Critics say that this formula does more to insure that African countries focus on repaying debt than on rebuilding basic economic structures. They wonder if the IMF approach has less to do with saving the continent than with writing it off. Perhaps financial leaders have concluded that Africa has little to offer to a capitalist world economy and that it is essential to delegitimate its high demands. Defenders of the IMF claim some success where IMF prescriptions have been followed, in Ghana and Uganda most notably, while the critics claim that this success is defined in self-fulfilling terms – that budgets have shrunk and debts have ceased to mount – while evidence that market-oriented policies are improving social welfare or building structures capable of sustaining growth is lacking. Further, the critics argue that if a major cause of difficulties was the overpayment of urban workers in relation to rural farmers, the precipitous decline in urban wages – greater than that of farmers' incomes – since 1980 should have resulted in economic advance. But the record of the low-wage 1980s was worse than that of the "high"-wage 1960s, which suggests that the so-called urban bias was a wrong target from the beginning. And while advocates of structural adjustment claim that privatization of state corporations and deregulation has given corrupt politicians less room for rent-seeking, critics argue that faced with shrinking resources politicians will cut necessary services and useful investments first and politically useful rents last, so that IMF policy has undermined the salaries of teachers and health care professionals and set back the development of a workforce able to develop their skills over a lifetime, but it hasn't stopped corruption. The World Bank has more recently urged combining financial rigor with a return to basic priorities, notably education, health, and the quality of government. Whether reform will merely push African states to export more of the commodities that already saturate world markets or help African states make more serious structural changes remains in question.

The argument takes on a special meaning if one remembers the debates in the 1940s and 1950s over "stabilization." The IMF program is an attempt to reverse a way of thinking that has been powerful since the 1940s, when colonial officials and leading international organizations argued that labor was a *social* phenomenon, that efficient and predictable contributions to production demanded that workers be able to live decently and support families who would be socialized into the world of work and urban life, that a working class with a future would serve the long term needs of capital and the state better than an army of the miserably employed – even if the latter could be made to work for lower wages. In this sense, the IMF argument was indeed for an end to the development idea. It elevated the immediate logic of markets above a social or political logic. But Africa's rulers, by not making the most of the development era, allowed themselves to become so vulnerable to outsiders' changing policies.

The misery of the poor urban worker or the impoverished farmer was multiplied in the war zones. The civil wars in Sudan and Somalia, the destructive predation of rebel gangs in Sierra Leone, Angola, and Mozambique, and the pointless combat of militias led by rival politicians in Congo-Brazzaville destroyed what infrastructure there was, made farming and commerce dangerous activities, and destroyed jobs as well as factories. But not everybody lost – and that was part of the problem. In Angola, Sierra Leone, and parts of Congo, civil conflict, whatever its root causes, took on a new dimension because certain groups gained access to diamond-rich areas and established smuggling networks to get the diamonds out and arms and consumer goods, including luxury items, in. Young men, some still children, whose alternatives have been extinguished by the violence and devastation, see enlisting in the fighting force as a sensible course; even those abducted into rebel armies had little alternative but to remain. In Congo/Zaire, government forces have also acted as a predatory network; in Angola, oil exports pay for government armies while diamonds bankroll the rebels, and neither side offers a way out to the people caught in between (see chapters 6 and 7). Such wars are run via specific networks, and the people who command them have much to lose from peace.

Africans have been told, by the most expert of the experts, what to do: that they should industrialize, or that they shouldn't; that they should maximize exports or build a balanced national economy; that they should minimize the role of the state or improve its functioning. They have not been in an equivalent position to tell rich countries what to do, although the allocation of a small percentage of industrial country GNP, the writing off of debt, or the favorable admission of primary products into European and North American markets would have big effects in Africa. African economic problems have long been coproductions; they have been shaped by the interaction of very different sorts of systems, horrifically so in the era of the slave trade, and with more mixed effects in the post-World War II era. Sharing of responsibility for the consequences is another story: to talk about "African" economies as if they were truly African, while international financial institutions and transnational corporations are "givens" to which Africans much adjust, is to stifle thinking about economic change from the start. At the same time, African governments have not been much better than western ones at listening to what small-scale cocoa farmers in Ghana or market women in Nigeria or the people who mysteriously supply Kinshasa with food have to say about economics. They might have learned a few lessons.

### Cities, countryside, and beyond

The African continent – however much the image of "tribes" has figured in outsiders' perceptions of it – can look back on a long history of movement: trade diasporas, religious pilgrimages, kingdoms incorporating their neighbors, the movement of expanding lineages into new regions, and labor migration, coerced and voluntary. The movement of people accelerated in the post-war era. Meanwhile, colonial officials, national leaders, and social scientists have tried to think through how the changes in people's lives could be analyzed. What was not in doubt was that this was an era of change; and that fact itself captured many imaginations, from street artists in Kinshasa to scholars in Cambridge.

Some intellectuals and scholars, outside and inside Africa, thought of themselves as part of a dynamic of "modernization." Modernization seemed like a complete package of transformations: nuclear families would replace extended ones, rigid social hierarchies would give way to openness and to individual achievement. Other African intellectuals saw modernization as "westernization" and as a danger to a uniquely African way of life. Still others thought Africans could adapt and change without become western. Meanwhile, ordinary people were trying to live their lives: to use resources that were new and others that were old, to struggle against the oppressiveness of the new by using the old and against the oppressiveness of the old by using the new. What they were producing did not fit a pre-packaged modernity, nor did it constitute "tradition" or "community." People were fashioning and refashioning forms of connections and association.

By the early 1950s, anthropologists were introducing concepts like "social situation," "social field," and "social network" to emphasize that Africans did not live within a bounded universe, but created new patterns of social and cultural relations as they moved into different sorts of places. Africans were not merely molded by being "urbanized"; they were bringing something to the city as well and weaving together city and country in different ways.

More recent scholarship has emphasized the vibrancy of urban social and cultural life: the wide range of associations that people formed among themselves; the importance of new patterns of leisure and consumption; the vitality of sociability and conversation in tea houses and bars; and the creativity of musicians, especially in a city like Leopoldville, which by the 1940s spawned a recording industry and influenced music throughout Africa and elsewhere in the world.

Africa certainly became a much more urban continent in the post-war years. As late as 1960, 15 percent of its people lived in cities. By 1975, this had passed 20 percent and by the early 1990s 30 percent. And given that the population had grown by over two and a half times, that meant a lot of people living in cities. In 1960 (see figure 7a), some countries were much more rural than others; by 1990, most African countries had substantial urban populations, in some a majority. Major cities were mushrooming (figure 7b).

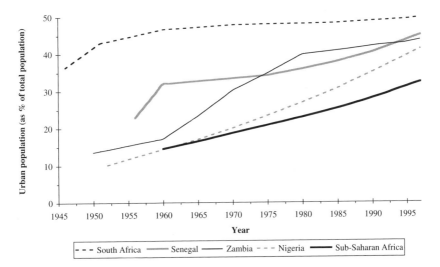

Figure 7a  Urban population as a percentage of total population for selected African countries and Sub-Saharan Africa, 1946–1997. *Sources*: World Bank, *World Development Indicators* (Washington, DC: World Bank, 1998); William H. Hance, *Population, Migration and Urbanization in Africa* (New York: Columbia University Press, 1970), p. 238; United Nations, *Demographic Yearbook* (New York: United Nations, 1948, 1951, 1960).

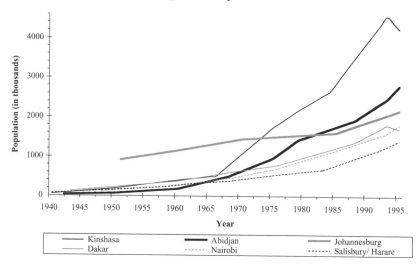

Figure 7b Population of selected African cities, 1940–1995. *Sources:*
John Hance, *Population, Migration and Urbanization in Africa* (New York:
Columbia University Press, 1970); Population Division, Department of
Economic and Social Affairs, *World Population Prospects: The 1996 Revi-
sion* (New York: United Nations, 1997); World Bank, *World Development
Indicators* (Washington, DC: World Bank, 2000); United Nations, *Demo-
graphic Yearbook* (New York: United Nations, 1986, 1991, 1993, 1996).

How can one think of the changes in urban life in the post-war decades?
The gap between what French scholars call the "legal city" and the
"real city" is a place to start: a distinction between the regulated, controlled space of planners' imagination versus the lived realities of city-
dwellers. Pre-war colonial cities were supposed to be nodes of government
administration and symbols of imperial power; they were more often
rude and haphazard. Africans were supposed to be temporary residents
with only a few exceptions: the old Yoruba cities; old trading cities along
the coasts with established urban elites; and certain South African cities
where the historic presence of an African population was grudgingly acknowledged. In reality, Africans had been making their own cities for
many years (chapter 2), and while the housing they built was usually insufficient and low-quality, settlements sprang up where they were not supposed to be and women entered spaces that were supposed to be for males.
The city was not the bastion of white society that colonial officials imagined, nor was it the haven of the "detribalized" native that they feared, for
what appeared chaotic to Europeans was often the fruit of well-organized
networks of rural-urban connection. Most urban-dwelling Africans in the
1940s were rural born, and cities were disproportionately male spaces
even if women had inserted themselves far more than intended.

After the war, French and British officials imagined a different sort of city, segregated more by class than by race and above all expressing their desire to concretize and symbolize the incorporation of Africans into a "modern" urban space, organized in accordance with the best ideas of sanitation and urban planning. There was much new construction, and this proved the model for the post-independence fashion in the building of downtown high-rises, grid-like urban layouts, and wide streets. Colonial regimes at times forcibly removed Africans from downtown neighborhoods to rebuild them in proper fashion. Sex ratios moved toward equality, both as women moved in from rural areas and as more and more urbanites were urban born.

Serious struggles took place in the 1940s and 1950s over restrictions on residence. Where center-city space was coercively modernized, periurban settlements – in Dakar, in Mombasa, in Lagos – spread outwards, sometimes on the basis of land that was simply occupied, sometimes on the basis of complex understandings between older and newer residents. The struggles were most severe in white-dominated cities in southern Africa. In Johannesburg, South Africa, in the late 1940s, where urban industry was expanding much more rapidly than housing, up to 90,000 people organized to occupy vacant land and build shack settlements, confronting authorities with a fait accompli. The state, especially from the 1950s onwards, removed Africans from other squatter areas or locations, where they had constructed too rich and threatening an associative life, and attempted to sort people into different sites within a racially defined urban space. Migrant men, meanwhile, were shuttled in and out of single-sex hostels on the mines and in Johannesburg.

If the space of the real city proved to be quite different from that of the legal or the planned one, so too did the kind of life Africans built for themselves within these spaces. Colonial thinking in the 1950s emphasized "stabilization" of urban labor. The reality, from then until the present, was that the regulated, relatively secure, unionized jobs were a minority, and by the 1960s, this kind of employment was not growing rapidly in most of Africa. In 1988, in International Labour Office estimates, "modern" wage workers constituted only 8 percent of the labor force.

Most people toiled in small-scale agriculture, but what was growing most rapidly was what colonial regimes had once feared and labelled as detribalized or floating populations. By the 1970s, there was a new name: urban informal sector. This wasn't specifically urban, for it referred to people moving into and out of cities, it wasn't literally informal, since a variety of relationships – from apprenticeship to Islamic brotherhoods to control by local power-brokers – regulated it, and it wasn't a sector, because people within it interacted closely with those in regulated employment, and state officials could exploit it precisely because these

7 Tailors working in a street, Mopti, Mali, 1962. Artisanal production and small-scale marketing remained the backbone of the "real" economies of urban Africa, even when colonial and post-colonial planners thought in terms of state-dominated economies or modern corporations.

8 Modernizing the African family; a nurse lectures mothers on infant feeding in a clinic in Lagos, Nigeria, 1959. To colonial officials – and many nationalists – women were the key to transforming African culture; if they could be taught lessons in child rearing and household management and were properly supervised, they would raise a new generation of Africans adapted to modern life.

activities were outside the law. The term refers to a domain outside state regulation, a world of small and often transitory workshops, of traders working in the streets, of illegal activities. An estimated 60 percent of urban jobs are "informal." Where official economies all but collapsed, as in Mobutu's Zaire or Sékou Touré's Guinea, the informal economy was what kept people alive.

In some ways the "illegal" city, whether in Mathare Valley outside Nairobi or Pikine outside Dakar, was better organized, because the legal insecurity of tenure required cultivating relationships with state officials. The informal economy delivered low-cost services, and in that sense it "worked", and some observers thought it was a model which the overregulated, corrupt, and inefficient legal sector should emulate. But it worked in particular ways. Such activities were organized more on the basis of relationships than routines. They were a sign that the project which independent states had taken over from their predecessors – of building a seemingly rational, modern economy, of making that economy and society truly national, truly incorporative of all its citizens – had failed, and that an Africa of less visible and more personal connections had emerged in its stead.

The stabilization concept had a particular gender ideology implicit in it: that of the male breadwinner, with wife at home. The worker would learn the ways of industry; his wife would be taught modern homemaking and childrearing. Trade unionists often drew on such notions to claim wages sufficient to support a family. But even where wages improved – or when, as in French Africa after 1956, workers received family allowances for each child – the effects of male wages were not necessarily as anticipated. As Lisa Lindsay has shown in regard to the "stabilized" railwaymen of Nigeria, better wages did not support a nuclear family so much as reinforce the notion of the "big man" who used his resources to make himself the center of a wider kin grouping. This might be polygynous, but more likely it involved the wage owner's contribution to a wider network of kin, whom he helped in a variety of ways and whom he expected to contribute to his social, and perhaps political, stature. Women did not necessarily adapt to roles assigned them; railway wives, using their own resources and those of their husbands, frequently followed the Yoruba pattern of engaging in marketing, which brought them not only into intense participation in the market but also into close association with other women. There were many variations on such patterns in West Africa, some involving cooperation between husband and wife, others considerable autonomy between spouses.

Stabilized labor never did conquer the labor market. The circulation of workers between villages and cities or workplaces was made possible by kinship groups wider than the individual family, and migration strengthened this extended family. People used family connections to find jobs in cities and to preserve access to farmland at home. Families – even husbands and wives– could thus have more than one residence and often live apart. Families had to think strategically about placing members in different locations. While kinship solidarity could help people cope with the precariousness of wage labor, and in the best situations lead to decent incomes from a combination of salaries, farm earnings, and trade, the risks were severe, above all to women and children. The ill-health or desertion of a male wage-earner could set a rural family spinning downward into poverty, or the breakup of family bonds in a city could leave children without support networks and with no state services to help. Child beggars, "parking boys," very young hawkers, and youthful petty criminals are a feature of every African city, as are youth gangs.

Most important is the historical sequence: to railway families of Nigeria or the mine families of Zambia stabilization and relatively high wages in the 1950s and 1960s seemed to offer new possibilities over the life cycle, giving a worker and his family the hope of living off of a pension and trade income late in life. But by the 1980s in both cases, men's wages and pensions eroded. The advance of "modernization" proved to be short-lived. What saved many – but not all – such families from penury was the continued viability of kinship and other forms of personal connection. Moreover, in cities from Accra to Dar es Salaam, the strong presence of women in "informal" economic activities, once the precarious flip side of men's privileged position in formal wage employment, became increasingly vital to family survival. The male wage-earner, despite the dreams of post-war colonial officials and African planners and trade unionists, has not led the African family into a 'modern' prosperity. Women and children have been hit hard by the reversals on Africa's economic pathway, while the persistence and diversity of social ties in African communities have softened, if only partially, the pain of an unrealized project of social change.

### Decolonizing gender?

Women remain the bedrock of food production: scholars claim that they do 90 percent of hoeing and weeding, 90 percent of processing food and hauling water and firewood, and 60 percent of the harvesting and marketing of food. In some areas, but far from all, women in the early colonial era extended their role in agriculture into cash crops and, for a time at least, acquired better access to cash, especially as younger men's roles in warfare, hunting, and porterage were undercut. Women's centrality to both agricultural production and household reproduction accentuated the pressures on them, especially from male elders, to leave out-migration to the more dispensable young males. Elder males guarded their power in village and kinship politics, while younger ones had more rapid access to the ways of the new order.

African and European gender biases intersected in slotting men into education and thus placing them in a privileged position as more roles in "modern" society opened to Africans after the war. While men's advantage in access to schooling persists to this day, the extent of the gap has slowly diminished (see table 1). Women's roles in crop production and food marketing are being complemented by a significant presence in teaching, health care, and other professional roles, a source of anxiety for "big men" as well of vital sustenance for the entire society.

The political openings of the 1940s and 1950s had ambiguous effects on women. Women participated actively in nationalist movements in places as varied as Tanzania and Guinea. In local politics in West African cities, women often played a political role stemming from their importance in marketing: female market leaders had a large and important constituency. But in other ways, politics in the 1950s became more of a male domain as it became an open, public one. Because men were predominant in "formal" employment, trade union leadership was virtually all male. Party politics might define certain roles for women, but in no case were women the top leaders, and in some cases as African men entered formal hierarchies, they saw their own status in relation to how "their" women maintained a respectable and deferential position. Susan Geiger, for instance, describes the importance of women in "performing nationalism" in Tanzania during the 1950s – playing a public role in rallies and organizing – but when it came to governing, the largely uneducated female activists were marginalized and their organizations subordinated to the national party.

Later, as more women became educated and professional, explicitly feminist movements developed in such countries as Senegal and Kenya, and forced public debate on issues of particular concern to women. Many have fought uphill battles against formidable male backlash. A Zimbabwe Supreme Court decision in 1999 declared that the integrity of African cultural norms outweighed constitutional provisions against discrimination and meant that women could not claim equal rights of inheritance to men. Legal efforts to restrict polygyny or to make men responsible for the children they have fathered by "outside wives" have run up against male legislators' refusal to surrender the prerogatives of the "big man." There have been advances, however. The post-1994 South African government has firmly advocated gender equality, and 30 percent of South African legislators after the 2000 elections were women and eight were ministers. That makes it all the more notable that in Africa as a whole, women are only 6 percent of legislators, and half of African cabinets have no women at all.

State regulation of reproduction became an acute issue at key moments. Before World War II, colonial states had sought to "retraditionalize" marriage, in order to strengthen the ability of indigenous elites and courts to regulate marriage and inheritance. In the 1950s they often stressed "modern" marriage, regulated by state law, hopefully producing the kind of monogamous household that would insure that children went to school and grew up to contribute to the market economy. Independent states sometimes acknowledged the intrinsic value of "customary" forms of marriage and inheritance, but insisted that those who chose other arrangements should be regulated by formal laws. But there has been another reaction, too, at the core of state power. The "big man" concept has far from died out; indeed, given the importance of building networks of clients to political leaders, the place of the patriarch in politics has been strengthened. Big men do not necessarily want to be constrained by the nuclear emphasis of "modern" marriage, and in Kenya and elsewhere have fought against legal regulations that might prevent men from doing what they wanted to do. Women have become adept at using kinship and informal social relations partially to redress the bias toward husbands in the bureaucracy and courts.

During the controversy over female circumcision in Kenya in the 1930s, many men spoke in the name of Kikuyu women. Whatever Kikuyu women thought did not enter into the political arena. That is no longer the case. Women's organizations have developed in many African countries, and feminists hold meetings and work with allies outside of Africa. Issues like polygyny, genital mutilation, child custody and support, property rights, and inheritance are the subject of political mobilization within Africa, not just do-good intervention from outside. That has changed the politics of reproduction. But gender equality remains a long way off.

### Religion in the age of progress and crisis

The relationship of religion to politics is often ambiguous. Around 1950, many Africans were worshiping in established Christian churches and trying to turn Christian universalism into an ideology of liberation and human progress. The Muslim brotherhoods of Senegal, having reached an accommodation with the French, were now forging relationships with the leaders of political parties. Leaders like Houphouët-Boigny and Kenneth Kaunda emphasized in different ways their Christian beliefs; Houphouët-Boigny, near the end of his life, built at enormous expense a basilica in his home town modeled on St. Peter's. Others, like Nkrumah, channeled Christian messianic imagery into a cult of the leader and his modernizing mission. Still others, Mobutu for instance, cultivated a reputation as men well connected with sorcerers.

But in other cases, prophets and cult leaders gathered followings that were highly personal and antagonistic to secular authority, be it that of Africans or Europeans. In Northern Rhodesia, the cult led by Alice Lenshina, known as "Lumpa," developed after 1953 from a mission station but broke away from Christian doctrine as much as mission organization, claiming it was building an instant millennium on earth and trying to separate itself from all other institutions. With some 65,000 followers living at the edge of the Copperbelt, the Lumpa church clashed with the leading nationalist movement, the UNIP of Kenneth Kaunda. After independence in 1964, Lenshina's attempt to control autonomous Lumpa villages challenged UNIP's desire to make clear its authority. The result was one of the bloodiest episodes of post-colonial state repression of the 1960s; some 700 Lumpa died and Lenshina was jailed for over a decade. Other newly independent countries cracked down on what they considered dangerously autonomous cults: the same worry that colonial regimes had about such activity.

9 The arrival of pilgrims from the Mouride Brotherhood at the holy city of Touba, Senegal, 1956. Although Mourides have migrated to cities in Europe and North America, their Islam is less universalistic than other versions. They focus the connection of the hierarchy of religious leaders (marabouts) to the founder of the brotherhood, Ahmadu Bamba, and his city of Touba.

What of religion in an era of crisis and decline? Perhaps the most important new trend, unevenly present from Angola to Kenya, was the proliferation of evangelical Protestant churches, some following American leadership but all emphasizing a direct relationship of individual to God. In Kenya, the more orthodox Christian denominations challenged the increasingly authoritarian regime of Daniel arap Moi, but the increasingly numerous evangelicals spoke of salvation and had relatively little to say about the inequities of the regime. Such churches both reflected and accentuated growing disillusionment with the national project. Building African or Kenyan or South African society was not the point; their concerns were salvation and another sort of community.

African Islam is as varied as African Christianity. The brotherhoods of Senegal tie their members, Mouride or Tijaniya *talibés*, into a religious hierarchy and network of connections closely linked to political and economic elites. This is not fertile soil for fundamentalist Islam; the social roots of Islam are too deep in local soil to be open to a universalist purism.

Originally a rural movement, Mourides moved into Dakar by 1945 and began to dominate the central marketplace. By the 1970s, the Mouride traders' diaspora was extending to Paris and New York. Transnational without being westernized, Mourides remained closely linked to a hierarchy of marabouts in Senegal itself. Mourides were once hostile to education, but by the 1970s Mouride student associations were strong in the University of Dakar. The marabouts had considerable influence on political parties, but also maintained a certain distance from the Senegalese state. Across the continent, in a part of Sudan where migrant men frequently go to Saudi Arabia in search of wage labor, such migrants return aware of a fundamentalist Islam that is more universalistic than the seemingly parochial Islam with which they grew up. What westerners consider to be sectarian appears in these Sudanic villages to be cosmopolitan.

As Stephen Ellis and Gerrie ter Haar comment, religious discourse has much to say about "manifestations of evil said to infest the main institutions of Africa's governance." This had led to critiques of human rights' abuse, as in the National Council of Churches of Kenya's attack on the Moi regime in Kenya in the 1980s, but it can also take the form of accusations that greedy or repressive politicians and businessmen are engaging in witchcraft or other occult practices. The discourse about abuses of state power is not dissimilar from the discourses of jealousy within kinship groups. Leaders may play on this discourse, claiming themselves to have access to dark powers, mixing claims to serve the public good with intimations of occult powers to get things done. But witchcraft accusations are not simply a critique of power and greed. The vertical linkages (see chapter 7) between leaders and followers produce much jealousy, and attempts to use spiritual means to gain influence on top or to project it toward the bottom are part of the maneuvering surrounding patronage systems.

Religious discourse often justifies patriarchy, but many of the cults, Christian and otherwise, that have flourished in post-war Africa have been led by women prophets. Parishioners in more conventional churches are disproportionately female. Spirit possession cults in a number of contexts allow a woman "possessed" by a spirit to make demands that would be seen as offensive to gender norms if she was in a non-possessed state.

Men and women alike are facing forces that seem more difficult than ever to control, and the fragmentation of religious and spiritual life is indicative of a situation where people's needs are great, their means compromised, and the solutions far from obvious. The 1950s and 1960s can no longer be seen as a time of giant steps forward in a linear advance of history, but as a very special moment when a solution, political independence, was visible. In subsequent years, cultural and spiritual institutions had to cope not only with the difficulties of survival, but with the pains of disillusionment.

## Conclusion: on blame and debt, on credit and trade

The continued poverty, the high indebtedness, the deteriorating infrastructure, and above all the absence of any clear trajectory towards a better future in Africa in the 1980s and 1990s have given rise to a blame game. Some argue that the damage colonialism did was permanent and that neo-colonial structures remain in place. Others blame African governments for turning development into a get-rich scheme for rulers and for unsound policies, too distrustful either of the pro-market wisdom of the experts or of the wisdom which peasants brought to environmental and community concerns.

One can also redefine the temporal boundaries of the question to say that what is being tested is not "colonial" or "post-colonial" economic policy, but the consequences of the development era, 1940–73. Arguably, both late colonial and African governments had real achievements after the stagnation of the previous decades: progress in building schools, roads, hospitals, and port facilities; progress in bringing Africans into positions in civil service and private employment where they could contribute more than menial labor and where they could help a younger generation advance. The blame, some would say, lies in the world economy that turned so decisively against Africa in the 1970s and the policies of the IMF and other international institutions that made it impossible for Africa to "develop" its way out of its limitations. Perhaps development did not go far enough, and an outside world which had long treated Africa as a zone of extraction did not devote sufficient resources to giving the continent a chance to find a different vocation.

But no, others argue, Africa benefitted from the favorable market conditions of the post-war era, and if it had left things to the market, it would have had better results than obtained by state-centered development in the 1950s and 1960s. And no, still others say, the developers did too much: their solutions were too dependent on technology and capital, too centered on a male-oriented formal economic sphere. These are counterfactual propositions, and one must ask what the imagined alternative was. Africans never had the choice of simply entering "the market"; they were up against real markets, some of them controlled by giant foreign firms like the United Africa Company or Union Minière or De Beers, which concentrated capital and power and had no interest in widening the narrow channels of African economies or building the institutions needed to build a diverse and self-sustaining society. Would the fate of Africa's millions of small farmers have been better if they had been left alone to bargain with the multinational giants, and how would those farmers' children have fared without self-conscious efforts to equip them with skills for new careers and access to a wider world? And would a "community" left in splendid isolation have been a force for collective fulfillment or for the reinforcement of the power of local patriarchs over young men and women of all ages? Such questions do not have neat answers; indeed, they point to the importance of asking more precise questions, moving beyond a stark choice between pro-market and pro-state policies, between an authentic and bounded African community and an opening to the world economy.

SUGGESTED READING

A full bibliography for this book may be found on the website of Cambridge University Press at http://uk.cambridge.org/resources/0521776007. It will be updated periodically.

Appiah, Kwame Anthony. *In My Father's House: Africa in the Philosophy of Culture.* New York: Oxford University Press, 1992.

Balandier, Georges. *The Sociology of Black Africa.* Trans. by Douglas Garman. London: André Deutsch, 1970.

Bates, Robert H. *Markets and States in Tropical Africa.* Berkeley: University of California Press, 1981.

Berry, Sara. *No Condition is Permanent: The Social Dynamics of Agrarian Change in Sub-Saharan Africa.* Madison: University of Wisconsin Press, 1993.

   *Fathers Work for Their Sons: Accumulation, Mobility, and Class Formation in an Extended Yoruba Community.* Berkeley: University of California Press, 1984.

Cohen, Abner. *Custom and Politics in Urban Africa: A Study of Hausa Migrants in Yoruba Towns.* Berkeley: University of California Press, 1969.

Cooper, Frederick and Randall Packard, eds. *International Development and the Social Sciences: Essays on the History and Politics of Knowledge.* Berkeley: University of California Press, 1997.

Enwezor, Okwui. *The Short Century: Independence and Liberation Movements in Africa 1945–1994.* Munich and New York: Prestel, 2001.

Fabian, Johannes. *Remembering the Present: Painting and Popular History in Zaire.* Berkeley: University of California Press, 1996.

Ferguson, James. *The Anti-Politics Machine: "Development," Depoliticization, and Bureaucratic Power in Lesotho.* Cambridge: Cambridge University Press, 1990.

   *Expectations of Modernity: Myths and Meanings of Urban Life on the Zambian Copperbelt.* Berkeley: University of California Press, 1999.

Geiger, Susan. *TANU Women: Gender and Culture in the Making of Tanzanian Nationalism, 1955–1965.* Portsmouth, NH: Heinemann, 1997.

Geschiere, Peter. *The Modernity of Witchcraft: Politics and the Occult in Postcolonial Africa.* Trans. by Peter Geschiere and Janet Roitman. Charlottesville: University Press of Virginia, 1997.

Grosz-Ngate, Maria, and Omari Kokole, eds. *Gendered Encounters: Challenging Cultural Boundaries and Social Hierarchies in Africa*. New York: Routledge, 1997.

Hunt, Nancy. *A Colonial Lexicon: Of Birth Ritual, Medicalization, and Mobility in the Congo*. Durham: Duke University Press, 1999.

Jamal, Vali, and John Weeks, *Africa Misunderstood or Whatever Happened to the Rural-Urban Gap*. London: Macmillan for International Labour Office, 1993.

MacGaffey, Janet. *The Real Economy of Zaire: The Contribution of Smuggling and Other Unofficial Activities to the National Wealth of An African Country*. Philadelphia: University of Pennsylvania Press, 1991.

MacGaffey, Wyatt. *Religion and Society in Central Africa: The BaKongo of Lower Zaire*. Chicago: University of Chicago Press, 1986.

Manchuelle, François. *Willing Migrants: Soninke Labor Diasporas, 1848–1960*. Athens, OH: Ohio University Press, 1997.

Mudimbe, V. Y. *The Invention of Africa: Gnosis, Philosophy, and the Order of Knowledge*. Bloomington: Indiana University Press, 1988.

Parkin, David J. *Palms, Wine and Witnesses: Public Spirit and Private Gain in an African Farm Community*. London: Intertext, 1972.

Robertson, Claire. *Sharing the Same Bowl?: A Socioeconomic History of Women and Class in Accra, Ghana*. Bloomington: Indiana University Press, 1984.

Vaughan, Megan. *Curing Their Ills: Colonial Power and African Illness*. Cambridge: Polity Press, 1991.

Villalon, Leonardo. *Islamic Society in Senegal: Disciples and Citizens in Fatick*. Cambridge: Cambridge University Press, 1995.

White, Luise. *The Comforts of Home: Prostitution in Colonial Nairobi*. Chicago: Chicago University Press, 1990.

World Bank. *Can Africa Claim the 21ˢᵗ Century?* Washington: The World Bank, 2000.

# 6    The late decolonizations: southern Africa 1975, 1979, 1994

The most important holdouts against the abdication of imperial power in the 1950s and 1960s were colonies with substantial white settlement. But despite the sustained efforts of settlers in Rhodesia and South Africa to retain power and the determination of the Portuguese government to retain colonies, their ultimate fate was determined by the regional and world-wide process which rendered empire indefensible. Take Rhodesia. In order to maintain white rule, Rhodesian settlers gave up their place in an empire that was intent on devolving power to black majorities. The unilateral declaration of independence in 1965 kept in place colonial institutions – a bureaucracy and police apparatus that enforced white landownership and racial segregation – but cut them off from imperial power. When African political movements, well aware of the rights Africans now had elsewhere, turned to guerilla warfare, the state fought back, but it faced a regional problem – armed groups finding sanctuary in now-free neighboring territories – and a global one, economic boycotts and isolation. In the end, colonialism could not be maintained without imperialism, not least because white Rhodesians vitally depended on their sense of participation in "European civilization" and in the comforts, securities, and opportunities of a worldly bourgeoisie. However divided and uncertain the guerilla movement, it won the international battle to be identified with self-determination and progress.

South Africa's 15 percent white population, with its long history, was more entrenched. But the white Nationalist government did crack by 1994, and for much the same reasons: although armed rebels could be killed, jailed, and exiled, its cities could not be made secure, and its white citizens could not participate in the western world of which they felt themselves to be privileged members. The revolutions in Rhodesia/Zimbabwe, Angola, and Mozambique dashed the South African government's strategy of supporting a "white" southern Africa as a buffer against a "black" Africa to the north. South Africa had the wealth and military might to harrow its neighbors, and it caused much death and dislocation, but it remained isolated in Africa and despised around the world until it conceded

power to an African majority. What surprised most knowledgeable observers was that the final stages of this political revolution were peaceful.

Like Southern Rhodesia and South Africa, Portuguese Africa had participated in the developmentalist process of the 1950s and its rulers
also tried to keep its benefits in white hands. Revolutionary wars in
Mozambique, Angola, and Guinea Bissau had such a negative effect on
Portuguese soldiers and civilians that a faction within the army overthrew the dictatorship in 1974 and withdrew from the African continent.
Africans who experienced Portuguese rule helped to bring democracy to
a part of Europe, at enormous cost to themselves.

Empires were thus a long time dying. By looking at this entire half-
century, one sees not only how fraught, long, and painful were the struggles to end empire and its racial consequences, but how much the process
involved cross-border connections within Africa and the engagement of
Africans with international organizations.

Then there is the role of the United States. Again, looking at late decolonizations in the context of the early ones is revealing. It is only slightly
too cynical to suggest that the high point of American contributions to
decolonization came in 1943, when the State Department pressed its
British allies to read the Atlantic Charter's invocation of a right to self-
determination in general terms, not just as words meant to apply to the
white victims of Hitler's invasions. The US pulled its punches, balancing its concern that the rising anger of colonized peoples could take a
radical turn and its desire to "open" imperial markets to American competition against its fears of weakening friendly powers. From the late
1940s, the US helped to internationalize imperialism by participating
(directly and through international financial institutions) in the development effort, and it hoped for gradual development and political devolution rather than sharp breaks that might aid the wrong side in the
Cold War. The US would provide aid, but not too much of it, to friendly
independent nations, and it would intervene, but not too often, when
instability or left-wing politics threatened its interests. Its involvement
in the Congo crisis and the assassination of Patrice Lumumba in 1961
signalled the American willingness to treat new African states as pawns
in Cold War conflicts, and its reluctance to eject racially exclusive states
from the community of democratic nations helped to allow the late decolonizations to occur even later. A low point of American post-war policy
came in 1986 when the Reagan Administration, citing communist powers' military support of the Angolan government, gave overt and covert
support to the anti-government guerillas of UNITA, putting the United
States on the side of South Africa's effort to destabilize a neighboring
country.

Within the United States, strong public sentiment linked the struggle against apartheid to the domestic civil rights movement, but government policy varied from official condemnation of apartheid to a "constructive engagement" that gave substantive support to the regime while claiming to influence it to behave like a normal state. American officials did little to aid the ANC in its quest for majority rule, but they celebrated the personality of Mandela when he came to power. Elsewhere in Africa, the United States has been eager to instruct African governments that they should support free markets and human rights, but not very eager to do anything about local tyrants (Mobutu, Abacha) who controlled important resources or to put much money behind whatever economic policy it favored at a particular moment. Africa was only intermittently on the map of what really counted. Meanwhile, American-based NGOs – from Human Rights Watch to church groups to African-American rights groups to advocates of sustainable, gender-sensitive development policies – were very much part of the African scene. They were a resource available to Africans who sought foreign connections but they also, whatever their intentions, tended to frame Africa as a region of famines, atrocities, and backwardness. That, too, is part of the story of a certain kind of decolonization.

## From Rhodesia to Zimbabwe

Southern Rhodesia, like other British colonies, was challenged by a combination of urban workers and western-educated elites in the late 1940s and 1950s. In the 1970s, its revolution was predominantly rural. Urban and rural politics were linked by a form of capitalist development which deprived rural Africans of land and kept urban Africans under police eyes, and by a high level of state repression which eventually forced nationalists into bases in neighboring Zambia and Mozambique, from which they attacked the adjacent rural areas of Rhodesia.

The big strike movements of post-war Africa hit Rhodesia in the form of a railway strike in 1945 and a general strike in 1948. Already, issues of family life, wages and housing for a male worker to support a family, were at the fore. Meanwhile, state efforts to limit the presence of women in town had the unintended effect of defining an illegal and unrespectable female element set apart from respectable city-dwellers. A populist trade union, the RICU (Reformed Industrial and Commercial Workers' Union), led by Charles Mzingeli, put issues of gender and urban life at the center of urban politics. The state, meanwhile, sought both to maintain racial segregation and to produce a trainable and tameable African working class in carefully policed quarters. There sprang up, however, communities led by charismatic leaders with an alternate vision of urban life in neighborhoods where the police didn't come. Meanwhile, maize, tobacco, beef, gold, and other minerals were part of the post-war commodities boom, and Rhodesia, in the footsteps of its richer and whiter neighbor to the South, seemed on the road to a racially repressive version of capitalist development.

African politicians in southern Rhodesia, as elsewhere, were also eager to establish their respectability and take advantage of the modest openings of the 1950s. This resulted in a loss of touch with the volatile politics of the neighborhoods, particularly in relation to women struggling at the margins. The RICU gave way in 1956 to the City Youth League, then to the National Democratic Party, and then to the African National Council of Southern Rhodesia in 1957. Meanwhile, the British creation (see chapter 4) of the Central African Federation – Northern Rhodesia, Southern Rhodesia, and Nyasaland – enhanced the influence of Southern Rhodesia's white settlers, concentrated industrial and agricultural development in that territory, left limited opportunities for African workers and farmers in Southern Rhodesia, and produced powerful waves of mobilization against the Federation in Nyasaland and Northern Rhodesia. The heated opposition eventually led the British to abandon the Federation and allow the two dissident colonies to become independent.

As Rhodesia's white settlers consolidated power, its black politicians slowly realized that the kind of orderly political organization – punctuated by strikes, urban riots, and other disorders – that had transformed politics in non-settler colonies would not work in Rhodesia. The ANC transformed itself into the National Democratic Party and then the Zimbabwe African People's Union (ZAPU), under the leadership of Joshua Nkomo, who had built his political career from a trade unionist base extended to the Ndebele region via Nkomo's strong evocation of religious symbolism and his connections to the shrines of regional cults. ZAPU had a more militant style and wider rural mobilization, but no effective counter to the repressive actions of the settler-dominated government. In 1963 the Zimbabwe African National Union (ZANU) split off from ZAPU under the leadership of the Revd. Ndabaningi Sithole and later of Robert Mugabe. Both organizations were considering armed struggle, and both were banned in 1964 (the year of Malawi and Zambia's independence) and their leaders jailed.

Ian Smith and his radical white party had a macho sense that settlers could do what soft colonial officials would not: keep their Africans down. The tension between London and Salisbury mounted until in 1965 Smith's government issued a Unilateral Declaration of Independence. Rhodesia would defend racial privilege in national rather than imperial terms. The Labour Government in Britain, convinced that the move would fail and loath to kill white people in the name of the empire, did little. The Rhodesian state, for about fifteen years, demonstrated that a highly motivated and unscrupulous minority controlling an army and a bureaucracy could maintain security in the urban areas, repression in the rural ones, and even foster a measure of industrialization and self-sufficiency in an economy that used cheap African labor to produce minerals and agricultural commodities for external markets.

ZAPU had guerilla bases just over the frontier in Zambia. ZANU's big break came when FRELIMO (Front for the Liberation of Mozambique) gained *de facto* control of neighboring parts of that colony, and especially after 1974 when FRELIMO defeated the Portugese and allowed ZANU to build bases from which it could work in the African reserve areas of Rhodesia where people spoke Shona, the language of the ZANU leaders. ZAPU guerillas working from Zambia and the more aggressive ZANU guerillas from Mozambique faced a common bind: they had to live off the land in the very place where they were trying to mobilize peasants. The consequences were complex: a mixture of embrace of the guerillas, who offered hope to rural cultivators impoverished and oppressed by the Rhodesian state; of fear of guerillas who raided, who themselves used coercion, and who exposed people to revenge by the Rhodesian army; and of possibilities for young men and women of all ages to find in the struggle alternatives to patriarchal domination.

The indecisive armed struggle proved costly to the increasingly isolated white government; as economic conditions in Rhodesia deteriorated in the early 1970s, guerillas recruited more effectively among young men who had little at stake in the white Rhodesian economy. Smith now began to cooperate with the British government to find a settlement that would bring black Rhodesians – hopefully of the less radical variety – into the government but protect the white minority. In a bizarre alternative to a vote, the British sent a paternalistic commission to see for itself whether Africans supported the proposed agreement. Even the white sages could see the hostility of most Africans to a denigrating compromise; religious leaders, released ex-detainees, and the African National Council, led by Bishop Abel Muzorewa, campaigned against the proposal. The war continued.

By 1977 Smith was trying to work with nationalists like Muzorewa to forestall the radicals like Mugabe. Negotiations resulted in the second of Zimbabwe's independences, a weak state with numerous guarantees for whites and little power for the new leader, Muzorewa. The white army continued to fight black guerillas and Muzorewa couldn't get either side to stop, let alone tackle the demobilization of armies, the rebuilding of a wrecked economy, and the underlying questions of economic justice. In the end, more negotiations finally led to real elections, with the result that in 1980 ZANU and Robert Mugabe came to power, with Joshua Nkomo and ZAPU uneasily and briefly cooperating with the new regime.

Some observers thought Zimbabwe would be different from those nations which had come into being fifteen to twenty years before. It had fought for its independence; its peasantry had been mobilized; its leaders were courageous, socialist, and self-confident. Zimbabwe inherited from wartime Rhodesia an economic infrastructure that emphasized self-sufficiency; it had a balance of agricultural, mineral, and industrial possibilities. Zimbabwe may well have had more economic and political options than other African states, but Mugabe chose not to use them.

Mugabe's socialist rhetoric ran up against his need for dependable revenue, not just for for projects to relieve an exploited population, but for patronage to keep ZANU's network of supporters content. Although some white-owned land was redistributed, the regime was careful to preserve the high-output agricultural sector, with its large, white-owned estates, and keep the white-owned business sector intact. Zimbabwe's elite has been Africanized by the kind of crony capitalism typical of gatekeeper states: the state does little to encourage an autonomous, African business class, but uses its own strategic location to provide opportunities to clients. The poor remain poor, and much of Zimbabwe's population remains in the badly eroded, badly supplied rural sectors.

Mugabe's freedom fighters, meanwhile, were dealt with carefully: their history of mobilization turned out to signify not so much that they were a vanguard of social transformation, but that they were an interest group – slow to give up its arms – that had to be placated. Most important was the regime's tendency to ethnicize issues of patronage and of opposition. Mugabe quickly fell into conflict with his fellow revolutionary and rival Nkomo, and he accused Nkomo's supporters of mobilizing Ndebele against Mugabe's primarily Shona base. Zimbabwe's security forces waged a repressive campaign in Ndebele regions, enhancing whatever animosity existed, until an uneasy truce was reached in 1987. Press censorship, detention of opponents, and the banning of political parties other than ZANU were severe in the 1980s, eased for a time in the 1990s, and worsened again, as the declining economy, increasing anger at corruption, and the ability of the opposition to make good use of even small openings in the press and electoral system have undermined the government's authority. Mugabe is now willing to make white landowners, whose role he once supported, the scapegoats for economic chaos, while he cracks down on domestic opponents and foreign journalists. The ZANU government achieved initial credibility for tearing down the race-specific obstacles to education and individual advancement, but it has largely squandered the opportunity, opting for repressive and demagogic politics while presiding over a deteriorating economy.

### Mozambique and Angola

Portugal's presence in Angola and Mozambique lasted from the fifteenth century to 1975. Mozambique and Angola had the misfortune to be colonized by one of Europe's poorest empires. The world-wide commodities boom of the post-war decade affected it in a particular way: a developmentalist colonialism directed by an authoritarian state, unmediated by the concerns for social progress and political stability in other colonies; and an influx of white laborers from Portugal, who took a large share of the skilled jobs and civil service positions which were so central to the new political and social dynamics elsewhere. In the 1960s, Angola's white population was similar in proportion to that of Rhodesia, but it was poorer and less educated. Roads, schools, and other services were miserable. Trying to adapt to the new international climate, Portugal asserted that its African territories were not so much colonies as an integral part of Portugal, and that Portugal had a special genius for Christianizing and assimilating indigenous populations into a nonracial people. The reality was otherwise: while Africans could theoretically aspire to the status of *assimilado* (the assimilated one), only one percent ever got there, and racism characterized every dimension of the system, from the judiciary to labor recruitment.

Angola was the better endowed of the two southern African colonies, and it suffered accordingly. It had been integrated into the slave-trade routes linking the central–western coast of Africa with Brazil; in the early twentieth century it was a source for coerced labor for offshore islands undergoing a cocoa boom; parts of its own interior were used, again via coercive methods, for cocoa and mineral production; and after 1975 its fate was shaped by oil and diamonds.

The nucleus of African organized opposition emerged among educated Africans who were either racially mixed or *assimilado*, and especially among educated Africans living outside Africa, notably through the founding in 1957 in Paris of the Movimento Anti-Colonialista, which included Agostinho Neto, Eduardo Mondlane, and Amilcar Cabral, who would lead radical movements in Angola, Mozambique, and Guinea Bissau. Peasant and worker unrest was for a time contained, until major peasant upheavals broke out in 1961.

Angolan politics was shaped by the sharp disarticulation of society. Whereas urban West Africans were linked by kinship networks and frequent movement to rural areas, the elite of Angola's capital, Luanda, constituted a small and isolated social category – Portuguese-speaking,

Catholic, educated. They stood in tension not only with Africans who had little chance of acquiring fluency in Portuguese, but also with the "new *assimilados*", whose education had not taken them into this social milieu. The old *assimilados* and racially mixed people were at the core of the Popular Movement for the Liberation of Angola (MPLA), founded in exile. The return of its key leaders in 1960 coincided with rural revolts and urban riots which they did not control.

The MPLA, led by Agostinho Neto, looked upon politics through nationalist and socialist lenses. Others, however, saw its leaders as mulattos who were remote from the social institutions and networks in which most people lived. Meanwhile, Bakongo living on the Angolan side of the border with the Belgian Congo, closely connected with Congolese Bakongo activists, also moved from exile into Angola. At the center of a rural insurrection in 1961, they eventually organized the FNLA (National Front for the Liberation of Angola) under Holden Roberto. Then came UNITA, organized by Jonas Savimbi, who was from an Ovimbundu-speaking region and had been in leftist student circles in Europe. His small cadre of followers, mostly from Protestant mission schools, had a thoroughly rural base. Savimbi at first espoused a Maoist ideology which emphasized peasant revolution, whereas MPLA's Marxism focused more on a vanguard leading the nation to modernization and social justice.

Angola's three nationalist factions were thus not "ethnic" rivals, only the FNLA being ethno-nationalist and that in a particular way. Conflict became, as Christine Messiant puts it, "ethnicized." UNITA developed its rural base among Ovimbundu-speakers in a region which had been left with few resources by Portuguese agricultural policy and extensive out-migration of laborers, and its effort to distinguish itself from the Luanda-based MPLA resonated to a significant extent there. The MPLA, in such a region, was perceived as ethnic and even non-African, although it saw itself as nationalist and internationalist. The three revolts went separate ways: FNLA getting support from now independent Zaire, UNITA from Zambia, and MPLA from the Soviet Union and Cuba.

The liberation struggle in Angola was long and harsh, and the three armed movements had limited military success. But Portugal was not rich and its conscript army was not motivated, while the settler population was too diverse, poor, and dependent on the state to go it alone, UDI style. The Portuguese empire came to an end when an army coup reversed the dictatorship and opened up a twisty road to democratization in Portugal itself. The coup leaders saw the war as draining Portugal of its strength, and they set their eyes on becoming more fully members of a modern Europe. To do so, they would wash their hands of colonies – and of Africans. They began a negotiation process with the liberation forces in

Angola, Mozambique, and Guinea Bissau which resulted in independence for all three in 1975. Independence also resulted in a mass flight – not anticipated by the Portuguese government – of white Portuguese from all three territories. Some 800,000 went to Portugal, including nine-tenths of the whites of Angola.

The anti-colonial war immediately became a civil war. The FNLA was supported by Zaire and the CIA, which saw it as the least Marxist of the three, but never got out of its ethnic confines and soon faded. UNITA had support from Zambia and then from South Africa, anxious to keep an independent Angola too weak to threaten its dominance over the region, especially in its dependency of Southwest Africa (now Namibia). Savimbi flipped his ideological stance from Maoism to Reaganism with scarcely the blink of an eye, and the United States added its support to UNITA in 1986. Savimbi's political style remained what it had always been: centralizing, personalized, and brutal. UNITA, although it had popular support within its regional base, was the tightly controlled and frequently purged satrapy of a warlord. In addition to garnering support from South Africa and the United States, UNITA organized diamond smuggling into Zaire, getting guns and spoils for Savimbi's henchmen in return. Most important for those in the region, UNITA provided rewards for young men who would smuggle and fight (and it coerced others into joining), and this provided the only means of earning a livelihood in an area otherwise devastated by terror and counter-terror.

The MPLA won the first round of the civil war by retaining Luanda and pushing outward, aided by Cuban troops and indirect Soviet support. It also enjoyed revenues from French and American oil companies, who were willing to pay "the state" regardless of its rhetoric. That rhetoric was Marxist-Leninist, and it represented, at some level and at least at first, the desire of an educated elite, familiar with the European ideals of socialist revolution, to be the agent of transformation of an impoverished, ill-educated population.

Instead, the MPLA combined the features of a Soviet party and the African gatekeeper state, whose power derives from controlling the interface of national and world economies (chapter 7). Its real source of power was oil revenue coming from militarized enclaves, and after gestures at revolutionizing agriculture, it did little in the countryside other than recruit soldiers. Education, health, and other services in the cities languished. The illegal urban economy supplied consumers, and rural distribution followed increasingly ethnicized lines of clientage.

When the Cold War ended, the United States and Russia lost interest and left Angolans with the mess their intervention had exacerbated. Cuba and South Africa pulled out their soldiers in 1988. A UN-brokered peace

10  The faces of war, a very young soldier for the MPLA, beneath a poster of the party's leader, Agostinho Neto, in the city of Huambo, Angola, 1976.

agreement in 1992 was patched together so incompetently that it soon failed. Meanwhile, the MPLA discarded its Marxism-Leninism in favor of cooperation with the neo-liberal west and it made gestures toward allowing multiparty elections. So the MPLA government, with its oil revenues, and UNITA, evading the state gatekeepers through diamond smuggling into Zaire and Zambia, continued their war. A small civic movement, associated with the Catholic church, is trying, without great success so far, to make Angola something other than rival clientage and enforcement networks. Yet the two elites have become entrenched in their mutually reinforcing relationship; it is the people of Angola, of all regions, who have been paying the price through nearly forty years of anti-colonial uprising and civil war.

Mozambique was once the preserve of European companies that administered large segments of territory on concessions from the government and built plantations for export crops, including sugar and cashew nuts. Victims of coerced labor sometimes fled to neighboring countries, but most had to bear a heavy burden. In southern Mozambique stints of migratory labor in the gold mines of the Witwatersrand, in neighboring South Africa, were preferable to coerced labor within Mozambique. The region's port, Lourenço Marques (later Maputo), also catered to the Witwatersrand's need for an outlet to the sea. In comparison to Angola, the lack of highly concentrated sources of wealth, the smaller size of the *assimilado* elite, and the way related languages and cultural patterns overlapped each other discouraged sharp rivalries among political movements.

FRELIMO emerged in 1962 in the northern region, where Tanganyika provided a haven and a base; northern peoples predominated in its membership. FRELIMO's advance was slow and painful, but it did establish liberated zones in the north, where it tried to involve peasants in their own governance, and infiltrated parts of the south. The uncertainties of guerilla warfare contributed to the demoralization of the Portuguese army and the 1974 coup. In 1975 FRELIMO came to power, under the leadership of Samora Machel, who had succeeded Mondlane after the latter was murdered by the Portuguese.

FRELIMO did not constitute an isolated state elite like the MPLA; it didn't have resources that could be produced and marketed without the active participation of a large proportion of the population. It did make similar mistakes: it assumed it would lead the way to remaking rural society, and it ignored the wisdom of people who knew their environments and their fatigue at having long been told by others what to do. It faced the basic dilemma of having to extract from agricultural production the resources it needed to improve education, health, and urban welfare. Independence was accompanied by destruction of materiel and the exodus of skilled workers; Portugal had done nothing to train its successors in running railway yards let alone ministries. Much of FRELIMO's attempts to rid urban areas of "marginal" people and revitalize agriculture seemed too familiar to people who had lived through colonial rule.

It also had South Africa for a neighbor. The apartheid regime engaged in economic sabotage; the plane crash which killed President Machal may have been caused by South African secret services. Because the FRELIMO government helped the rebels fighting white Rhodesia, Rhodesia worked with South Africa to develop a rebel movement to destabilize Mozambique. Although RENAMO began that way, and was continually supported by South Africa until the 1990s, its relative success also reflected FRELIMO's failure to build support in parts of the countryside. Many peasants saw themselves not as committed and loyal participants in FRELIMO's democratic experiment but as people beset upon by government troops on one side and rebel troops on the other. Where the latter were strong enough, rebel rule could become a reality, and then government counterattack became another menace. War and underlying political and economic weakness had devastating effects: GNP per capita declined 30 percent between 1982 and 1985.

The collapse of apartheid in South Africa ended outsiders' interest in ripping apart the region, and neither FRELIMO nor RENAMO could play the oil and diamond games that UNITA and MPLA did. There was, at least, a basis for a settlement, and in 1992 the two sides agreed to stop fighting, to allow participation of both movements in government bodies, and to hold elections. FRELIMO had, since 1989, dropped its Marxist-Leninist label (the substance had long been a mixed bag), won reasonably fair elections, privatized much of its state enterprises, reconnected its economy to South Africa, and cooperated with the World Bank and development agencies. Mozambique has crawled back from the brink; it remains poor, but not without hope.

### South Africa

Since World War II, South Africa had been both the epitome of and a mockery of the development idea. Its post-war boom entailed serious industrial development and the production of great wealth, and it left millions in misery. The government called its policy in the 13 percent of the country reserved for African cultivators and families, into which millions of people removed from cities were dumped, "separate development." Whereas around 1950 the ANC seemed like other African parties, the latter were organizing for real elections that would soon confer real power, and the former could organize but not campaign and frequently saw its members jailed. In South Africa blacks got to vote in their first meaningful election in 1994 – thirty-seven years after Ghana became independent.

The 1960s were grim years for South African politics. The escalating militance of the ANC and the Pan-African Congress (PAC) – mass demonstrations and mass violations of pass laws, boycotts of buses and shops – culminated in March 1960 in an anti-pass demonstration in the town of Sharpeville, upon which police fired, killing scores of Africans. The government response to the ensuing international outrage – coming at a time when other African colonies were going free – was to ban the ANC and the PAC. These parties moved their bases into exile, mostly in Zambia and Tanzania, and founded armed branches, the ANC's Umkhonto we Sizwe and the PAC's Poqo. Nelson Mandela and many other leaders were soon arrested; Mandela would reside in prison for twenty-seven years. After faltering for a time, the South African economy began to race forward; it, unlike almost all African countries, profited greatly from gold sales during the troubled years of the world economy in the 1970s. Its industrial products didn't break into international markets, but its relative self-sufficiency prepared it for the boycotts and sanctions that were to come. Whites in South Africa lived like Europeans. Blacks and Coloureds did not.

This was not a state run by racist fanatics. The apartheid state's ability to monitor the movements of Africans, via pass laws and residential controls, enabled it to balance demands for labor against the desire to exclude from "white" areas those Africans who were not immediately of service. Under the Group Areas Act, some Africans born in cities had a right to live there permanently; others could in specified circumstances stay for long periods; others lived in single-sex hostels. The best-paid, best-housed Africans still chafed at the impossibility of obtaining the rights of citizens; the fivefold expansion of African high school enrollments between 1965 and 1975, as the industrial economy demanded more educated labor, still left students with an inferior curriculum, inferior job opportunities, and few legal means of political expression; the migratory system still divided families; and the combination of bitter rural poverty and urban discrimination left a large number of young men and women excluded from opportunity or hope, likely recruits to criminal gangs, the "bo-tsotsi."

Few people in the early 1980s would have thought that apartheid would soon be dismantled, fewer still that it would end via negotiations. Revolution seemed one possibility, continued oppression a more likely one. How did this come to pass?

Not because of armed struggle – a point Mandela himself has made. One has to understand the multiple basis of mobilization as well as the particular vulnerability of the white elite. The multidimensional

11 Forced removals, Soweto, South Africa, 1987. A family in Soweto, near Johannesburg, collecting its belongings after police evicted them from their dwelling following a rent boycott.

engagement of African political actors, as noted earlier, has deep roots: the politics of chieftaincy, of peaceful petition, of Gandhian peaceful resistance, of Christian universalism, of Pan-Africanism, and of labor militance could coexist in a single township or rural district. These efforts could be conflictual or complementary, but they enhanced the possibility of different networks among South Africans and different linkages outside of South Africa. After the 1958 All-African People's Congress in newly independent Ghana, other African countries became a source of inspiration, while independent southern African states could serve as guerilla bases, places of exile and organization, and sources of support. South African leaders, from the 1950s, traveled to other African countries, to India, to the 1955 Bandung conference of "Third World" nations, to the UN, and to states in both the "western" and the "Soviet" bloc. Soviet support was particularly crucial to the ANC's exile bases in Zambia and Tanzania. Even when repression within South Africa seemed solid, political and labor leaders had reason to believe that maintaining hope and sustaining effort were not acts of insanity.

A decade after Sharpeville, the South African and international threads were spinning together in new ways. Take labor. For all the state effort at insisting that Africans were not really "of" the city, the growth of industry in places like Durban proved otherwise; families were part of the city too and needed shelter, food, and schools. Underground organization of the workplace in Durban surfaced in January 1973 when workers – to the last man – at a brick factory went to a field instead of to work, beginning a series of strikes in automobile and other advanced industrial sectors. In the absence of recognized unions, officials did not know with whom to negotiate or whom to jail. Zulu chiefs as well as unknown labor leaders became involved, and negotiated with employers. The strike wave occurred at a time when capital had been prospering for years, when wages were held in check and prices rising, and when African's rural resources were severely compromised by the forced removals of the 1950s and 1960s. In 1974 there were 374 strikes involving 58,000 African workers. They won substantial wage increases. There were strikes and disturbances on the gold mines in 1975–77, and wages went up elevenfold in the 1970s, after decades of stagnation, even as the mineowners tried to draw on the wider southern African region for labor. African miners broke into whites' control of more skilled positions, their share of semi-skilled and skilled roles moving from 22 percent to 39 percent. After recognition of the mineworkers union in 1982, 60 percent of miners had joined by 1988.

12 South Africa on strike, August 1987. Members of the National Union of Mineworkers at ERGO, a gold refinery near Johannesburg, during the major mine strike of 1987. Although this strike was not successful, it was one of many events in the 1980s that convinced the white government that it was not fully in control.

The government hesitated between repressing the labor movement and trying to co-opt it into a system that would give it a measure of recognition and orderly channels to negotiate. It opted more for the latter, hoping that an organized working class would be held distinct from other segments of the urban population and would be an element of stability. Parts of the business elite feared that repressive industrialization was reaching its limits and that it would be better to channel militance into known channels when it could not be stopped. African unions became major actors from 1979 onward. The new policy echoed the policies of France and Britain thirty years before, which had been rejected in South Africa. It would – as it did in British and French Africa – have consequences more far-reaching than the calculations of officials.

The second thread came from youth, urban youth in particular. They were part of the city, but the city was not offering them a future. The Bantu Education system was humiliating, and the segmentation of housing and jobs meant that many stood little chance of getting even where their parents were. It was not just the city that was in question: the migratory system had spread urban culture and the appeal of urban life styles into the most remote parts of South Africa. The political significance of youth was by no means homogeneous. Some were satisfied with the pleasures and the expressiveness of music, drinking, and dance; others gravitated into gangs that often preyed on African workers.

But in the schools and universities there developed a more specifically politicized tendency known as Black Consciousness. Steve Biko split off from a multiracial student organization to form the South African Student Organization (SASO) in 1969. SASO picked up the Africanist thread of all-black political movements, thoroughly nationalist, from the banned PAC. It was in the high schools, however, that Biko and SASO caught on most strongly, appealing to young men and women who were far from the worst off in South African society, but whose imaginations and hopes were ground down by Bantu Education.

Biko was arrested in 1973 and SASO banned; he was murdered by the police three years later. In 1976 the most violent outburst of youth occurred: the Soweto rising, in the biggest township outside of Johannesburg. Its immediate cause was an attempt by the Bantu Education authorities to make Afrikaans the language of instruction, which students took to be a wanton demand for submission to the culture of their most immediate oppressors, but its underlying causes were everything described above. In the townships, the students forced the schools to close; they blockaded streets; they attacked police stations; they tried to force their elders not to work. Police fought back with bullets as much as tear gas. In official figures – grossly understated – 575 people died and over 2,000 were injured. Riots took place in other cities as well. They not only shook the white population's sense of being in control, but defined an event whose anniversary would be marked every year and which would serve as a symbol of collective anger at police violence and at the entire system that underlay it.

South Africa at the beginning of the 1980s remained a police state: banning organizations and individuals, jailing people for political offenses as well as for violations of pass laws and other apartheid regulations, killing opponents. It remained a sophisticated police state, hoping that creating different categories of residential access would separate an elite interested in stability from others, and that with the iron fist in the background a small incentive to cooperate would go a long way. But apartheid also meant that very few black South Africans would more than grudgingly accept the status quo, and the elaborate attempts of the state to build an ideology of acquiescence were ridiculed.

The apartheid system had tried to channel urban dwellers into townships like Soweto, where it distinguished long-term residents in their small houses from short-term, male migrants in hostels. Some illegal settlements, like Crossroads, near Cape Town, vigorously defended themselves and were tolerated; others were bulldozed. But all this was breaking down as people poured into the crevices of the system, driven by the overwhelming degradation of rural conditions and the especially precarious condition of women, caught between the illegal status of most of them in the cities and the impossibility of survival in the countryside. People moved into backyard shacks, into squatter settlements, into rooms in other people's shacks. In the 1980s, official strategy was to regain control by widening the zone of tolerance of shack settlements, while keeping them confined to certain areas. But shack dwellers also organized themselves; they provided another urban constituency of considerable volatility, a source both of gang violence and of organized, careful protest. Women leaders in shack settlements organized against lawless gangs as well as against the police.

The cracks were getting wider. The recognized trade union movement, above all its umbrella organization the Congress of South African Trade Unions (COSATU), founded in 1985 but building on another organization founded in 1979, was vigorous, and not confined to the narrow terrain of "industrial relations." As Gay Seidman argues, "social movement" unionism came into being in a situation where the problems workers faced were not specific to their place of employment. The state's regulation of housing and of schooling, and its policing of migration were all issues that a labor movement had to raise. With the ANC underground, COSATU became a surrogate political party as well, using its legal status to make claims and to threaten collective action, from strikes to mass demonstrations. The government had to live with COSATU, for it feared that the alternative was worse.

The urban order – never as neat in reality as on paper – was cracking as well, and despite waves and waves of arrests for pass law violations, the movement of people between cities, townships, shack settlements, and rural areas was not really under control. When the South African economy entered a recession in 1982, many people who had been drawn into the segmented wage-labor system, including high school graduates, were left jobless. Urban violence escalated around 1984 and 1985 – some of it organized, some of it a mark of despair. The underground ANC was trying to channel it, calling on city-dwellers to make the cities "ungovernable." The reality may well have preceded and exceeded the intention.

The apartheid government's attempt to make rural reserves (once "bantustans" or "homelands") into nominally independent polities convinced hardly anyone. The one rural leader who appeared to be more than a stooge was Mangosuthu Buthelezi, the head of the KwaZulu administrative district. By refusing independent status for KwaZulu, he kept enough distance from the government to retain autonomy and plausibility, while controlling a tight hierarchy of chiefs who had considerable power over returning migrants' access to land. He also drew on a form of Zulu neotraditionalism developed by the bilingual elites of a previous generation, who in the 1920s gathered into a Zulu cultural organization called Inkatha – the name Buthelezi took for his revived Zulu association. For a time, Buthelezi positioned himself as an anti-apartheid leader, and while it has since been proven that in the 1980s and 1990s his organization cooperated with the secret police, including in the murders of opponents, he kept a certain public autonomy.

The ANC underground clashed more and more with Inkatha. In the Johannesburg area, where most Zulu workers were short-term migrants still dependent on the power apparatus in KwaZulu, young Zulu hostel-dwellers (known as impis) frequently clashed with young ANC supporters, children of long-term residents for the most part (known as comrades). Gang violence got worse in the early 1990s. In Natal, near the Zulu homeland, much of the violence was Zulu on Zulu, for Inkatha's appeal was far from uniform across this group, and particularly those Zulu well ensconced in Durban's strong industrial culture were likely to be COSATU and ANC supporters. Inkatha thugs tried to police the "exit" option of Zulu who were not willing to remain in the confines of a system of rural political authority linked to control of access to land (via chiefs) and periurban housing (via "shacklords"). As the government secret police intrigued with Inkatha against common enemies, the violence got uglier and uglier.

The constitutionalist, nonracialist, nonviolent side of the ANC tradition, which had absorbed the "Africanist" initiatives of the 1940s and 1950s rather than give way to them, remained important even when the ANC itself was underground or in exile. In 1983, many of the local and regional organizations fighting apartheid founded a national, coordinating body, the United Democratic Front (UDF), initially aimed at combating a new constitution that would have given Indians and Coloureds a small electoral presence and Africans none. The UDF was strongly shaped by its ordinary members, notably Africans of working-class origin, radicalized in high school, then trapped in the segregated, stifling economy. The UDF, nevertheless, had a multiracial membership and was committed to the ANC's democratic goals. "People's power" became a slogan at the national level, but neighborhood networks, consumer boycotts, school boycotts, rent boycotts, and attacks on African agents of local government made the UDF an important presence in the townships, which was not entirely eliminated by the government banning order and declaration of a state of emergency in 1986. Meanwhile, the South African Communist Party, long linked to the trade union movement and the ANC, stood on the left flank, emphasizing both organization and the call for economic justice. The ANC itself, from exile, organized a new round of armed attacks, more important for marking its continued presence than for their actual effects.

The international picture was opening up, too. Since 1959 organizations in England had organized boycotts of South African products, with limited economic effect but an important political one: underscoring that newly independent African countries constituted the international norm, while South Africa was a pariah. African states maintained a steady critique at the United Nations and other international bodies and tried to deny South Africa a place in international commercial, cultural, and athletic organizations. South African goods were at times refused entry by dockworkers in European or American ports; American campuses were enlivened by demonstrations against endowment fund investments in companies doing business with South Africa; religious organizations raised money for exiles and protested racial exclusion and violence; the African-American organization TransAfrica continuously publicized South African issues and campaigned, with partial success, for official American sanctions against South Africa. The Communist world provided aid and arms to the ANC, as well as a platform for some of its leaders and connections to other revolutionary movements.

South Africa had taken itself out of the British Commonwealth when it ceased to be white enough, and at Commonwealth meetings Africans painted the apartheid state as abnormal. South Africa tried to influence conservative African leaders like Mobutu and Houphouët-Boigny to share in mutually beneficial trade relations, but others kept up the pressure to quarantine the apartheid state. The founding of the Southern African Development Coordination Conference (SADCC) in 1980 was intended to cement, through closer economic ties, the solidarity of southern African states against South Africa.

Two points are fundamental to understanding why this led to the unravelling of apartheid in the mid-1980s and a negotiated resolution between 1990 and 1994. First, the old radical line that the key to revolutionary mobilization is polarization – that things should get as bad as possible so that the most radical possible response will emerge – is wrong. As in Gorbachev's Soviet Union, and indeed in the British and French empires a few decades previously, a little reform led to the breakdown of a system of domination. The legalization of trade unions for Africans in 1979 and the easing of some restrictions on urban residence in the mid-1980s were a start. The attempt of the government to gain ground or time by allowing Coloureds and Indians to vote only revealed that the regime was casting about for a way out of endless insecurity, isolation, and escalating repression. Business was finding the cost excessive when there was no resolution in sight. In 1986, the regime – beset by riots, student protests, and strikes – tried to ease the burden on itself and gain a little legitimacy by abolishing the hated pass system. That gave the urban poor, both women and men, a better chance to set up shack settlements in bits of vacant land and to carry out the entrepreneurial (and sometimes criminal) activities typical of "informal" economies elsewhere in Africa and which provided alternatives to the officially regulated economy. Meanwhile, COSATU and the UDF offered a democratic, apparently peaceful alternative. The South African regime was losing its ability to frame political action.

The other point involves the nature of the South African elite itself. For a time, Afrikaners could set themselves against English-speakers and enjoy the pleasures of thinking themselves a struggling community; but Afrikaner politics had always emphasized the "Christian" nature of their society, and by that they evoked a connection to the history of western civilization. By the 1970s or 1980s, many Afrikaners had become too rich and too worldly to be satisfied with proud isolation. They had become like most other participants in global capitalism. White South Africans wanted to travel, to have a national team in the Olympics, to have access to all the cultural and consumer resources to which their prosperity entitled them. Business leaders needed international sources of credit. They were hemmed in overseas for the same reason that there were demonstrations every week and a chronic atmosphere of crisis. The boycotts may not have actually isolated South Africa economically, but they did affect foreign investment and credit, and above all moral discourse. In terms of coercive power, the regime could have gone on for years, maybe decades, but without international legitimacy and domestic order it is not clear for how long it could have carried along the majority of whites.

Probably the most important point to remember about the late 1980s and 1990s is that political change is a process, not an event. From the first conditional offer to Mandela that he could be freed in 1985, to the cautious contacts between the famous prisoner and officials of President Botha's administration, to Mandela's meeting with Botha in 1989, to Mandela's release in February 1990 – simultaneous with the unbanning of the ANC and the latter's renunciation of armed struggle – the National Party (NP) government went from trying to regain control to trying to get concessions from the ANC. When F. W. de Klerk succeeded the aging Botha, he seems to have thought he could manage this process, but he had four things going against him: the demoralization of the white elite; the alternative of endless strife and global isolation; economic difficulties; and the quiet self-confidence of Mandela, who could wait in prison for a while longer to get what he wanted and what ANC and UDF leaders and the "comrades" in the street would accept. By 1990 he not only had the organization of the ANC in exile to back him, but also COSATU and UDF, and able leaders like Cyril Ramaphosa, the mine union leader, COSATU official, and UDF activist who became General Secretary of the ANC after it was legalized. With Mandela's release, the UDF passed its torch back to the ANC, which took up negotiations with a South African state that had lost control of local government, national politics, and international discourse.

The NP did not obtain what it thought it could out of negotiations, but settled for what it could get: the protection of minority rights, and guarantees that property rights would be respected and certain electoral rules followed. It may be that the NP actually believed its own reasoning behind the previous reforms: that it had separated out from the dangerous African masses an elite conservative enough to vote for it. But in the end, the NP leadership could only bargain on how it would give up power – a long and complicated process from late 1991 to early 1994. The ANC accepted to work with the NP in insuring interim government, and trying to stop violence and capital flight only when the latter had agreed to a date for elections, April 27, 1994. The NP became so involved in its *pas-de-deux* with the ANC that it all but dropped its earlier connections with Inkatha, which for a time seemed to prefer violent confrontation in quest of regional autonomy to participation in the constitutional and electoral process. But it realized just in time that electoral fever was high in KwaZulu, too. So, late in the game, Inkatha decided to contest the election as well. The violence in Natal-KwaZulu abated, and the last weeks of the campaign were both calm and enthusiastic.

In the end the National Party learned that its status as the lone defender of white civilization was precisely what its voters could no longer accept; they had to be part of an international system, and only majority rule would get them that. After years of denying Africans fair trials and access to property, whites' future prosperity now depended on whether the ANC majority would continue to take seriously a discourse on the rule of law and human rights which it had espoused since its founding in 1912. Mandela and his colleagues understood the irony: in offering to the NP the rights long denied the ANC, they could complete the long march to freedom.

When on April 27, 1994, black South Africans lined up in queues stretching around city blocks to cast their ballots, they revealed just how meaningful the act of voting can be. The ANC government then faced the burden of reforming one of the world's most unequal societies in an era of worldwide economic uncertainty. There would be no immediate economic miracles to complement the political one of 1994 (see chapter 8). The stuttering economy, the lingering poverty, and the devastation of AIDS – not to mention the precedents of shortcircuited democratization elsewhere in Africa – make it all the more remarkable that South Africans' commitment to democracy has proved a powerful one. In 1999 South Africans had their second chance to vote in a general election, and this too was open and fair, and approached with the same seriousness of purpose. Mandela took his retirement and Thabo Mbeki became South Africa's second President. Mandela achieved something that only a few of the first "fathers of the nation" ever did: he passed on power to an elected successor.

SUGGESTED READING

A full bibliography for this book may be found on the website of Cambridge University Press at http://uk.cambridge.org/resources/0521776007. It will be updated periodically.

Birmingham, David, and Phyllis Martin, eds. *History of Central Africa: The Contemporary Years since 1960*. London: Longman, 1998.
Gerhart, Gail. *Black Power in South Africa: The Evolution of an Ideology*. Berkeley: University of California Press, 1978.
James, Wilmot. *Our Precious Metal: African Labour in South Africa's Gold Industry, 1970–1990*. London: Currey, 1992.
Kriger, Norma. *Zimbabwe's Guerilla War: Peasant Voices*. Cambridge: Cambridge University Press, 1992.
Lodge, Tom, Bill Nasson, Steven Mufson, Khehla Shubane, and Nokwanda Sithole. *All, Here, and Now: Black Politics in South Africa in the 1980s*. London: Hurst, 1992.

Ramphele, Mamphela. *A Bed Called Home: Life in the Migrant Labour Hostels of Cape Town*. Athens: Ohio University Press, 1993.

Ranger, T. O. *Peasant Consciousness and Guerilla War in Zimbabwe*. Berkeley: University of California Press, 1985.

*Voices from the Rocks: Nature, Culture and History in the Matopos Hills of Zimbabwe*. Bloomington: Indiana University Press, 1999.

Van Onselen, Charles. *The Seed Is Mine: The Life of Kas Maine, a South African Sharecropper*. New York: Hill and Wang, 1996.

African states were successors in a double sense. First, they were built on a set of institutions – bureaucracies, militaries, post offices, and (initially) legislatures – set up by colonial regimes, as well as on a principle of state sovereignty sanctified by a community of already existing states. In this sense, African states have proven highly durable: borders have remained largely unchanged, and virtually every piece of Africa is recognized from outside as a territorial entity, regardless of the effective power of the actual government within that space. Even failed states – those unable to provide order and services for their citizens – are still states and derive resources from outside for that reason.

Second, African states took up a particular, and more recent, form of the state project of colonialism: development. African political parties in the 1950s and 1960s generally insisted that only an African government could insure that development would serve the interests of "their" people. Here, continuity is less striking. By the 1970s in most African states, the development slogan had become either tragedy or farce, and people now viewed such claims with either bitterness at the politicians who developed their own wealth at the people's expense, or a continued yearning for development in the form of schools, hospitals, marketing facilities, and a chance to earn money and respect.

The early governments thus aspired both to define their authority over territory which, however arbitrary its borders, was now theirs, and to build something on that territory. But the dual project was born into the limitations of the old one, the colonial version of development. African states, like their predecessors, had great difficulty getting beyond the limitations of a gatekeeper state. Their survival depended precisely on the fact that formal sovereignty was recognized *from outside*, and that resources, such as foreign aid and military assistance, came to governments for that reason. Like colonial regimes, they had trouble extending their power and their command of people's respect, if not support, inward. They had trouble collecting taxes, except on imports and exports; they had trouble setting economic priorities and policies, except for the distribution of resources like oil revenues and customs receipts; they had trouble making the nation-state into a symbol that inspired loyalty. What they could do was to sit astride the interface between a territory and the rest of the world, collecting and distributing resources that derived from the gate itself: customs revenue and foreign aid; permits to do business in the territory; entry and exit visas; and permission to move currency in and out.

Colonial states had ultimately derived their authority from the movement of military force from outside; their coercive power was more effective at staging raids and terrorizing resistors than at routinizing authority throughout a territory; they had built garrison towns and railways to extend their capacities for such deployments; and they had come to rely on localized systems of "traditional" legitimacy and obedience. Their successors faced similar limitations and often hesitated between alliances with the same decentralized authority structures, with the risk of reinforcing ethnic power brokers or breaking them via another deployment of military power likely to provoke regionalist opposition. Colonial states could turn to the armed forces of the distant metropole to insure control of the gate. Their successors could not call in such support. Keeping the gate was more ambition than actuality, and struggles for the gate – and efforts of some groups to get around it – bedeviled African states from the start.

What independence added was the possibility of weaving patron-client relationships within the state, something colonial officials did too, but not so well. One also has to avoid the temptation of being overly institutional in one's analysis–to look for a "state" (bureaucracy, executive, military, legislature) attempting to rule over and interact with "civil society" (interconnections and collectivities formed among the people of a territory). At least as important were the vertical ties formed by a political elite, the connections between a "big man" and his supporters, who in turn had linkages to their own supporters. A person might hold an office – for example as a commissioner in charge of a region – with certain duties and powers, but his daily reality might be to distribute rewards and cultivate support, shaping vertical ties that did not quite coincide with his official role. It is too simple to call that corruption, although many Africans as well as outsiders would do so.

Not all manage vertical ties successfully, for one of the origins of instability in Africa is the inability of gatekeepers to keep the gate. Traders bypass customs collection; oppositional networks establish connections with outside powers and get arms and support; and people often try to live their lives within and across territorial borders as if the state had limited power over them. Some states, Senegal for instance, have managed patron-client systems with relative stability, whereas others, like Zaire, turned them into crude machines by which a single leader and

13 Self-representations of power, Zaire, 1984. President Mobutu Sese
Seku sitting on a throne, with the leopard skin that was his personal
symbol at his feet. Mobutu cultivated an image of the all-powerful ruler,
blending symbols of European power (the throne) and African power
(the leopard).

his shifting entourage extracted resources arbitrarily from poor peasants and rich merchants to such a degree that the formal dimension of state rule collapsed. In Sierra Leone or Angola, rivals developed cross-border networks that smuggled out valuable resources, notably diamonds, and smuggled in arms and luxury goods for the gate-evading leadership.

During the struggles for independence, leaders of parties, trade unions, farmers' organizations, merchants' groups, students, and intellectuals aspired to a view of state-building with a strong "civic" dimension: the state would act in the interest of citizens as a body, through institutions accessible to all. Once in power, African regimes proved distrustful of the very social linkages and the vision of citizenship which they had ridden to power. Nkrumah set a dangerous and revealing precedent when he attacked trade unions and cocoa farmers' organizations in his first years in office. New presidents and prime ministers used their control of access to import-export markets and revenues to reward followers and exclude rivals.

The gatekeeper state was vulnerable: it made the stakes of control at a single point too high. Politics was an either/or phenomenon at the national level; local government was almost everywhere given little autonomy. Leaders often saw opposition as "tribal," which could encourage regional leaders to accuse the "national" elite of being tribalist itself. Gatekeeper states' insistence on the unity of the people and the need for national discipline revealed the fragility of their all-or-nothing control; they left little room for seeing opposition as legitimate. All states, undoubtedly, function via a mixture of personal ties and formal structures. That African history has encouraged people to form rich webs of connections, based on kinship, trading diasporas, religious networks, and so on is not necessarily a political liability; it was most often a strength. A combination of predictable state institutions, a civic-minded political culture that emphasizes the accountability of leaders to the citizens, and a measure of personal politics and networking may produce tensions, but also balance civic virtue and personal connections. What is problematic about gatekeeper states is the focus of patronage systems on a single point and the undermining, in the midst of intense rivalry for that point, of alternative mechanisms for influencing decisions and demanding accountability.

Western governments and international institutions were only too willing to work with gatekeeper states, which were permeable to their influence and useful in cold war rivalries. Even a modest amount of economic or military aid could be a major patronage resource to a leader, or to an insurgency trying to evade the gatekeeping state, when other forms of access to the world economy were weak. From the moment of independence, notably in the Congo crisis of 1960 (see below), western states signalled that they might intervene against a radical *national* policy because they judged that its international implications were unfavorable to their interests. Some of Africa's most conflict-ridden states in the 1980s and 1990s had been among the largest recipients of economic and military aid intended to foster Cold War alliances: Angola, Zaire, Somalia, and Ethiopia. Both sides sometimes left in place former proxy combatants, either ruling cliques or insurgent movements, which continued to reap havoc – in Angola and Somalia for instance – after the Cold War ended.

Even more important, the huge disparities in the world economy accentuated the importance of gatekeeping to state elites: they could not bring their domestic economies to the level of Europe, North America, or East Asia, but they could try to police their citizens' access to the wealth that lay outside and find a profitable niche for themselves. Even a small quantity of resources – a marketing deal, remittances from migrant labor, foreign aid, automatic weapons – could make a decisive difference to whoever could control the asset. Hence the importance of guarding the gate to those who possess it or of building networks to get around state-regulated export-import institutions to those who do not.

When African states proved unable to cope with the difficulties of the post-1973 world economy, western development institutions were quick to blame the corruption and ill-considered policies of African governments. The remedies proposed, under the rubric of structural adjustment, do not necessarily address the structural or historical conditions that gave rise to gatekeeper states. Both African rulers' fear of the kinds of mobilized citizenries through which they challenged colonial rulers and the diminished resources which African states have to offer their citizens in the age of structural adjustment make gatekeeping and patronage more attractive strategies of rule than the democratic bargain by which governments ask for votes and taxes and provide needed services. Gatekeeper states are thus not "African" institutions, nor are they "European" impositions; they emerged out of a peculiar Euro-African history.

What follows is a series of short case studies of different African states from their emergence from colonial control until the mid-1990s. They illustrate both how hard it is to escape effects of the historical trajectory this book has brought out and the variety of forms these processes have taken. One of the hazards in talking about African politics in the United States and Europe is that news stories about violence in Rwanda, Liberia, or Sierra Leone turn into a single set of images applied to Africa as a whole. African realities should not be contrasted to an idealized picture of "democracy" elsewhere in the world; there is not a polity on earth where every member has an equal chance to have his or her political opinion heard or where patronage and corruption are absent from political life. But there are vast differences, within and beyond Africa, in the degree to which people can express their views openly and without reprisals, in the capacity of government institutions to implement policies demanded by a voting public, and in the fairness with which government services and protection are provided to citizens. In many places across the continent, African people are posing demands on government as citizens; Claude Ake considers this a call for a "second independence." What one does not yet see is an example of a government which both guarantees civil rights and choice of leadership and has a long-term record of delivering economic growth and widespread opportunity. No one has found the magic formula.

## The trials and tribulations of states

*Ghana: the pioneer guards the gate*

There is a particular poignancy to the history of Ghana because it was the pioneer. Kwame Nkrumah was more than a political leader; he was a prophet of independence, of anti-imperialism, of Pan-Africanism. His oft-quoted phrase "Seek ye first the political kingdom" was not just a call for Ghanaians to demand a voice in the affairs of state, but a plea for leaders and ordinary citizens to use power for a purpose – to transform a colonized society into a dynamic and prosperous land of opportunity.

But even when Nkrumah became Leader of Government Business in 1951 and prime minister of an independent country in 1957, he was operating under serious constraints. His government, like its colonial predecessor, depended on cocoa revenues for its projects to diversify the economy. A clash with cocoa farmers was virtually inevitable, as the government retained in its Cocoa Marketing Board accounts up to half of export earnings. As described in chapter 4, Nkrumah had by 1959 suppressed the cocoa farmers' own organizations; he had also banned all regional political parties, and hence eliminated the Asante-based National Liberation Movement. Meanwhile, the world price of cocoa was falling, farmers' income plummeting, and incentives to maintain and replant cocoa trees diminishing. After 1965 cocoa production fell by over half as farmers turned to growing food crops, depriving the Ghanaian state of its main source of revenue for everything it was trying to do. Meanwhile, Nkrumah's biggest project to challenge the "neo-colonial" monocrop export economy, the Volta River dam and aluminum processing industry, actually put much of the Ghanaian economy into the hands both of multinational aluminum companies, which had the needed technology, and of international financial institutions, which had the money.

14 Demonstration of workers in the streets of Accra after the military *coup d'état* which overthrew President Kwame Nkrumah, March 1966. Note the signs saying "Ghanaians are now free" – nine years after the country had become independent of Great Britain – and the sign portraying him as *Sasabonsam* super demon.

By 1958 Nkrumah was ruling by decree. He changed his political underlings frequently. His stature abroad, as the pioneer of African independence and as a spokesman against imperialism, was high, but his most principled and ardent supporters at home were disillusioned. Wage workers, in the eyes of the CPP, went from allies to sources of subversion. The autonomy of the trade union movement was severely curtailed; leftist trade unionists were detained or forced out, strikes all but made illegal. Nkrumah told workers that their "former role of struggling against capitalists is obsolete" and that their task now was to "inculcate in our working people the love for labour and increased productivity." In 1961, nevertheless, a general strike erupted, led by railway workers. By the mid-1960s, the export agricultural economy was in collapse. In 1966, a military coup overthrew Nkrumah while he was abroad.

For many years afterwards, Ghana underwent a cycle of military coups, of governmental efforts to deal with basic problems which neither the

British nor Nkrumah had solved, of frustrated military governments turning rule over to civilians and frustrated civilian leaders falling to military coups, and of each generation of rulers accusing the previous one of corruption and failure to help the common people. Ghana was ruled by military governments in 1966–69, 1972–79, and 1981–92. Flight Lieutenant Jerry Rawlings finally made a successful and apparently stable transition from military ruler to civilian and elected president. First taking power by force in 1979, he allowed elections and a civilian government to take office, then staged a new coup in 1981. In 1992 he again allowed elections and was himself the successful candidate for president, as he was in the next election in 1996. After his term was up, Rawlings stepped down, and he accepted the defeat of his party's candidate for the succession, allowing a peaceful governmental transition to take place.

Government policy swung from Nkrumah's statist orientation in 1957–66 to a market-oriented economic approach under military and civilian rulers from 1966–81, and then in a populist direction under Rawlings between 1981 and 1983. Rawlings was critical of wealthy Ghanaians and their foreign partners, using socialist rhetoric and seeking policies aimed at helping the poor. In some ways, he followed a cyclical pattern started by Nkrumah: an invocation of the common citizen and an opening toward participation, followed by fear of the exercise of citizenship and repression. But unlike Nkrumah, Rawlings changed his policy as well as his mode of governance, and he received considerable outside support for doing so. He became the favorite of the International Monetary Fund for his willingness to cut back government expenditures, discard subsidies aimed at fostering urban consumption, privatize state-run corporations, and in general follow the rules of the structural adjustment policy. He had something to show for this: Ghana's debt burdens have been reduced, its growth rate has turned modestly upward after years of stagnation and regression, and it is attracting outside investment. Critics argue that the ultimate question – whether years of curtailing government services have made the common citizen any better off – remains unanswered. Rawlings implemented these policies in a period of tight control; a critic dubbed them an experiment in neoclassical economics "untroubled by popular democracy." That Rawlings could in 1996 make a case for his re-election on the basis of market-oriented economic reform, and that in 2001 a reasonably open campaign and honest election could take place in Ghana, provide a ray of hope that such serious issues can, at last, be debated.

### Congo-Zaire: the unguardable gate

The disastrous decolonization of the Belgian Congo in 1960 attached the word "crisis" to Africa in much of the world's press. Forty years later, this vast and potentially wealthy territory remains as far removed from stability, democracy, and social progress as it seemed in the summer of 1960. Yet if the breaking up of this state has appeared to knowledgeable observers, for the same forty years, to be imminent, the borders of the state remain the same.

This story crosses the frontier of independence. Belgium's hasty decolonization, in the footsteps of France and Britain and following the 1959 Leopoldville riots, came on the basis of inconclusive elections involving two regionally based political parties, the Bakongo Abako and the Katangese Conakat, plus Patrice Lumumba's MNC (Mouvement National Congolais), which was at least trying to offer a national vision and a critique of Belgian colonialism. The independence deal-making made Lumumba the Congo's first prime minister and Joseph Kasavubu, the Abako leader, its president.

Whatever chance there was for Lumumba's national vision to be translated into concrete policies is hard to know, for he had no time. Some want to see him as a revolutionary hero, but his views fell within the more liberal politics of 1950s African nationalism: a man who sought liberation from an oppressive colonial regime and who sought some kind of social and economic liberation beyond that, but was not quite sure what that concretely meant. He was catapulted to leadership without the experience of an Nkrumah or even a Sékou Touré. His speech at the ceremonies of independence, in front of the King of Belgium, which spelled out a devastating – and accurate – portrayal of the violence and exploitation of Belgian colonialism, encouraged Belgian intrigues against him and helped attach the labels of radical or communist to his name in western capitals.

Lumumba had little room to maneuver. Within two weeks of independence, the Congolese army mutinied, largely in revolt against the continued presence and arrogance of Belgian officers. Belgian civil servants left the central government *en masse*, having done nothing to train Congolese successors. Then Katanga, whose leading political figure Moïse Tshombe had excellent Belgian connections, seceded, and in this case, Belgians stayed to help the secessionists. Lumumba's unwieldy state depended vitally on the revenues of Katanga's copper. Here was a gatekeeper whose gate was about to become irrelevant. Lumumba scrambled for outside support, including from the Soviet Union and its allies, which proved of little help except to tie the label of Marxist more closely around his neck.

Within a month, then, a war of secession had started, alongside urban riots, the army mutiny, threats to Europeans, and the undermining of government capacity to act. The UN, with Congolese consent, sent troops to restore order, but Lumumba and Kasavubu represented two different Congos. Kasavubu soon fired Lumumba, whether legally or otherwise,

15 Patrice Lumumba under arrest in the Congo, December 1960. After being ousted from the office of prime minister and placed under house arrest, Lumumba escaped and tried to flee to his home region in eastern Congo. He was captured by government troops and shortly thereafter murdered.

and the UN – pressed by the United States and western European powers – worked with the president, not the prime minister. Lumumba was placed under house arrest, but he escaped and fled towards his home base in eastern Congo. By then Joseph Mobutu, an army officer who had initially worked with Lumumba, was becoming the real strong man in the Congo. He played a decisive role in Lumumba's arrest and later in the effort to track him down. In January 1961 Lumumba was captured and murdered with the connivance of Belgium, the CIA, Mobutu, and local henchmen. Mobutu acted in the background behind a series of weak prime ministers, and he displaced Kasavubu. UN troops played a crucial role in stabilizing this kind of state. By 1963 they defeated Tshombe and restored Katanga, renamed Shaba Province, to the Congo. A semblance of order, albeit of an authoritarian sort, returned, and the copper revenues began to flow again.

The Congo's tradition of millenarian movements blended with its radical, Lumumbist one in the form of rebellions led by Pierre Mulele in 1964. Other regional rebellions broke out. The Congo was clearly not working as a nation-state. But the fact that it was a state was crucial, for outside interests feared a power vacuum in so large, central, and well-endowed a space within Africa; Belgian, American, French and UN military resources were used in various ways to quell rebellions that threatened the territorial integrity of the state. Algeria, Egypt, and Cuba helped out rebels, particularly Lumumbists in the eastern region. The rebellions between 1960 and 1964 are thought to have cost a million people their lives.

In 1965, Mobutu put an end to the masquerade of the prime ministers. He ruled for the next thirty-two years as dictator. He did so with a great deal of western support, both military and financial, from those who knew how corrupt and undemocratic his regime was but saw him as a bastion against communism or other destabilizing forces. Thomas Callaghy argues that Mobutu went from running a "typical military autocracy" to another level of despotism. Formally, his system was "prefectoral": top-down rule by appointed representatives, hired and fired in order to keep them loyal and intimidated, plus efforts to attach each ethnic group, each locality, and each region directly to presidential authority. This version of state-building was not without its achievements; even opponents saw Zaire, as Mobutu renamed the country in 1970, as a unit to which to aspire. "Mobutuist" ideology emphasized the personality of the ruler and Zairian "authenticity," with everyone ordered to drop European names in favor of African ones. Mobutu renamed himself Mobutu Sese Seko. Frequent and arbitrary changes of administrative personnel, and the taking of a personal cut out of all sorts of business activity, were his hallmarks; he is thought to have sent billions of dollars into personal investments in Europe. He was shrewd at staying just one step away from the behavior western powers would not tolerate, and he was bailed out by France, Belgium, and the United States in 1978 when exiles invaded Shaba Province; projects of dubious economic merit were financed by western banks.

Over time, the state became less like a state and more like a mafia. Its weak point was money, for not only did Mobutu loot the treasury, but his security depended on his licensing others to do likewise. By the late 1970s, as copper prices fell, he was in trouble. The formal institutions of Zaire, from health facilities to transport, failed long before the system of clientelism and redistribution of spoils did. But by the 1990s, Mobutu could no longer pay very much of his army, which for a time kept functioning by using its "state" authority as a license to pillage. For a time, the gatekeeping function of the state kept going: copper revenues were funnelled through the state, which took its official and unofficial cuts. That became less reliable as prices fluctuated and industry capacity faltered. Zaire both provided a way around other states' gatekeeping efforts (allowing diamonds to be smuggled out of Angola) and saw its own wealth smuggled out in other directions – notably, gold through East Africa.

Most people lived off their own production and networks of social relations independent of the state. The other side of the parallel economy was a parallel society: a cultural dynamism in Kinshasa, with rich and critical forms of expression, particularly in painting and music.

Mobutu's downfall might not have happened if Mobutu had not lost his ability to insert himself into the social relations by which people survived. It might not have happened if he had kept paying his army, which stopped fighting before it stopped pillaging. Student protests in Lubumbashi in 1990 led to massacres by police; riots and looting took place in Zairian cities in 1991 and 1993. There was pressure starting in the 1990s from western human rights organizations and then from governments; financial institutions wanted him to clean up corruption. Mobutu probably could have survived all that: his gestures toward allowing opposition, debate, and political contestation opened a little space, and he outmaneuvered his domestic opponents and his foreign interlocutors. He turned an outside threat to his advantage, as the influx into Zaire of refugees from the crisis in Rwanda in 1994 (chapter 1) meant that relief agencies had to deal with Mobutu. Sovereignty, once again, had its compensations.

But he could not control the situation. The presence of Hutu militias that had been involved in the Rwanda genocide in the refugee camps led to clashes with Zairians from groups related to the Rwandan Tutsi, who organized to defend themselves. With multiple oppositions in eastern Zaire to the exactions of Mobutu's prefects and soldiers, this proved to be an important catalyst, and the rebellion was supported by the new Tutsi-led regime in Rwanda, backed in turn by Uganda. For reasons little understood, a man with a strange history put together the diverse elements into a coherent fighting force focused not on the border region but on the state of Zaire itself. Laurent Desiré Kabila, originally from Shaba, had been a Lumumbist and then a regional warlord, running a small fiefdom isolated enough that Mobutu's army couldn't get him, connected enough to run smuggling operations and to survive for decades. His rag-tag army, with Rwandan and Ugandan support, expelled Hutu refugees and militias alike from camps, at terrible human cost, and began an odyssey across Zaire. The long march was at least made possible by the unwillingness of the Zaire army to resist and much of the population's hope, after three decades of predation, that the young soldiers of Kabila offered something.

Kabila's dramatic entrance into Kinshasa in May 1997 was extraordinary. He was welcomed by a populace where an anti-Mobutuist popular culture had taken strong root, but without ties either to Kabila's Shaba or eastern Zaire, where his soldiers and backers came from. They were soon disappointed. Kabila was dubbed Mobutu II; even his renaming (again) of the country as the Democratic Republic of Congo had a Mobutuist tinge to it; he made similar deals with foreign mining firms to pass out the country's wealth for uncertain long-term development prospects; he showed no patience with political debate and alternative organizations; he had few scruples about human rights; and he was not the man to turn personal and clientalistic authority relations into routine performance of state functions. His inability to control violence – including that of surviving Hutu militias – cost him the support of Uganda and Rwanda, and another rebellion, with parallels to the one Kabila himself led, took over much of the eastern part of the country, while Zimbabwe and Angola provided key support to Kabila. In 2001, Kabila was killed by one of his bodyguards, and he was succeeded by his little-known son, who like Kabila himself was notably detached from the society he was trying to rule.

Kabila's rebellion aimed at transforming Zaire, not breaking it up. While Mobutu was skilled at using the western desire for stable states to maintain his fragile internal hold on the country, Kabila made use of similar desires on the part of rulers of Zimbabwe and Angola to maintain the sovereignty system and have a share of the spoils of Congo. And despite the unwieldiness of Congo and the inability of the state to monopolize outside outlets, the gatekeeping state still controls potentially large export revenues and access to the international system that gives its leadership real resources to distribute and to use.

### Senegal: managing the gate

Senegal is a state with few natural resources; its most important export has, literally, been peanuts. But its history reveals that gatekeeping itself can be managed by an astute elite.

Senegal, whose leading city, Dakar, was once the capital of French West Africa, lost its special position from France's territorial approach to decolonization (chapter 4). Léopold Sédar Senghor's attempt to salvage a smaller federation by uniting with Mali had failed as both leaders realized the risks they ran of challenges to their carefully built political machines. Senegal ended up a small, resource-poor country whose major assets remained those of connections: Dakar's attractiveness as a headquarters to business and development agencies; an educated urban population; and a good harbor.

Senghor's rise to power had come from his understanding of the French citizenship law of 1946; by working through Islamic brotherhoods, he had obtained the allegiance of former "subjects" in rural areas neglected by his urban rivals. But he still appealed to educated Senegalese with a new vision of politics, simultaneously appropriating the best of European science and culture to aid economic and social progress and insisting that African culture had something of value to offer the rest of the world.

The territories of French Africa acquired local self-government in 1958 and independence in 1960. Senghor and the left-leaning Mamadou Dia, his second-in-command in the Bloc Démocratique Sénégalais, planned to emphasize education and Dakar's linkages, but they also commissioned an economic study that instead of assuming that a prefabricated model would be imposed on all of Senegal, asked what resources and possibilities each community within the country possessed. Senghor and Dia saw rural community mobilization as a new way forward.

But they had little room for maneuver. Dakar's commercial establishment was divided between old colonial firms and Senegalese entrepreneurs connected to the Mouride Islamic brotherhood. These were conservative forces, and they fit poorly with Dia's "rural animation." Senghor's politics was one of drawing fine lines. He did not, unlike Nkrumah, seek to dismantle the organizations which had brought him to power, most especially the Mourides, and he did not want to break his French connections, which Senegalese were now in a position to take advantage of. Senghor moved back and forth between a politics that was at times authoritarian and at times open to dialogue, sometimes oriented toward mobilizing a population toward national progress, and sometimes tending toward rule by experts.

In 1962 Senghor, feeling threatened from the left, fired Dia and imprisoned him, along with some of his allies. From 1963 to 1976 Senegal was a one-party state, under Senghor's Parti Socialist. In 1968 a wave of strikes and student uprisings brought harsh crackdowns and imprisonments. The autonomy of trade unions was undermined and student organizations dismantled. In 1974 Senghor was challenged from the rural areas, as Mouride leaders helped to organize peanut farmers to resist the government's setting of the purchase price of peanuts at a low level. The government gave in. The regime slowly returned to allowing a measure of debate and electoral contestation. Senghor allowed other parties to organize in 1976 and, in 1978, elections were finally held.

In 1981, in one of Africa's few legal, orderly successions, Senghor retired in favor of his long-time protégé Abdou Diouf. Diouf came up through the bureaucracy; he had built his legitimacy on claims to be a skillful technocrat and loyal follower, not the "father of the nation." He allowed – and won – elections in 1983, 1988, 1993, and 1998; the press has mostly been open enough to allow political debate but threatened enough by the possibility of censorship to keep the debate within limits. If certain opposition leaders spent time in jail, some of the same ones spent time in Diouf's cabinet, as he attempted to build coalitions. However, low peanut prices, poor harvests in Senegal's arid rural areas, and IMF-imposed structural adjustment policies limited the state sector when Diouf needed to strengthen his networks of clients. Opposition parties drew on students, teachers, health care workers, and a few other public-sector employees with a populist message. Many people built their trading relationships and communities outside of official channels, while strikes, student rebellions, and peasants' periodic refusals to grow market crops kept up an oppositional ethos.

Until the election of 2000, the state – and the Parti Socialist – controlled all the patronage, so that competition at the level of ideas took place, but only one political apparatus offered concrete rewards. Minority parties could aspire to few resources by competing for municipal or provincial offices, and because the state controlled a large percentage of salaried employment, party control of patronage signified more than it did within a more varied capitalist economy. The Diouf regime was better at containing opposition within its "vertical" patronage system than addressing the overburdened school system, high unemployment, the failures of agriculture, and the impossibility of industrialization.

Diouf's grip failed because both the state's and the party's resources diminished in the era of structural adjustment and atrophied export markets; people had less to lose by voting for the opposition. Its criticisms of Diouf's ineffectiveness rang true. Whereas Diouf needed the support of the Mourides, successful Mouride traders had less need of the state, and they ceased to be an automatic source of electoral support for the Diouf regime. The victory of Abdoulaye Wade, a long-time, populist opposition leader, over Diouf in the 2000 election, signifies a real change in politics; whether it will in policy remains to be seen.

The art of politics in Senegal is more about building connections than mobilizing ethnic or other forms of solidarity. The Islamic brotherhoods cross lines of region and ethnicity for the 80 percent of the population who are Muslim. Moreover, the relationship of religious leader (marabout) to follower (*talibé*) is similar in some respects to that of patron and client – personal and long term, with broad mutual expectations rather than contractual ones, and with both sides having to take care to maintain the other's enthusiasm for the relationship. Political and socio-religious connections reinforce each other, but provide enough distance so that neither can impose its will on the other. The co-existence of these two sorts of vertical relationships has helped keep Senegal from the extremes of state efforts to exclude all nonclientage relations or of religious organizations to promote a "fundamentalist" alternative to the state's role in society. And because people expect something from their vertical relationships, they expect less from horizontal – that is, class – relationships. Rich and poor interact with each other but not as equals.

The relationship between Senegalese remaining in Senegal and those abroad has also been crucial. Many young men from the arid regions of the country and from its inland neighbor, Mali, have migrated to Dakar and then onward to France. For a time, they, along with North African immigrants, became vital components of the French working class. Since 1974, immigration to France has been severely restricted and harsh measures of deporting illegal migrants have been taken, but a West African population is well established in European cities. This population is not cut off from Senegal, and indeed particular villages along the Senegal River Valley have close links to particular neighborhoods outside of Paris, and Senegalese in Europe send regular remittances "home." Mourides, meanwhile, have been at the core of a commercial diaspora extending from Rome to New York, giving street sellers a strong social base in the cities where they work and strong links to Senegal. The horizons of Senegalese are thus quite broad, and their contribution to keeping their arid country of origin going is a vital one, despite the pain of separation and the harshness of American and European immigration regimes.

### Nigeria: the excesses of the spigot economy

Africa's most populous state has been doubly constrained, first by an administrative structure of British design which turned its social and religious divisions into a politically deadly polarization, and then by the discovery of oil, a blessing which became a curse. Nigeria's educated elite had roots extending to the nineteenth century and a cosmopolitan outlook, from its linkages across much of West Africa and to Pan-Africanist circles in England. Its lawyers, teachers, and clerks had experience in state services for decades and familiarity with local, regional, and national deliberative councils, under limited self-administration programs. Nigerian cocoa farmers and commercial entrepreneurs, like urban lawyers, teachers, and clerks before them, constituted a politically aware class, with the means to support an active press and political organizations. The human resources which Nigeria brought to independence were thus considerable.

It also faced all the weaknesses of colonial economies and political structures. By the 1950s, the British policy of allowing African involvement in government at the regional, rather than federal, level was having divisive consequences (chapter 4). In each region, a single party, dominated by members of the majority ethnic group, obtained office and used it to provide services and patronage within its bailiwick. In each region oppositions developed, to some extent (notably in the north) as populist challenges to the governing elites, but most importantly among regional minorities.

This kind of politics took place both before and after independence in 1960. In the late 1950s and early 1960s, exports of cocoa from the

Western Region and a variety of other agricultural products from the Eastern and Northern Regions were sufficient to allow politicians to play their patronage games, for real progress to be made in education, and for Nigeria to build the symbols of its national independence. The modest powers of the federal government, from independence, were in the hands of Alhaji Abubakar Tafawa Balewa, leader of the Northern People's Congress (NPC). All regional parties worried that their rivals would intrigue with other regional groups to gain solid control of the federal government. The east and west feared the north, which was populous and tightly controlled by an Islamic elite, while the north feared that east and west would gain control by insinuating their better-educated population into the bureaucracies that actually ran the state. But Nigeria's worst luck was that it was lying atop one of the world's largest pools of high-grade oil, and by the mid-1960s it was coming into production.

Oil can turn a gatekeeper state into a caricature of itself. Unlike agriculture, which involves vast numbers of people in the production and marketing of exports, oil requires little labor, and much of it from foreigners. It also entails relationships between the few global firms capable of extracting it and the state rulers who collect the rents. It defines a spigot economy: whoever controls access to the tap, collects the rent.

Nigeria plunged into civil war soon after oil exports began. Oil came from the east, and potential oil revenues threatened a shifting regional balance. The diaspora of educated Igbos to Western and Northern cities was also causing tension. In January 1966, the Balewa government was toppled in a coup and Balewa was assassinated. General Johnson Ironsi soon took over from the coup leaders. Ironsi's government was one of Africa's outbursts of military populism: a military elite, trained to get things done, perceiving a government of elected politicians as self-interested, corrupt, and incompetent, announcing its determination to restore competence and regularity to government. It was not seen that way in the north, where Ironsi was less the national reformer than the Igbo power grabber. There had been anti-Igbo riots in the north in the 1950s, but the pogroms that broke out in the Igbo ghettoes in northern cities – with the connivance of local elites – killed tens of thousands and made many more into refugees. In July northern officers instigated Ironsi's overthrow and assassination, and he was replaced by another officer, Yakubu Gowon, who was to rule for the next nine years.

In Eastern Nigeria the second coup was seen, in the context of the pogroms and the tensions over oil revenues, as an anti-Igbo move. Eastern autonomy seemed the only way to keep regional hands on the spigot. Eastern Nigeria declared itself independent and named itself Biafra. What followed was a horrific war: a small regional army, convinced of its righteousness, fighting a larger one which claimed the legitimacy of a nation-state. Biafra had its outside supporters – France, most notably – and as the war and blockade had a devastating impact, particularly on children, the publicity generated sympathy for Biafra and deepened the image of Africa as a land of starving children victimized by wars that seem a product of irrational tribal enmity. That it was a war of maneuvering politicians, as much to do with geographic region as with ethnicity, was more difficult to convey than the stark images.

The federal government won the war, and Gowon tried to avoid a retributive peace. Gowon had earlier divided Nigeria into twelve states, blurring the correspondence of region and ethnicity of the British three-state system. Each region would have its own governmental institutions, services, and educational system. Building twelve universities in the years after the war, for example, created numerous jobs and diffused ethnic competition. The patronage structure was pyramidal, going down to urban neighborhoods, with the head of each pyramid jockeying for access to the next level. At the heart of politics were personal, vertical relationships, as individuals sought help from local "big men" who had access to information, jobs, and construction permits, and as brokers sought state funds for roads, clinics, and meeting halls for their areas. Women turned their active role in running markets into participation in municipal politics. The possibility of using vertical ties provided alternative strategies to organizing horizontally – by the working class, for example – and while patron–client ties reinforced in some ways ethnic and regional affinities, they were not the same as dividing the population into ethnic groups. This did not prevent certain moments of mobilization on a class, ethnic, or religious basis – Nigeria witnessed general strikes from the 1960s to the 1990s and severe flashes of ethnoreligious conflict.

Oil revenues made this distributive logic possible, but they also entrenched Nigeria in its gatekeeper role. Instead of providing capital for the diversification and the industrialization of the Nigerian economy, oil revenues were used above all for the primary task of the political elite: patronage. Having so much to distribute provided some political stability and a model of uneconomic spending. The building boom, focused on schools and roads, sent the cost of labor so high that cocoa farmers could no longer hire, and they themselves saw little reason to invest in developing their farms, when getting their children an education and contacts in the provincial or federal capital were far more likely to bring them prosperity. Oil became the only significant export; agriculture collapsed (see figure 3); industry developed in only the narrowest of niches; port facilities choked on imports; and the dream of a balanced, integrated economy went nowhere. With the fall of oil prices in the 1980s, Nigeria had much less money to throw around so inefficiently. Nigeria could no longer maintain roads, electricity, or hospitals; it became an oil producer with gasoline shortages. Its oil-producing zones, receiving little from foreign oil companies other than disruption, pollution, and heavy-handed security interventions, became discontent, and the government's execution of the regional activist Ken Saro-Wiwa in 1995 dramatized to Nigerians and others the politics of neglect and repression in the oil-rich region.

There was, however, no repetition of the Biafran war. Ethnic tension and violence there has been, much of it between groups within the old regions, some between Muslims and Christians. The most important tensions have been over control of the gate. There were successions of coups, tentative attempts at civilian rule in 1979–93 – no less dishonest than the military variant – and reimposition of military rule. The military's annulment of the 1993 election was a bitter disappointment to the democracy movement, and the ensuing dictatorship of Sani Abacha was particularly harsh, brought to an end only by Abacha's fortuitous early death in June 1998. The Nigerian labor movement, especially during the huge general strike of 1994, was one source of organized opposition; the efforts of lawyers, doctors, students, and others in the Campaign for Democracy to forge links between Nigerian democracy activists and over-seas human rights organizations were another. The election in 1999 of Olusegun Obasanjo, under conditions that were less than ideal but better than anything in recent memory, is another of those moments that just might turn out to be a turning point.

### Kenya: a capitalist alternative?

In the late 1970s, some Kenyan and foreign scholars thought Kenya might be moving beyond the political economy of the gatekeeper state. They saw a Kenyan elite actively buying up farms, including those left by departing British settlers, investing in industry and commerce, and founding joint ventures with multinational corporations. Marxist scholars thought that a property-owning, labor-employing – that is capitalist – class seemed to be taking root. Market-minded observers thought agricultural investment of particular significance too, for it seemed an antidote to the biases of urban-dwelling state elites. Other scholars were skeptical of the "Kenyan exception": they thought that multinational firms still controlled the most crucial sectors of the economy and that the new bourgeoisie was more statist that bourgeois.

With independence in 1963, Jomo Kenyatta tried to reassure foreign investors that Kenya was not still the land of Mau Mau. With British loans, elite Kenyans bought property from departing settlers and so ac-quired a vested interest in maintaining the security of private ownership of land and other resources. The government was challenged from the left, and alternated between cooptive gestures – making designated portions of land available in small units to the landless poor, bringing union leaders into the government, and providing a measure of services to poor urban zones – and repression, banning populist opposition parties, arresting or assassinating threatening leaders, suppressing free speech, and trying to paint opponents as "tribalists" standing in the way of national advance. Official political culture focused around meetings ("barazas") where politicians made their distributive gestures in public: putting money into a school or road and encouraging local self-help projects. But the politicians around Kenyatta who were enriching themselves were largely Kikuyu, and it wasn't clear in the late 1970s whether the central issue was the emergence of class divisions – bringing potential economic growth as well as exploitation – or the more typical instance of the clients of a gate-keeper state enriching themselves. In Kenyatta's Kenya, modestly sized businesses did have a certain autonomy, which they did not in Nkrumah's Ghana or Nyerere's Tanzania, and the civil service was relatively effective, but it is not clear that business ever broke out of the limits of an economy dominated by peasant producers, multinational firms, and a government that policed the gate between the two.

Doubts became stronger when Kenyatta died in 1978 and was succeeded by his vice president, Daniel arap Moi, who was from the Kalenjin region. Moi set about dismantling the Kikuyu-centered patronage system, enhancing the position of Kalenjin clients, and working with other small ethnic groups to redress the regional balance. He had the disadvantage of doing this in a time of global economic contraction. His methods ran to the heavy-handed, including imprisonment and assassination as well as harsh ethnic politics, such as the use of security forces to remove Kikuyu from land coveted by Kalenjin. But he also tried to strengthen Kenya's single party, KANU. His regime was opposed, especially since 1986, by Kenyan activists, notably in the legal profession and in established churches, as well as by international human rights organizations, who now worked more closely with Kenyans than they had before. International financial organizations, concerned with the regime's corruption and economic mismanagement, on occasion suspended aid. Student demonstrations and strikes have been frequent; professionals, like doctors and nurses, have struck as well against the state's degradation of working conditions in public service. Kenyan business people hurt by the reconfiguration of the patronage system helped to finance and organize opposition parties when they were legalized.

The KANU government has had to respond to internal and external pressure by gestures towards democratization, including the legalization

16 Personality and politics: President Jomo Kenyatta watches the un-
veiling of his statue at a ceremony in Nairobi, December 14, 1964. The
statue is being unveiled by Oginga Odinga, then the vice president, but
who later became a populist opponent of the Kenyatta regime and was
isolated and at times detained for his political actions.

of multiple parties and the holding of elections in 1992, which were
open enough that Moi won only a narrow plurality of the votes. Moi has
been helped by the fact that opposition parties, notably the two different
branches of the Forum for the Restoration of Democracy, were as much
built around the personal networks of their leaders as was the apparatus
of Moi himself. Kenya's economy, meanwhile, has moved between stagnation and periods of modest growth; it remains dependent on exports
of coffee and tea; it is still highly penetrated by foreign capital; and its
indigenous capitalists remain closely linked to the state and vulnerable to
the whims of its leadership.

*Tanzania: a radical alternative?*

In the abstract, the leaders of African states had choices beyond those
described in the narratives above. The very thinness of the social basis of

the regimes – the absence of powerful pressure groups – gave leaders flexibility in how they would represent their goals. At some level, independence movements had been popular mobilizations, and given the small size of the property-owning classes could hardly have been anything else. So "development" was a near universal watchword and building schools and clinics a near-universal policy; and many regimes called themselves socialist, including some (Senegal) whose policies were not very different from those who represented themselves as "pro-market" or "pro-west." The stakes of ideological positioning could be high, mainly because the Cold Warriors rewarded their friends and punished their enemies. But that would not necessarily translate into differences in how regimes actually operated domestically.

A few governments, either at the moment of liberation or with a change of regime, proclaimed themselves to be "Marxist-Leninist" and espoused a Soviet-style version of scientific socialism. The self-proclaimed "people's republics" of Bénin and Congo-Brazzaville and the revolutionary regimes of Angola and Mozambique set forth programs of radical economic reform stressing state ownership of industries and commercial organizations, rural cooperatives or collective farms, the expansion of educational and health facilities, and also attacks on the wealthy and on traditionalist chiefs. But in practice, how much did they differ from other gatekeeper states, with their tendencies to eliminate autonomous sources of wealth and power and to try to control key commercial institutions? It is not clear that any African state had the capacity to plan on a national scale or control production in a truly Soviet fashion. The "Afro-Marxist" states were not run by parties solidly rooted in working-class or peasant movements; the radical impetus was more likely to come from urban intellectuals, students, young soldiers, and bureaucrats. The reformist projects in these states most often focused on education and on involving rural people in the national economy and national political institutions. They sent students to the USSR or East Germany rather than to France or the United States, and they received aid workers and military attachés from the Soviet bloc in their cities.

But in their Marxist phases, Bénin or the Congo could do little more than populist, but non-Marxist, governments to provide education or reform agriculture. The Soviet Union provided little capital and dubious expertise. It did provide some of its allies with military support, but whether that provided a real alternative to western "imperialism" is another question. If some of the Afro-Marxist regimes made stronger efforts than others in the realms of education and health, none achieved significant breakthroughs against poverty.

There was still another alternative: to work out an ideology and a program that were original and focused on conditions in Africa, and that might resonate outside the universities and capital cities. Tanzania's "African socialism" was a notable example of such a quest, positing "self-reliance" against the trade-and-aid model of development and emphasizing the engagement of rural communities with a national project.

Tanganyika, which was to join with Zanzibar in 1964 to create Tanzania, had a few zones of export potential: the sisal growing area inland from the coast and, above all, the coffee growing area near Mount Kilimanjaro and other highland regions, surrounded by much larger areas where a culturally diverse population lived in resource-poor environments. Tanganyika was led into independence by a former school teacher, Julius Nyerere, a small educated elite, and a modest trade union leadership. In the few tense years before independence, TANU forged ties with a variety of rural movements, particularly those aggrieved by heavy-handed British development and soil conservation programs. At first, TANU's development policies were close to the orthodoxy of western experts. But given Tanganyika's spread-out and meager resources, it was not attractive to investors.

In 1964 Tanganyika negotiated its union with the island nation of Zanzibar, which had recently undergone a revolutionary struggle that threw out its substantial land-owning class of mainly Arab origin, and sought to install a radical, self-consciously African regime. Taking stock of the post-independence years in 1967, President Nyerere argued that trying to base development on "money" had failed. We will not get the money, he concluded, and moreover, the danger of eroding fundamental African values and community solidarity was all too real. Nyerere's "Arusha Declaration" called for togetherness and self-reliance, a strategy based on the allegedly communal nature of African society. The state, and the party in particular, would breathe dynamism into Tanzania's communities, and they would bring shared values to the nation.

The new plan entailed nationalizations, particularly in banking and commerce. The government improved education and tried to emphasize rural clinics over fancy urban hospitals. At the heart of its strategy was the building of *vijiji vya ujamaa* – solidarity villages. Intended to turn African values into practical cooperation, the program envisioned bringing people who were living in scattered homesteads into villages that could be provided with schools and clinics – and party offices. The program promised peasants a voice within the single party. By 1972, 15 percent of the rural population had been brought into the *vijiji vya ujamaa*, by 1976, 91 percent. But the results were disastrous. Many, probably most, peasants did not want to move. The government was able to force them into villages, but not to produce in accordance with its plans. Bringing them closer to a disliked political party did not make Tanzanians more active participants in "self-reliance." The nationalizations in the commercial

17 A "village of solidarity" (*kijiji cha ujamaa*), Tanzania, 1974. Women hoeing a communal plot. These villages were heralded by the social-ist government of Julius Nyerere as a way of integrating farmers into the fabric of the nation, but the farmers resented a new form of state imposition.

sector had equally bad results, so that Tanzania fell into a pattern of de-development – less production, less trade, less integration into a truly national economy. The standard of living fell 40 to 50 percent between 1975 and 1983. And self-reliance never meant what the words implied: heavily supported by Scandinavian countries and even the World Bank, Tanzania became one of the world's biggest per capita consumers of for-eign aid, and it needed every penny to stay afloat. Ironically, the *vijiji vya ujamaa* bore a considerable resemblance to colonial programs of "vil-lagization," intended to bring dispersed rural populations under closer surveillance.

Nyerere, architect of the one-party state imposed in 1965 as well as of socialism and self-reliance, had the wisdom to recognize that things had gone wrong. Having done his share of arresting opponents and stifling dissent, he was one of few heads of state who willingly passed on the torch (in 1985), remaining as party head and elder statesmen, and in 1990 he was willing to admit that the one-party state was not a good idea. Multi-party, competitive electoral politics was reinstated in 1992. Tanzania backed away as well from its collectivist economic strategies. With the loosening of control of production and prices a semblance of economic order returned, coffee exports rose, and a wider range of goods became available. Cooperating with the IMF's structural adjustment strategy, Tanzania allowed its budget allocations for education and health to be cut, and literacy rates fell. Tanzania's economy came back from the nadir; it slowly returned to being a conventional impoverished country.

### Can the gatekeeper state become democratic?

Fifteen years ago, some observers thought that pro-trade, agriculturally oriented countries like Kenya and Côte d'Ivoire were exceptions to the rule of African economic stagnation; they were "miracles of the market." Since then, they have proven to be less than miraculous, constrained by their inability to do more than produce larger quantities of primary commodities which world markets want less of and by their leaders' perceived need to put their own control of patronage ahead of economic growth and diversification.

At the other end of the policy spectrum, African states like Nkrumah's Ghana tried to restructure a colonial economy radically, but had little other than mounting debts to show for the effort. The disasters of African political economy range from the self-proclaimed market-oriented (Zaire, Nigeria) to the self-proclaimed socialist (Tanzania, Guinea). The grossest violations of human rights have occurred in states whose formal ideologies have covered a wide spectrum (Zaire on the right and Guinea on the left), and in others where ideology was less important than the *folies de grandeur* of a leader (Idi Amin in Uganda or Jean-Bedel Bokassa in the so-called Central African Empire). Some states have broken down nearly completely, Somalia notably, where not only basic institutions – bureaucracy, judiciary, army – have failed but where rival warlords construct distinct patron-client systems.

Ideology is not the theme around which the most important variations occur. But gatekeeper states can be managed so tightly that they destroy all sources of social cohesion and economic dynamism other than that which can be controlled from the top, as in Mobutu's Zaire, or they can be more flexible, allowing somewhat diverse economic and social relationships to develop, as in Senegal. As I have argued, gatekeeper states are distinguished not by effective control of the gate, but by the intensity of struggle over it, which has had varying outcomes. While it is clear that it is a mistake to turn the worst failures of gatekeeper states – Liberia, Sierra Leone, Zaire, Guinea – into stand-ins for all of Africa, it is harder to look at the other end of the spectrum, to find clear paths for a way out.

In the classificatory scheme of political scientists Michael Bratton and Nicolas van de Walle, there were in 1989 only five multiparty regimes in Africa, compared to eleven military oligarchies, sixteen one party-regimes that gave people no choice but ritual ratifications of pre-selected candidates, and thirteen one-party systems that allowed some choice of candidates within the party. In the 1990s, there seemed to be an opening, and some commentators spoke of a "wave" of democracy pushing aside dictatorships and military governments across the world, including Africa. Was this a conjuncture in which the exercise of national citizenship was reinvigorated, perhaps comparable to the post-1945 conjuncture in which the notion of imperial citizenship opened up and then exploded the very idea of reformist colonialism? Some elements were coming together that shook up the gatekeeper state:

1. Over a decade of economic contraction eroded the patronage resources of ruling elites and left them searching for new ways to obtain support.
2. Key categories of African societies, notably professionals and students, found their paths to the future blocked and little outlet for their talents.
3. Workers and the urban poor may have remained desperate enough to keep trying to use whatever personal connections they could, but were doing so badly that many were *available* (as with youth in the 1940s) to be mobilized in strikes, demonstrations, and sometimes anti-regime violence.
4. Donor agencies like the World Bank were frustrated at the dissipation of aid via corruption and were demanding "good governance" as a condition for the assistance which rulers desperately needed.
5. An expanding range of nongovernmental organizations, concerned with human rights, legal reform, women's empowerment, and ecology, were involved in Africa, and they were interacting more closely than before with African activists.

Just as the revolution which overthrew colonial rule came about not as the bottom overthrew the top but as interaction became more intense and the path of change less controllable by rulers, the uncertainties within African regimes seemed to promise an unfolding dynamic of political restructuring. Movements for multiparty elections and increased freedom of speech can be infectious; a contested election in one country suggests a possibility in another.

But the results were mixed and short of the dynamic of the 1950s and 1960s. A wave of national conventions, of rewriting of rules of electoral competition, of legalizing multiple parties, and of elections with at least a measure of fairness took place after 1989, starting with Bénin's calling of a national convention to write a more democratic constitution. In the 1990s, there have been more elections – some of them offering genuine choice – than in any time period since the early days of independence. In Bénin, Zambia, and Senegal, old-guard leaders were voted out of office; second rounds of more or less open elections have occurred in several countries. Bratton and van de Walle claim that between 1990 and 1994 progress toward democratic elections occurred in sixteen African countries (out of forty-seven), and limited transitions in others, and civil liberties improved at least a little in thirty-two countries.

The degree to which electoral choice and freedom of expression and organization have progressed varies, but there are only a few clear models – Botswana, Mali, and newly "free" South Africa – of the institutionalization of political reform and new expectations of ordinary people that their voices will be heard. Leaders remain wedded to winner-take-all models of government, fearful of allowing rivals to have access to provincial or local patronage and other resources. If they concede multiple party elections, they still use patronage and coercion to maintain control of the process. Opposition parties, meanwhile, have tended to be built around the same kind of patron-client ties as the ruling party. Moi's Kenya remains a clear example of a regime facing all the pressures cited above, but manipulating a multiparty system as it had a single party system, as a divided and clientelistic democracy movement fails to bring together professional and popular opponents of the status quo. In Bénin and Zambia victorious oppositions soon replicated the regime they had replaced. Nigerian political scientist Julius Ihonvbere fears that "elections and more elections" have "recycled" old leaders, old ideologies, old political styles, and old suspicions. They have neither ended the politics of patronage and suppression of dissidence nor put in place governments capable of addressing fundamental problems.

At first glance, pressures to "liberalize" politics – to reduce rulers' arbitrary power, foster electoral competition, and encourage debate – may seem congruent with pressures to "liberalize" economies – to reduce the size and power of government, privatize public enterprises, and stimulate market competition. But the effects of such double liberalization can be contradictory. Decreased government services, under pressure from the IMF, are not the best selling points for democracy. Thandika Mkandawire fears that without more resources, African states will become at best "choiceless democracies." Privatization of state enterprises may not release assets into an open "market" but put them into the hands of leading politicians and their clients, who in their "private" capacity as businessmen do what they did as "public" managers.

Indeed, the private-public distinction is a misleading one, where politics depends on the "big man" who controls a range of resources, from money to kinsmen to clients to state office. Downsizing the state might do less to reduce clientalism than to reduce the effectiveness of those institutions, including the civil service, which provide services to the population as a whole, making the search for a patron all the more necessary. At an extreme, public service can collapse altogether and the "state" loses control of even the gate, leaving in place a series of power brokers who acquire followers and weapons and transform themselves into warlords. This has happened most clearly in Sierra Leone and Somalia and was resisted where state institutions retain at least some respect and effectiveness, as in Senegal or Kenya. At the positive end of the spectrum is Botswana, where a relatively coherent leadership, with traditional legitimacy, education, and business acumen, has maintained a strong civil service, governed through recognized institutions rather than personal deals, allowed room for debate and decision-making at the district level, bargained firmly with foreign corporations to insure adequate state compensation and control, aided private enterprise, and insisted that state enterprises be commercially viable. Electoral democracy has remained intact, and Botswana has maintained one of Africa's highest rates of growth – 9.9 percent annually in 1960–80 and 5.6 percent in 1980–91 – although the distribution of income and wealth is wide and growing.

Despite the variations, the widespread sense of frustration after the era of "democratic experiments" in the early 1990s should be no surprise, for the historical patterns and global conditions which gave rise to gatekeeper states in the first place have not fundamentally been altered, and the political economy of an African state cannot necessarily be remade by an act of will of even the most enlightened leadership. But the fact that economic and political reform have been debated and attempted in different African countries is itself of great importance. Such debate has, perhaps in a way unseen since the 1950s or early 1960s, enhanced among ordinary citizens a sense that citizenship entails multiple possibilities: that officials can be held accountable for their actions; that constituencies for reform can be built; that associational life and public discussion can be enriched; and that trade unions, women's associations, and political parties can be organized.

## Other Africas: connections beyond the nation-state

As emphasized in previous chapters, the national focus of African elites in the mid-1950s represented a shrinking of spatial perspectives. Senghor, for one, regretted the narrow territorial focus of politics in the late 1950s, but his broad defense of equality within the French Union and even within smaller federations in West Africa proved untenable. By hosting the All-Africa Peoples' Congress in 1958, Nkrumah tried to revive

Pan-Africanism, which had lost ground to territorial politics since the Manchester Congress of 1945. Pan-Africanism, however, was becoming a relationship of states, not of people. Nkrumah's hope for a United States of Africa achieved little support from African leaders intent on protecting the sovereignty they had so strenuously fought for.

State-centered Pan-Africanism became institutionalized as the Organization of African Unity (OAU). It met regularly, discussed common action on various fronts – above all seeking global economic policies more favorable to developing countries – but its possibilities were constrained by what it was: an assembly of African heads of state, many of whom were part of the anti-democratic trends of their own countries. The OAU failed its most obvious moral test, failing to act in the name of values shared across Africa against those leaders who were the most egregious violators of them.

Economic cooperation, as described in chapter 5, had its failures, such as the East African Federation, and also its moderate successes in regard to tariff reduction, shared banking institutions, and other interstate arrangements, notably the Economic Community of West African States (ECOWAS) and SADCC. ECOWAS also has a political and military component, which performed more credibly than previous efforts in its interventions in Sierra Leone, where it contained a rebellion against an elected government. But after 1994, African institutions failed to contain the worst border-crossing conflict, when Uganda, Rwanda, Angola, and Zimbabwe fanned the flames of conflict in Central Africa and became involved in the trafficking of Congo's resources of gold and diamonds. Charles Taylor, once a rebellious warlord in Liberia, laid successful claim to recognized sovereignty over that country, while intriguing with shadowy movements in Sierra Leone, Guinea Bissau, and other neighbors in pursuit of the diamond trade. In short, intra-African cooperation has sometimes taken the form of covering up the vices of gatekeeper states and participating in the vices of cross-border networks that bypass the gate. Constructive interaction of African states remains an elusive goal.

African states have been more likely to be the targets of intervention from outside than active participants in international regulatory processes. Their need for periodic financial bail outs has made it hard for them to pose alternatives to IMF policies. Africa has been the focus of operations by refugee and famine relief organizations, whose services have been desperately needed, as in the aftermath of the Rwandan genocide of 1994 or the Sahelian famine of 1974. International humanitarian organizations have given Africans a means to find allies in their struggles against abusive regimes, in obtaining support for sustainable agriculture, or in combating AIDS, but some have defined the problem in terms of African helplessness – its need of outside help to feed starving babies – rather than that of cooperating with Africans to address issues of injustice and impoverishment.

At the same time, Africans have actively participated in international organizations which address the continent's problems. A Ghanaian, Kofi Annan, heads the UN. The United Nations Development Program (UNDP), where "Third World" economists and other specialists play important roles, has been instrumental in keeping alive the idea that growth and structural change in Africa require participation of its citizens in the process. The United Nations Educational, Scientific, and Cultural Organization (UNESCO), which for many years was directed by Mochtar M'Bow of Senegal, has called attention to the diversity of historical and cultural contributions of peoples throughout the world, and while opponents have criticized it for wastefulness, intellectual and cultural innovators have made use of its resources to promote the idea that not all literary, artistic, and musical contributions fit within canons derived from European experience. The UNESCO-sponsored history of Africa has its virtues and its flaws, but the fact that a substantial portion of its editorial board have spent time in detention or in exile reveals clearly that African intellectuals can both argue for specifically African perspectives and criticize the nation-states which claim to embody Africa's uniqueness.

Cross-border relationships take more forms than this. Every border gives rise to specialists who figure out how to cross it; they constitute a "community" as much as any people located firmly within a given set of boundaries. Islamic networks link much of Africa to other parts of the world, through annual pilgrimages, the training of religious leaders in Egypt or Saudi Arabia, and financial support from oil-producing states in the Middle East. Islam, as in Senegal, may mean participation in a brotherhood deeply rooted in local social and political relations, and it can mean participation in a universalistic faith with adherents around the world. Christian churches, as noted in other contexts, participated in a variety of transnational linkages. The numerous Africans who have obtained higher education in Europe and North America, who participate in international professional organizations, and who work for NGOs, participate in world-wide networks. The extent of labor migration and the fact that African communities are now well established in European countries shape other sorts of connections.

All this suggests that political imaginations of Africans, from poor migrants to sophisticated professionals, have multiple roots and may provide alternative models for changes. Some forms of political organization have been – for good, one hopes – excluded from the realm of possibility: the empire and the white supremacist state, for instance. The 1950s and

1960s witnessed an opening of opportunities for Africans to participate in politics, but the very possibility of attaining power focused imaginations on the units in which power was available.

Some argue that the problem is the nation-state itself. Basil Davidson, a stalwart supporter of African nationalism in its heyday, now sees the nation-state as the "black man's burden," an imposed institution inappropriate to the conditions of Africa. We have, however, seen something worse than the nation-state: its absence. The collapse of state institutions in Somalia, and their weakness in the face of warlordism in Sierra Leone, Liberia, and Zaire, reveal how much, in today's world, we depend on state institutions to regulate conflict and provide basic infrastructure. Anthropologists can celebrate the ability of the Somali clan structure to balance the relative strengths of different kinships, foster equality among males, and settle conflicts within the kinship system itself, but once – following the cynical manipulations of both the United States and the Soviet Union – Somalis got access to AK-47s and truck-mounted artillery, clan conflict took on an altogether different aspect. Seeing the possibility of actually dominating others, clan leaders carried warfare to a more devastating level, tearing down state structures altogether. The effects of vacuums in state power in Sierra Leone and Zaire are no less devastating.

It may also be too simple to lament the "western" character of the state, for states as they exist throughout the world reflect a history shaped by the struggles of once-colonized people, and state institutions take new forms when they are used in different contexts. But the history of decolonization did foreclose alternatives that were once the object of attention – supranational federations and Pan-Africanism – and it put in place a particular kind of state as well as a ruling class conscious of its own fragility. The devolution of sovereignty by European states was accompanied by a denial of responsibility for the historical process which had put in place this institutional nexus. This leaves the question of whether in the future the range of possible forms of political action can be expanded as well as constricted. Here, the question is not whether Africa should maintain or abolish the nation-state, but rather what kind of state can be constructed, what kinds of relationships can be forged across state lines, and what kinds of recognition within states can be given to the variety of forms of affinity to which citizens subscribe.

The tragedy of Africa's decolonization lies in the foreclosure of possibilities that once seemed genuine: of a citizenry choosing its leader; of a socially-conscious citizenship, in which education, health services, and other services are seen as a duty of government; and of cooperation across borders against the injustices of imperialism and for recognition of Africa's contributions to global culture. That states are units of electoral politics and territorial administration does not preclude a politics of larger and smaller units, of activism across borders. If some see sovereignty as a barrier against any questioning of the good or evil done within borders, others argue that sovereignty is a part of an effort to share the planet and that the abuse of sovereignty concerns people everywhere. African states will probably remain stuck within the limitations of the gatekeeper state – with its brittle and heavily guarded sovereignty – unless nation-states in Europe and North America as well as Africa acknowledge a shared responsibility for the past which shaped them and the future to which they aspire.

## Other Africas: popular culture and political critique

One of the mistakes of western critics of African governments and their policies, coming from journalists and international financial "experts" alike, is to think that they were the first to diagnose problems. The fact is that African intellectuals became aware of fundamental difficulties within their countries while most of their western counterparts were still celebrating the arrival of Africans into the "modern" world. In city after city and village after village, even under oppressive conditions, popular discontent has found powerful forms of expression.

A key moment in the emergence of a critical intelligentsia was the publication in 1968 of Ayi Kwei Armah's novel *The Beautyful Ones Are Not Yet Born*. Armah evoked the disillusionment of young Ghanaians who had been captivated by the idealism and dynamism of the new state, only to see their classmates and families caught up in the greed and corruption of the new order. The book ends with the chaos of a coup, in which the hero helps his corrupted former classmate escape; an ending which evokes the shared humanity of people whose political and ethical decisions differ and which opens the possibility that a new generation will have another chance. Other novelists and playwrights of that era – Mongo Beti, Chinua Achebe, Wole Soyinka, Ngugi wa Thiong'o for example – developed a politicized fiction written for Africans literate in French or English and for foreigners as well, and which brought out the moral dilemmas of people who had struggled against colonialism and were facing new struggles. Other writers refused to be typecast into the mold of writing political fiction and saw themselves opening up a wide variety of imagined worlds, as writers in many contexts have done. But most important were the efforts of intellectuals familiar with a variety of oral and written literary forms to perform in ways accessible to a wider populace. The emergence of a Yoruba popular theater in western Nigerian cities is a case in point, as was the performance of plays in Kikuyu by Ngugi wa Thiong'o, an effort which, unlike his equally critical writing in English, landed this distinguished writer in prison.

Critical artistic creation took more forms than the literary. The Nigerian singer Fela Ransome Kuti, the scion of a family active in the Nigerian nationalist movement, developed a politicized and highly popular musical style in Lagos, for which he was harassed and detained by the police. In Kinshasa, renowned for decades for its musical creativity, a subtle form of criticism of Zairian society under Mobutu crept into what at another level were love songs and dance music. The café/club/bar scene was entertainment, but it was also part of forming new kinds of sociability, which as in the 1940s and 1950s was not without political content. Zairian musicians – including Papa Wemba and Franco – were influenced by African-American jazz and Ghanaian high life, and they in turn influenced music throughout Africa, Europe, and North America. So, too, with visual art. Kinshasa was the home of a vigorous community of painters, Cheri Samba and Kanda Matulu Tshibumba the best-known of them, who were influenced by comic book art as much as by formal schooling in painting to create a style that was in part moral lesson, in part political critique, and in part a colorful, visually appealing form of self-expression.

African writers, artists, singers, and film-makers have long debated what it means to "decolonize" African culture as well as to distance the artist from the rigidities of the post-colonial successor states. Does it mean rejecting European ideas of what constitutes a novel, a painting, or a film as much as refusing Eurocentric content? Does it mean searching for some sort of African "authenticity"? Or does it mean that the artist is open to whatever influence he or she wishes to turn to, to whatever themes he or she wishes to engage?

It would be a mistake to see African urban culture, in Kinshasa, Lagos, or elsewhere, as simply a popular, critical form standing in stark opposition to a detached form of "power." Power is much more ambiguous than that. Achille Mbembe finds a culture of "vulgarity" in African cities. The "big men" of the regime are seen literally to "eat" the country, to have huge sexual appetites as well, to flaunt their wealth and power. Popular culture is at one level angry at this, but at another level desirous. The vulgarity itself marks both an evil – dangerously close to witchcraft, for supernatural forces are also seen to "eat" their victims – and a sign of power, something deeply desirable as well as immoral.

The insight is especially crucial when one is not limited to seeing society divided into categories – elite versus popular classes or ethnic, racial, or gender divisions – but rather stresses *relationships*, and in particular vertical relationships. Rich and poor see each other not just in terms of antagonism, and not just via the desire of the latter to become the former, but by interaction and mutual expectations between the two. The poor seek access not just to wealth, but to the wealthy. The rich have access to many poor – who can provide political support, muscular action, and cheap services – while poor people have limited access to the rich. The jockeying for access gives rise to both connection and antagonism and gives African political culture, particularly in cities, a high degree of volatility. Outbursts of popular rage, whether riots against price increases in Zambia or strike action against the Abacha regime in Nigeria, alternate with periods when patron-client networks offer at least a possibility for vulnerable members of society to get something – even if most will end up disillusioned.

The importance of the quest for a rich relative, a marabout, a former classmate, or a well-placed fellow-villager is thus incorporated into popular culture, even as patron-client relationships are also crucial to the very summit of power. Patron-client relationships are part of any political system, but a particularly big part of African polities. And the reason is partly that of the structure of the world economy, above all the enormous gap between the resources available within African countries and those in Europe, North America, East Asia, and parts of the Middle East.

Africans as much as outsiders have expected state institutions to perform certain functions: to organize schools and clinics; to deliver mail; to guarantee security of persons and of transactions; and also to promote a common sense of affinity and shared responsibility among the nationally-defined community. States can and should be judged on whether they can perform such basic tasks for the benefit of the large majority of citizens. But states consist of people and people build networks. The institutional strength of states and the networks of its most important leaders may reinforce each other or stand antagonistically to each other. A political leader may benefit from fostering economic growth in which many people share, adding to his political capital, or he may also try to deny potential rivals access to resources and insure control by eliminating alternatives. One process fosters institution-building and resource generation; the other weakens institutions and consumes resources. Both are rational strategies, and both are used by leaders of African states in various combinations. Nothing guarantees that the virtuous circle will triumph over the vicious one. It helps little to point out the failings of governments without understanding the constraints and their causes, but historical reflections should deepen discussions of accountability, not foreclose them. Governments, oppositions, and concerned citizens have choices, and their consequences are enormous.

SUGGESTED READING

A full bibliography for this book may be found on the website of Cambridge University Press at http://uk.cambridge.org/resources/0521776007. It will be updated periodically.

Armah, Ayi Kwei. *The Beautyful Ones Are Not Yet Born*. Boston: Houghton Mifflin, 1968.
Bayart, Jean-François. *The State in Africa: The Politics of the Belly*. London: Longman, 1993. Trans. by Mary Harper. (Originally published as *L'état en Afrique: La politique du ventre*. Paris: Fayard, 1989.)
Bratton, Michael, and Nicolas van de Walle. *Democratic Experiments in Africa: Regime Transitions in Comparative Perspective*. Cambridge: Cambridge University Press, 1997.
Callaghy, Thomas. *The State-Society Struggle: Zaire in Comparative Perspective*. New York: Columbia University Press, 1984.
Hutchinson, Sharon. *Nuer Dilemmas: Coping with Money, War and the State*. Berkeley: University of California Press, 1996.
Joseph, Richard, ed. *State, Conflict and Democracy in Africa*. Boulder: Lynne Rienner, 1999.
Mbembe, Achille. *On the Postcolony*. Berkeley: University of California Press, 2001.
Reno, William. *Corruption and State Politics in Sierra Leone*. Cambridge: Cambridge University Press, 1995.

# 8    Africa at the century's turn: South Africa, Rwanda, and beyond

April 1994. In that month, the planned extermination of Rwanda's Tutsi population began, and South Africans of all colors and origins voted for the first time to select their government. This book began with these two events, which seemed to reveal Africa's two futures: one of electoral democracy, the other of ethnic violence. Viewed statically, those labels convey hopes and fears in many parts of the continent. Viewed historically, they are inadequate, and this book has explored the past that has shaped this present.

Rwanda turns out to be one of the least culturally divided former colonies of Africa. Difference will not explain the genocide, nor will "ancient hatreds." A particular historical trajectory was described in chapter 1: a history of inequality of power and wealth in the pre-colonial kingdom, of the ethnicization of difference under colonial rule, of growing tension as the possibility of African autonomy became clear, of Belgian indifference to anti-Tutsi violence as a Hutu-led government came to power. It is a history of that government's inability to manage the politics of a gatekeeper state in the face of diminishing resources, of conflict with refugee Tutsi whose only recourse was to try to get access to the state on the battlefield, and of government officials and clients building a propaganda machine and militia organization to stir up hatred and prepare for the slaughter of Tutsi.

That story, even in schematic form, gets us closer to the still unfathomable process of how the leadership of a state could organize the killing of an entire category of its population and how many citizens could hack their neighbors – Tutsi and Hutu deemed moderate – to death with machetes and loot their belongings. It doesn't begin to explain how the UN, democratic states in the rest of the world, and the Organization of African Unity allowed such an event to become imaginable, let alone to let it unfold. The genocide in Rwanda was unique in Africa; that is, slaughter intended to *eliminate* people categorized in a certain way was unique. But mass killings have not been, from the anti-Igbo pogroms that preceded the Biafran war of 1967 through the still ongoing brutality

191

of a Tutsi-led, minority government in Burundi against Hutu. Ethnic cleansing – including exemplary killing, rape, and destruction of houses and cattle to force people to leave a specific area – has occurred in parts of Kenya with the apparent connivance of the Moi regime; a brutal war by a northern-dominated regime, run as an Islamic state, against non-Muslim populations to the south has been going on in the Sudan for twenty-five years. The common thread here is not just "ethnicity," for that is a label that glosses many different phenomena and processes, but a form of politics that makes an all-or-nothing struggle for inclusion or exclusion to access to state resources conceivable. In chapter 7, I argued that gatekeeper states are particularly at risk for this kind of excess, but even so sequences of decisions which human beings need not have made are responsible for turning tension into civil war or systematic murder.

Within the borders of post-1994 Rwanda, there has been no counter-genocide. Settlings of accounts against Hutu, raids by Hutu militia who had hidden themselves in neighboring Zaire/Congo, and coercive government attempts to concentrate rural populations into more easily monitored villages have continued. Rwanda has made progress in restoring basic institutions. What has not been done is to resolve the issue of responsibility in the genocide. Both international and national courts are at work, but seven years later neither has provided justice. In Rwanda, suspects rounded up for ill-defined reasons languish in squalid prisons alongside the most vicious killers. The thorniest question of all is how a Tutsi minority, the victim of a horrific attempted genocide, can feel secure if majority rule were restored.

Outside of Rwanda itself, the aftereffects of 1994 continued as massacres and war. The rebellion led by Kabila against Mobutu, supported by Rwanda and Uganda, engulfed Zaire in 1997. The Hutu – whether hostile militias or fearful refugees – were victims of atrocities by Kabila's forces and the Rwandan army in Zaire, while Hutu militias continued bloody raids into Rwanda and sometimes Uganda. When a new rebellion erupted in eastern Congo against Kabila, Rwanda and Uganda – having broken with their ally – supported it, while Angola and Zimbabwe intervened against the rebels. All outside parties, and the Congo state, had interests in trafficking gold and diamonds, not just in protecting borders and supporting allies. The consequences of this regional war included thousands of deaths and the paralysis of a large region in dire need of reconstruction. All this testified to the unpredictable and horrific consequences of the collapse of state institutions, to the extent of cross-border networks, and to the ambiguity of the distinction between warlords seeking spoils and states defending borders.

And South Africa? If the problem were simply race, one could declare it solved. Apartheid is dead, and not just in the sense that a black president elected by all voters is head of state. The once-white universities have for years had a black majority among the students (but not the faculty); the desirable neighborhoods are no longer all-white; and corporations are hiring Africans into managerial positions and trying to make African capitalists part of the business world. The elite of South Africa is no longer exclusively white, and a substantial black middle and working class has access to decent salaries and pensions, but income inequality among *black* South Africans is amongst the highest within any population in the world. Still, the ending of apartheid means a great deal to the daily existence of even the most downtrodden: they no longer fear arrest or deportation to a barren "homeland" for walking down the street without required documents. What has proven most elusive since majority rule is ending the grinding poverty affecting so much of the black population.

Not long before 1994, a white South African with good leftist credentials told me that he feared South Africa would become another Nigeria. That a series of political and economic failings of states have been coded as "African" is the unstated premise of the remark, but the anxiety that it reveals about the possibility of a state coming under the control of a small group of gatekeepers is real enough. The variations recounted in chapter 7, from the extremes of Nigeria or Zaire to the abortive capitalist transition of Kenya, give little precedent for optimism. But one has to be careful about what – other than the fact of being African – the implicit comparison presumes.

There remains a fundamental difference. South Africa, in its brutal and racialized way, did effect a process of capitalist accumulation going beyond anything elsewhere on the African continent. This meant not just the extension of market relations – which have spread across the continent – but the monopoly of usable land and productive resources in the hands of a small number of property owners, their acting together in defense of property and competitively toward the accumulation of profits. In South Africa, a white elite's control of land was mediated by the allocation of a small portion of land as "reserves" for Africans not actually at work. But since the massive urban expulsions of the 1950s to 1970s – building upon earlier expropriations in rural areas – those reserves have become dumping grounds, incapable of providing even modest support to families. African families with small amounts of land get little income from it; they rely on the wages remitted or pensions of relatives who have jobs, be they in legal or illegal sectors of the urban economy. Other African countries have landless people, but not the large majority of the once rural population. In Kenya, for example, most people "straddle," combining farming and wage resources in various sorts of ways, with varying degrees of success. Wage-labor capitalism, in most of Africa, takes place on islands in a sea of other sorts of socio-economic relations; in South Africa, wage-labor capitalism pervades the economy. And, therefore, the most salient fact regarding the economy of the post-apartheid state is that the unemployment rate is over 35 percent.

The unsettled question in South Africa is not whether it will remain capitalist or not. It is whether capitalism will be dynamic, growing, and open to the inclusion of new capitalists, rather than insular, parasitic, and exclusive. Balancing capitalists' demands for investment and growth against workers' (and nonworkers') demands for security and opportunity, against the need to remedy the effects of bad schooling and living in homes without water, and against the cost of fighting AIDS are central issues facing the nation. There have been programs to build homes and improve services, but 73 percent of Africans in South Africa still live without tap water in their homes and 69 percent without electricity. The ANC government promptly made education compulsory and got 95 percent of school-age children into classrooms, but the quality of the facilities and the teachers, especially in the poorer districts, remains in doubt. So far the government has leaned toward reassuring investors and maintaining economic "discipline."

But at least such issues can be talked about in South Africa without someone ending up in jail. Most encouraging – in comparison with what happened earlier elsewhere in Africa – the labor movement, COSATU notably, has refused to be absorbed into the ANC, although it has lost the influence over government policy it once had. The 1994 election did not come about because someone pronounced the magic words "electoral democracy"; and the strength of what can too easily be called "civil society" came from associations of neighborhood women, of factory workers, of high school students, of church members doing a lot of hard work in the crevices of an oppressive system for many, many years. It would be hard for the government, in the style of Sékou Touré or Nkrumah, to use the fiction of unity to insist that such organizations have no place in a liberated South Africa.

South Africa, for all its social inequities, has a chance to avoid two debilitating aspects of the gatekeeper state: the winner-take-all nature of competition for control of the state (the loser of an election in South Africa can still aspire to get rich), and the elimination of strong organizations capable of defending an open political system and a fair judiciary. It is not the strength of capitalism *per se* that fosters such possibilities; South Africa's past shows that some forms of capitalism can develop via racial oppression and exploitation. In Kenya, Zimbabwe, and other states, a crony capitalism associated with the state uses mixtures of market, kinship, and authoritarian relations to keep out competition, aligning patron–client politics with monopolistic capitalism. But South African capitalism is neither monolithic nor uncontested. Social progress and equity will likely remain objects of mobilization and argument within a political culture that values its newly found freedoms. South Africa's achievements and ongoing struggles are a reminder that it is the structural constraints of gatekeeper states and extraverted economies that have dashed hope elsewhere, not something inherent in being African.

Another pitfall, emphasized by Mahmood Mamdani in his comparison of South Africa and "tropical" Africa, is that while supplanting racial divisions, liberation may retain "tribal" ones. Mamdani emphasizes that "tribe" in Africa means not just a sentiment, but institutions of authority, a reality that people must confront even if their sentiments pull them in different directions. In South Africa, Zulu migrant workers are particularly dependent – if they are to have any chance of maintaining ties to their rural home villages – on the patronage system established by Zulu chiefs and their political leader, Buthelezi. The question is whether ethnic entrepreneurs like Buthelezi can harness cultural difference into a powerful political force, something that in all parts of Africa has required hard work and favorable (or rather unfavorable) conditions. Buthelezi is the only "tribal" leader of pre-1994 South Africa to have kept sufficient distance from the apartheid regime's efforts to avoid being discredited. More important, the intensity of urban–rural migration has spread urban youth culture widely in South Africa, crossing although not eliminating more local cultural traditions, and the deterioration of land has diminished the power of rural brokers; even Zulu are divided and often ambivalent, not necessarily ardent tribalists or captives of an ethnic demagogue. And *process* – how the revolution of 1994 unfolded – matters too. The possibility of acting as citizens captivated South Africans in 1994, Zulu included. Buthelezi, who initially wanted to boycott the election, had to accommodate himself to this reality and join the electoral process. South Africa's constitution gives more autonomy to regional governments than do the systems of most African countries, and the fact that the ANC's impressive national popularity is countered by slim provincial majorities for Inkatha in Natal-KwaZulu and for the National Party in the Western Cape gives opponents a stake in the system. The tensions remain but the mechanisms to contain them are in play. Institutions that strengthen associational life, debate, and public participation in decision-making could make a difference elsewhere in Africa, too.

Difficult issues remain about the relationship between South Africa's universalistic, progressive constitution – one of the most rights-conscious in the world – and its citizens' perceptions of cultural difference and their desires for spaces of partial autonomy. Should the rights of women over-rule particular groups' "traditions" of patriarchy and marriage rules that give women unequal voice and access to resources? So far the answer is a qualified yes, but debates continue. The resolutions are not necessarily either/or. South Africa's second election witnessed neither the spread of ethnic particularism nor a revival of "Africanist" politics, a quest for an entirely black nation, despite the fact that black poverty remains enormous and white privilege remains visible. The unanswered question is how much the government of Thabo Mbeki can address the basic issues of access to water, schooling, jobs, and a decent standard of living. The danger is less that South Africa will become another Nigeria than that it will become another Brazil, a large, potentially prosperous country, where the gap between rich and poor is enormous and the racial dimensions of inequality are kept in obscurity.

One can reverse the question: is there much chance that Nigeria's future could come to resemble South Africa's present? Can Nigeria obtain electoral democracy and chart a plausible, if uncertain, route to economic development? Writing in 2001, I can be more optimistic than I could have been in 1998, for after the unexpected death of Nigeria's dictator Sani Abacha, a courageous general, Abdulsalam Abubakar released political prisoners from jail, eased press restrictions, and eventually superintended a relatively fair election in which he was not himself a candidate. But can a state with a forty-year history of conflict, oppression, and corruption, transform itself by the accident of a clot in one ruler's coronary artery and an act of will by his successor? Will the resources of the oil spigot be used for purposes other than patronage and elite consumption? Will Nigerians' entrepreneurial skills, much in evidence for many decades, be used in diverse agricultural units, in industrial projects, and in small-scale marketing free of state harassment? Will unions, trade associations, and professional bodies be able to develop themselves and represent different points of view? And will government itself be decentralized enough so that meaningful political organizing, with real resources to use and distribute, can take place at municipal, regional, provincial levels?

One needs to remember that the gatekeeper state is neither a choice made by current political actors nor an automatic response to a given situation in terms of the world economy or the global system of states. Such states – with their considerable range of effectiveness, repressiveness, openness to countervailing pressures – are the product of an historical process.

The constraints and possibilities of that history have been the subject of this book. Africa was systematically conquered but not so systematically ruled. The pre-1940 colonial system was able to function because it had limited transformative ambitions. Colonial power was a combination of gatekeeping, bastion building, and the state's effort to make itself into the patron of patrons, particularly of chiefly elites who brought coercion and the distribution of rewards to the village level. But chiefs and commoners found numerous niches and crevices in the system. Trading diasporas, labor migration networks, associations of school graduates, churches, mosques, and shrines cut across tribal cages and territorial borders, even as islands of wealth and influence developed among cash crop producers in various regions.

By the 1940s, the reality of Africans in dynamic agricultural systems, in wage labor, and in cities could not be contained within this system of rural power and patronage. The preservationist colonialism of the 1930s became the developmentalist colonialism of the 1940s and 1950s. Ironically, the radical claims of developmentalist colonialism – that it would revolutionize the backward ways of African economies, creating a new African as much as new wealth – translated into a focus on those more bounded areas of the economy that the state could in fact remake. The state revenue base remained shallow, export-oriented, and vulnerable to the vagaries of the world economy. Politically, the developmentalist state undermined provincial and chiefly administration and became more centralized: representatives of the state claiming technical and bureaucratic knowledge, rather than white men who "knew their natives" or chiefs who knew their traditions, tried to rule the countryside.

The constraints of the post-colonial era were not those of "colonialism" *per se*, but of an entire process, including the form of African political and social mobilization. This was true in a double sense. First, the shift in the colonial state towards an activist, centralizing, modernizing direction presented a particular target to the budding nationalists of the 1950s: the possibility of an activist, centralizing, modernizing *national* project. National officials often partook of the same arrogance toward peasants and small-scale marketeers as their predecessors, but they were more concerned with the implications of development for patron-client relations, with providing resources to people loyal to them and keeping resources away from potential opponents. Second, the first generation of leaders knew from their own experience the potential of claims made on the basis of citizenship. The reformist colonialism of France and Great Britain had been beset by demands – for equal wages, equal social services, and an equal standard of living – based on a notion (explicit or implicit) of imperial citizenship; their successors faced such demands from mobilized groups on a national level, and they had more meager resources with which to meet them. Efforts by African states to augment the vertical relationships they could control and to undercut people who could make claims upon them or develop autonomous power bases added a new dimension to the bastion-making, controlling, and gatekeeping qualities of the late colonial state. Subsequent generations of leaders were caught up in competition for control of the gate itself.

Not the least of the losses dating from the 1970s has been the national imagination: an excitement once found in many parts of the population as colonial rule collapsed, as national institutions and symbols seemed to express a sense of people controlling their own destiny. Although protests calling for the accountability of rulers to citizens can still be heard, national ideals are at times replaced by a bitter sense of betrayal and of the necessity of finding a patron inside the governing elite who can send some of the fruits of the gatekeeper state in one's direction. Or people have focused their collective imaginations on neighborhoods and religious affiliations, on kinship relations and on other sorts of personal ties. Such affinities had been important all along. But for a time, claims could be made as citizens, in the name of common interest. The very process of claim-making had helped to define a national imaginary. The repressive actions of African leaders, starting with Nkrumah, not only damaged associational life and expression, but the very national ideal which the leaders themselves asserted.

Those leaders inherited from colonial powers the institutions of state, even if not the spirit of the nation: bureaucracies, armies, customs houses. The nation-state gave leaders access to international resources. Heads of state could draw on the intellectual, moral, and financial resources of the United Nations, international financial organizations, and the development agencies of industrial states, who were concerned with making the international system at least minimally functional. Rulers like Mobutu proved skilled in manipulating Cold War and other rivalries. Whereas state elites tried to guard the gate, regionalist movements, smuggling networks, and rebels tried to get around it, and the complexities of international business and rivalries of nations, as well as the possibilities of cross-border networks within Africa, made gate evasion a feasible possibility, at least if the rebels had resources worth buying. What was crucial was the struggle to control the nodes in a pattern of resource movement.

The gatekeepeer state thus emerged out of a peculiar history of decolonization, itself a product of the desire of European powers to work with African states of limited size and influence, of the first generation of independent leadership to consolidate the political apparatuses they had built up in the late colonial years, and of the limited imaginations of all concerned. The peculiar history of decolonization, for better or worse, gave rise to a series of states which stood at critical junctures in a highly unequal world.

The question of constraint becomes more difficult if one asks the counterfactual question of whether in the absence of activist state projects, colonial and post-colonial, more dynamic forms of capitalism could have emerged. The most likely answer is, with great difficulty. It is not clear that the goose which gatekeeper states killed was capable of laying golden eggs; indeed, the obstacles facing capitalist development within a capitalist world economy were themselves an important reason why state leaders tried to find other means of expanding national wealth. Even before colonization, Africa presented unfertile ground for capitalist expansion. It offered many places where people could survive and if necessary hide; it offered closely woven social networks that could foster movement across certain routes and solidarity in certain places; and it offered relatively few places where an elite could try to exclude all others from access to crucial assets – notably land – and thereby create a permanent workforce subordinated to their task. African kings had themselves faltered in their quest to turn power into systematic extraction from their own populations and had looked to external connections – trade, conquest, and enslavement – to set themselves apart. The would-be capitalists of the colonial era, with the notable exception of South Africa, were only a little more thorough. They could build islands of wage-labor capitalism, and mostly had to live off less direct extraction from peasants who were both spread out geographically and connected to each other socially. Colonial capitalism focused on the extraction of a few commodities and on the building of narrow commercial structures, not on wide and inclusive commercial interaction or diversified and long-term investment.

The rulers of independent Africa found themselves in the same bind, so that their takeover of the development project of late colonialism also failed to produce systematic transformation of production and exchange, but instead reinforced narrow channels which the would-be rulers could try to control and much larger areas which they could not. By then, countries exporting primary products faced an international economy dominated by powerful corporations with a wide choice around the world of where they could find primary products, cheap labor, and investment opportunities.

From the late 1940s through the 1960s, expanding crop and mineral exports plus development efforts in their most expansive phase seemed for a time to promise more varied economies. Some cash crop producers, despite the tendency of states to confiscate a significant portion of export earnings, acquired significant wealth. The best organized workers achieved better wages and the possibility that a career could provide a family with a decent house, education for the next generation, and a pension.

These hopes fell victim to world economic trends that turned viciously against primary product exporters in the 1970s and 1980s. But even in the best years of export growth, few African countries got much beyond increased primary product exports and import substitution industrialization; and the most successful, such as the Côte d'Ivoire, still faced steep declines later on. Neither the most market-oriented African economies nor the most nationally focused achieved notable breakthroughs, even if for a time many were able to finance substantial improvements in education, health, and other basic services. Internally, African states had already run into the limitations posed by gatekeeper elites who feared both the claim-making capabilities of organized farmers and workers and the danger that pockets of wealth could produce regionally based opposition. Small-scale entrepreneurs, from market women to cross-border traders, were often harassed by African governments, as they had been by colonial regimes, unless they could be incorporated into the leadership's patron-client structure.

Such restrictiveness contradicted governments' desire to promote economic activity in their national territories, and the balance between these tendencies varied greatly. But the absence of long-term trends toward the emergence of strong business communities and the reversal of the 1950s pattern of developing a stable, decently paid labor force reflected back on the political process itself, making politics more of a winner-take-all situation, where both wealth and power depended on keeping control of the central government. Local and regional government were discouraged, leaving little space for those out of power to retain a stake in the system independent of the patron-client system. States discouraged the activities of civic as well as political organizations, from unions to women's associations to organizations advocating ecologically responsible development.

This historical sequence, a limited opening followed by a narrowing of political and economic possibilities, trapped African states in a vicious circle: the resources of the gate had to be all the more protected because resources were so limited. Such a situation encouraged intrigue – in the army, among regional power-brokers – to take over the all-important institutions attached to sovereignty and the linkage with the outside world. The rash of *coups d'état* of the late 1960s in Africa revealed the extent of the problem; the Congo crisis and the Biafran war indicated the extremes to which it could go. The diamond-smuggling warlords of Sierra Leone and Angola reveal how prevalent struggles to evade gatekeeping authority remain at the dawn of a new century, while Moi's Kenya and Mugabe's

Zimbabwe continue to illustrate the economic failures and disillusioning politics that even long-lasting gatekeeper states entail. Some gatekeeper states possess civil services and state institutions that function moderately well, allow a degree of debate and civic organization, and more rarely – as in Senegal in 2000 – allow open enough politics for an incumbent leader to be defeated and to accept defeat. In quite a few states, including Kenya, Senegal, and Nigeria, the media and public debate are becoming more open. In a number of countries, the weakening of state economic control, under pressures of structural adjustment and leaders' realization of their own policy failures, has led to expanding entrepreneurial possibilities, misleadingly labeled "informal," and that has produced a rather different sort of market economy from that imagined in the 1960s; one where women traders and artisans play a bigger role and male wage workers a smaller one. At the other extreme, some regimes have become little more than the most powerful warlord among others, each trying to keep together a set of followers and reward them with the spoils of certain export revenues or from predation against the citizenry.

Is there a way out to get beyond the historical sequence that produced the limited possibilities and the horrific dangers of the gatekeeper state? Here, first, are some *false* ways out, the kind of one-size-fits-all solutions to Africa's problems that are often imposed on the continent:

1 Privatize as much as possible, shrink the state, and let the market work its magic.

   Markets certainly have their virtues, but they are specific ones: markets are institutions, systems of power, and personal networks whose effects can only be understood by examining them in all their specificity. It is not clear now, any more than it was in the 1940s, that the rag-tag army of the miserably employed has much to offer to Africa's future, that Africa can achieve a breakthrough merely by making exports for which demand is weak a little bit cheaper, or that reducing government expenditures might not hurt the long-run expansion of human capital via, above all, education.

2 Let's get serious about African capitalism. Perhaps an African capitalist class should kick peasants off the land and create a capitalist economy that will grow, prosper, and employ everybody.

   The problem here is that at best this would produce a nineteenth-century proletariat for the twenty-first century and at worst leave only the pain, oppression, violence, and insecurity of other capitalist transitions without producing the benefits. Such a tendency is hardly compatible with building states with stable, democratic, and legitimate governments: people do not vote to be expropriated.

3 Give up on the rest of the world: build an economy, national or regional, with minimal outside connections; make African economic life an expression of Africa's uniqueness.

Africa's experiments with economic nationalism – import substitution industrialization, state corporations in key sectors of the economy – have gone badly. Uncompetitive, insulated producers are inefficient and their products expensive; it is the poor who bear the burden.

Are there more constructive ways of broaching the reform question? Here are some suggestions, not for prepackaged solutions, but for historically based ways of thinking about the future:

1 First, to think realistically, we need explanations. It may be true that most African states are ineffective, prone to corruption, and follow unsound economic policies, but such observations mean little without explanation. Gatekeeper states in fact have something to fear from networks or collectivities able to pose a challenge or from African cultivators who use social connections to make the state irrelevant. This leaves the question of whether certain kinds of policies by governments or outside institutions can encourage "going with the flow" – taking advantage of social systems that keep options open – instead of imposing yet another single-minded solution. We might do well to think about the small-scale cocoa producer in the Côte d'Ivoire and the market women of Ghana, about the ways in which urban wage-earners invest their savings in rural communities. What can states and outside agencies do to encourage such processes?

2 We need to think more subtly than the opposition of state and market or of a dichotomy between state and civil society. Some political economists have pointed out that keeping a market economy functioning requires more state capacity than maintaining a centralized economy; the latter may work badly, but it functions in the interests of the rulers. Shrinking government may do less to shrink the capacity of bad rulers to steal than to weaken the basic institutions that permit workforces to be trained and to stay healthy, or to provide the predictable services which domestic and foreign investors need. Patronage politics blurs the line between public and private resources and depends on the vertical relationship of an elite and the individuals and groups which make up society; privatizing ownership may redirect rather than reduce the importance of patronage. Indeed, all systems contain mixtures of personal connections and institutions that play by a set of rules. The problem is to make institutions rule-bound and transparent enough that all citizens can obtain services or make claims upon them, while avoiding their becoming distant and alienating. Rejecting the state in the name of civil

society or the market is likely to be no more effective than assuming that the state can solve all problems in the name of the people. All this requires careful attention to the institutional capacity of states; it requires thinking in the long term. Whatever the failings of African governments that claimed to be "socialist" – and which were typically variations on the gatekeeper state – a democracy that is not in some sense "social" will garner little support. Voters need to sense that their decisions will bring them predictable services and opportunities that improve their lives.

3 We need to ask what are the implications of the fact that "African" problems are actually Euro-Afro-American co-productions, emerging from a history that included the slave trade, colonization, and international support for rulers like Mobutu. In the literal sense, the indebtedness of African countries, and in a more figurative sense, the accumulation of bad habits and the failure to solve basic problems, the burden of this co-production lies heavily on Africa. We are caught in a dilemma: on the one hand is the fact that young Africans are saddled with the multiple costs of the illegitimate rulers who built up big debts and bad structures. On the other hand, the writing off of debt encourages irresponsibility. The international system recognizes the latter danger, but not the former; even Mandela's and Mbeki's South Africa is expected to pay the debts the apartheid state incurred to oppress its African population. If a new generation of Africans is to get out of the difficulties their elders – with lots of help from outside – got them into, all of us need to take a more balanced view of responsibility. Let us realize that international banking, transnational corporations, donor agencies, and international institutions are not some impersonal embodiment of the "world economy" but are specific institutions, particular kinds of power relations, and they should be scrutinized just as carefully as the behavior of African politicians. International corporations and foreign aid can help or harm; they – not just the behavior of Africans – deserve examination. Africa has been told endlessly what it should do to conform to the world market; the more difficult question is how the institutions which constitute the world market can be restructured to give the world's poor and excluded more of a chance.

4 From the days of anti-slavery movements to opposition to colonial rule to mobilization against apartheid, successful political action has depended on the resonance between the concerns of "local" people and their networks of supporters in other regions and in other countries. Such connections have turned slavery, colonialism, and racial domination from facts of life into political impossibilities. Political change does not come simply from do-good outsiders getting their way or from authentic local communities bringing down the all-powerful. Time and time again,

change has happened by interaction. Africa has its scoundrels who speak in its name and its thoughtful critics who were the first to warn that governments were failing to live up to their promises, well before western journalists and academics made their transition from credulous to judgmental. Outsiders need to know the difference: to listen and to think about what they hear. The future of purely "western" intervention is likely to be no better than its past, but the prospects of thoughtful cooperation remain open. As the experience of past cross-national social movements makes clear, the possibility that large-scale institutions can be changed is not entirely a utopian one.

Africa, under colonial rule or independent administration, has not had the opportunity to develop multiple, diverse, and dense economic linkages to the rest of the world. Its conquerors wanted certain things from Africa, and they constructed an infrastructure and incentives for them to be delivered. Faced with these forms of colonialism and capitalism, Africans struggled to hold them at arm's length. They had considerable success and paid a frightful price for it. Are Africa's choices between the poverty of marginalization and the devastation of exploitation? Or are there other ways to organize agricultural production, small-scale industry, and regional markets? Are the moments, from the 1940s to the 1990s, when Africans demanded the benefits of citizenship, doomed to be fleeting, as rulers fearful of the tenuousness of their own power repress forms of association and communication that might counter their singular hold on limited political and economic resources? Or do the experiences Africans have had over the past fifty years in forging associations and alliances among themselves, of imagining new forms of religious, cultural, and political action, offer possibilities for the future?

# Index

Abacha, Sani, 135, 174, 189, 196
Abako, 81, 164
Abidjan, 120
Abubakar, Abdulsalam, 196
accountability, 159, 183, 187, 189,
    191–92, 198, 202
Accra, 50, 51
Achebe, Chinua, 187
Action Group, 69
Africa
    asserted unity of, 11–14, 66, 71, 79–80,
        159, 183–84, 202
    connections within, 14, 25, 27, 44, 48,
        80, 104–05, 118, 143, 146, 159,
        183–87
    and diaspora, 12, 24–26, 58
    diversity of, 11, 13
    geography of, 14, 99, 101
    images of, 18, 23, 57–58, 64, 71–74,
        77, 83, 104, 135, 173, 180, 184–85,
        193
    international connections of, 11–14,
        24–26, 105, 118, 129, 131, 134, 152,
        156, 159, 183–87, 203–04
    Subsaharan, in relation to North Africa,
        11–12
    *See also* African Americans, and Africa;
        international opinion; Pan-Africanism
African Agricultural Society (Société
    Agricole Africaine), 45
African Americans, and Africa, 10, 12, 24,
    54, 61, 135, 151, 188
African Mineworkers Union (Southern
    Rhodesia), 74
African National Congress (ANC), 9–11,
    56–57, 135, 144–54, 194
African National Council of Southern
    Rhodesia (ANC), 136, 137
Africanism (South Africa), 57, 151,
    196
Afrikaans, 148
Afrikaners, 32, 53–55, 152

agriculture
    African initiatives in, 18, 21–24, 72,
        92, 107, 174, 202
    collectivization of, 97, 177–80
    and European export firms, 22–23, 67,
        131
    failures of, 98, 105, 107, 162, 168–70,
        173, 178–79
    growth of, 21–24, 69, 86, 93–97, 106,
        199
    and plantations, 143
    and rural political mobilization, 8,
        45–46, 48, 59–60, 71–73, 93, 135,
        137–38, 140, 143
    and rural wealth, 21–24, 68, 93–96, 174,
        199
    and smallholder production, 21–24, 86,
        93–97
    and social differentiation, 21–24, 72, 74,
        93, 96, 174
    state controls over, 67–68, 93, 97, 143,
        161, 168, 178–80
    white farmers and, 23, 36, 45–46,
        53–54, 63, 72–73, 86, 136, 138, 139,
        147, 193
    *See also* cocoa; coffee; peanuts; sisal;
        sugar; labor, wage; labor migration;
        land; squatters, rural
Ahidjo, Ahmadu, 76
AIDS, 109–111, 184, 194
Ajayi, J. Ade, 15
Ake, Claude, 161
Algeria, 63, 77, 166
All African People's Congress (1958), 81,
    183
aluminum, 67, 97, 161
Amin, Idi, 103, 180
Angola, 62, 117, 133–34, 139–43, 159,
    160, 168, 177, 184, 192, 200
Annan, Kofi, 185
apartheid, 1, 10, 55–58, 135, 145, 149–53,
    193, 195, 203